P9-EDI-609

DATE DUE

Demco, Inc. 38-293

THE HIDDEN NATIONS

THE HIDDEN NATIONS

The People Challenge
the Soviet Union

Nadia Diuk and Adrian Karatnycky

WILLIAM MORROW AND COMPANY, INC.
New York

Library of Congress Cataloging-in-Publication Data

Diuk, Nadia.
    The hidden nations : the people challenge the Soviet Union / by
  Nadia Diuk and Adrian Karatnycky.
       p.   cm.
    ISBN 0-688-08849-X
    1. Soviet Union—Ethnic relations.   2. Nationalism—Soviet Union.
3. Soviet Union—History—Autonomy and independence movements.
4. Soviet Union—Politics and government—1985-   I. Karatnycky,
Adrian.   II. Title.
DK33.D58   1990
323.1'47—dc20   90-39501
                                                                              CIP

Printed in the United States of America

First Edition

1 2 3 4 5 6 7 8 9 10

BOOK DESIGN BY PAUL CHEVANNES

To Irene and Petro
and
To the memory of Mariyka and Bohdan

Acknowledgments

We began to discuss this project in the winter of 1988, as mass demonstrations were erupting in Armenia and as the independence movements in the Baltic states were beginning to take shape.

When we initiated our inquiry into national ferment in the Soviet Union, we could not have predicted the rapid pace of events. Nonetheless, we were certain that the mass demonstrations in Armenia, as in Kazakhstan two years before, were but the first signs of the reemergence of the hidden nations of the Soviet Union onto the stage of world history. Many years of thinking and writing about the Soviet Union and its predecessor, the Russian empire, had long before convinced us that the USSR was in its essence an unstable, conflict-ridden entity.

Much of the research that led to this book was conducted during the nearly two months that each of us spent in the USSR in the winter and summer of 1989 and in early 1990. During our several journeys we were the beneficiaries of the assistance, encouragement, and generosity of many of the protagonists in the unfolding drama of national ferment.

We are particularly grateful for the kindnesses shown us by Ghia Nodia and his wife in Tbilisi, Georgia; by Evhen Sverstyuk and Ivan Drach in Kiev, the Ukraine; by Rostyslav Bratun, Stefania Shabatura, Ihor and Iryna Kalynets in Lvov, the Ukraine; by Najaf Najafov, Leyla Yunusova, and Arif Yunusov in Baku, Azerbaijan; by Fouat Ablamov and Abdurrakhim Pulatov in Tashkent, Uzbekistan; by Sherhan Murtazayev in Alma-Ata, Kazakhstan; Tunne Kelam in Tallinn, Estonia; Eduard Bekrlavs in Riga, Latvia; and the helpful staff of the Lithuanian Popular Front "Sajudis" in Vilnius.

In the months since we were with them, many of these leading voices for national rights and democracy have been elected to high office, in a dramatic vote of confidence for the movements that espouse national autonomy and outright independence.

There are many friends, colleagues, and acquaintances who generously shared their views and offered advice. All cannot be named. But we are especially grateful for the help given us by Ludmilla Alexeyeva, Leon Aron, Peter Bejger, William Bodie, Vladimir Bukovsky, Ginte Damusis, Milovan Djilas, William Fierman, Devon Gaffney, Carl Gershman, Paul Goble, Eduard Gudava, Mykola Haliw, Paul Henze, Ojars Kalnins, Roger Kaplan, Marta Kolomayets, Taras Kuzio, Vytautas Landsbergis, Nancy Lubin, Konstantin Mishev, Viktor Nakas, Dr. Jaroslaw Padoch, Will Pyle, Leonid Plyushch, Mari-Ann Rikken, Ayshe Seytmuratova, Maria Rozanova, Ivan Sierany, Andrei Sinyavsky, Alexei Sobchenko, Nadia Svitlychna, Kazimieras Uoka, Enders Wimbush, Volodymyr Yavoriwsky, and Mykola Zhulynsky.

Above all, we are most grateful to Arch Puddington of Radio Free Europe/Radio Liberty, who encouraged us to pursue this endeavor and with whom we were able to regularly debate concepts and ideas.

We express our gratitude as well to our employers, who were generous in affording us the flexibility to travel and work on a time-consuming project that debilitated one of the authors with a bout of hepatitis of Central Asian origin.

To Barbara Lowenstein, our literary agent, we owe a debt for her painstaking advocacy, constant encouragement, and firm belief in the importance of this project.

We are grateful as well to the Shevchenko Scientific Society of New York, which made possible our research in the Soviet Union. The Society finds itself in enforced exile, having been suppressed and banned after Stalin's takeover of Western Ukraine. After we began our research the Society resumed its activities in the Ukraine.

To Sherry Arden, formerly at William Morrow, who took a chance on our book long before the disintegration of the Soviet empire became a popular topic, we owe thanks.

We thank Margaret Talcott, our patient and hard-working editor at Morrow, who has been a tireless worker and thoughtful reader. She helped us shape arguments about often arcane matters more precisely and has assisted us in stating our ideas more concisely. She has worked with us with diligence, dispatch, and intelligence.

David Falk, our precise copyeditor, has eliminated lapses in grammar, corrected stylistic inconsistencies, and has dug deep to verify the accuracy of arcane names.

What remaining obfuscations and imprecisions the reader finds are, alas, the products of our own stubbornness.

It is a timeworn verity for authors to claim their work to be a collaborative effort. In our case, the term is literally correct. As husband and wife, our lives have long been collaborative. Our venture into collaborative writing has proved, much to our surprise, to have been remarkably smooth and agreeable.

Although we made no conscious effort to achieve a single voice, the process of writing was such that each of us had a hand in the fashioning of the other's chapters. In the end, we hope that the process of collaboration has helped to mute the differences in literary style that are as signatures to authors.

Nadia Diuk and Adrian Karatnycky
New York and Washington, D.C.
June 1990

Contents

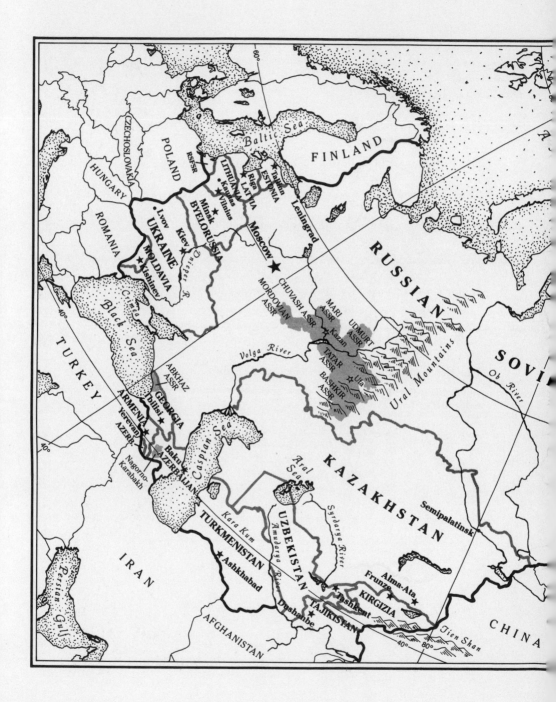

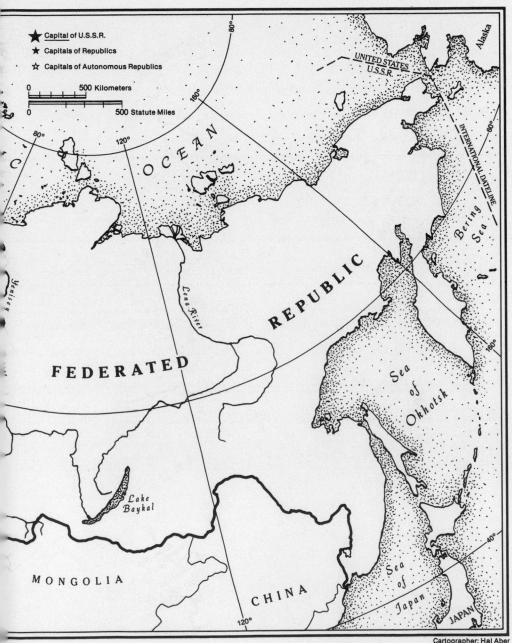

Capital of U.S.S.R.

Capitals of Republics

Capitals of Autonomous Republics

500 Kilometers

500 Statute Miles

80°

180°

120°

80°

UNITED STATES
U.S.S.R.

Alaska

INTERNATIONAL DATELINE

60°

O C E A N

Bering Sea

Yenisey

Lena River

R E P U B L I C

60°

F E D E R A T E D

Sea
of
Okhotsk

Lake
Baykal

MONGOLIA

CHINA

120°

Sea
of
Japan

40°

JAPAN

Cartographer: Hal Aber

THE HIDDEN NATIONS

The National Question:
A History of Peoples

And empires gleam, like wrecks in a dissolving dream.
—Shelley, *Hellas*

O<small>N THE</small> basis of Western news stories, it is difficult to piece together what has happened in the USSR in the last few years, even in the last few months. Since December 1986, millions upon millions of Soviet citizens— Ukrainians, Georgians, Lithuanians, Byelorussians, Crimean Tatars, Estonians, Turkmenians, Azerbaijanis, Uzbeks, Armenians, Latvians, and Moldavians—have taken to the streets in an outpouring of popular discontent. Additional millions have taken part in general strikes to protest the ethnic, economic, and political policies of the Soviet state. These mass protests have shaken the very foundations of the Soviet state and altered Western conceptions about the stability of the "indissolvable union of socialist states."

Hundreds have died, and thousands have been injured, in fierce interethnic conflicts, in large measure the consequence of the denial of sovereignty and of appalling economic misery. Hundreds, too, have perished as a consequence of army and police actions in such places as Azerbaijan, Armenia, Georgia, and Kazakhstan.

News dispatches on the non-Russian peoples seem to lurch from crisis to crisis. In Armenia and Azerbaijan, territorial disputes are said to be at issue. In Uzbekistan and Kirgizia, interethnic hatreds are reported to be at the root of violence. In Byelorussia and Moldavia, deep-seated resentments over native language rights are said to inspire unrest. In the Ukraine, mass protest is said to be fueled by unhappiness with local Brezhnev-style bosses. Yet all these current tensions arise from a common source—the imperial nature of the Soviet Union. The unprecedented unrest springs from the impatience and urgency of the USSR's non-Russian subjects. They feel that now, at long last, is the time to press for change, and for freedom.

An Empire Quakes

For some seventy years, the totalitarian Soviet system has been single-mindedly devoted to crushing all independent organization. Under Khrushchev, Brezhnev, Andropov, and Chernenko, non-Russians made up the vast majority of political prisoners—even before national dissent was permitted to blossom into mass movements. From the 1920s to the late 1980s, individual dissenters were trapped in a web of repression spun by the internal espionage network of the KGB and its string of informants and by the Ministry of Internal Affairs (MVD), with its uniformed militia and dreaded Sixth Detachment armed with rubber truncheons and ferocious guard dogs. An extremely regimented system of controls made it well-nigh impossible for most independent organizations to rent a meeting place, much less photocopy a statement or print a leaflet, without official approval. For decades, the absence of a free press contributed to the weakness of independent life and the resultant atomization of the Soviet public.

For nearly three quarters of a century, the USSR's citizens kept their most deeply held views to themselves. Their outward passivity had even led many Western experts to conclude that the traditions, values, and bonds of the past had been irretrievably lost and sundered—that a new type of docile citizen had been shaped by totalitarianism and mass repression.

Even prominent Soviet dissidents joined in this pessimistic chorus. In a book published in 1984, the brilliant Russian writer and philosopher Aleksandr Zinoviev characterized national issues in the USSR in his deeply cynical book *The Reality of Communism:*

> The Communist regime deals successfully with national problems, as Soviet experience has shown. In particular it has been extremely effective in raising the educational, cultural and living standards of the more backward peoples and groups of the population to a comparatively high level. These peoples become a bulwark of the new society.

According to Zinoviev, the Communist system had a strong capacity to destroy national barriers and eliminate ethnic differences. Communism created a new, bland, homogenized community of people who, Zinoviev argued, were "beyond nationality." Those features of the Soviet system led the writer to wrongly conclude that *"any expectation that conflicts between nationalities will cause the ruin of the Soviet Empire derives from a total misconception"* (italics added).

These words are written by one of the most acute analysts of Soviet life, an insightful man who spent more than half a century living under Soviet Communism. Today, his assessment has been disproven by the remarkable national rebirth that is sweeping across the USSR.

Zinoviev had good reasons for skepticism and cynicism based on the status quo of the Soviet Union in the 1970s and early 1980s. Much of the national spirit and energy of the USSR's peoples endured beneath the surface, repressed by the police state and hidden under the superficial and glib assertions of the self-confident totalitarian media. The recent rise of widespread and wide-ranging national movements marks an astounding shift in the consciousness of the peoples that make up the Soviet Union.

Since the accession of Mikhail Gorbachev to the pinnacles of power and the emergence of the policies of *glasnost* and *perestroika*, the institutions and instruments of repression and control have been forced to work under new constraints and rules: Regulations governing the use of force have been promulgated; many of the best-known political prisoners have been released; the psychiatric prison system has undergone some revisions; and overzealous security *apparatchiks* have been chastised and, on occasion, have even been brought to trial and punished. More important, the array of the state's mechanisms of social control has become the subject of limited but often very real and honest scrutiny in the official press.

Such press scrutiny and shifts in regulations are all part of the upheaval that has accompanied the reforms required by perestroika and glasnost, as well as by the much ballyhooed campaign for the "humanization for the KGB." Military actions against protesters, as in Soviet Georgia, now often result in unwanted parliamentary commissions of inquiry and embarrassing, highly public denunciations of military and security personnel. Illegal interceptions of mail can sometimes result in the loss of livelihood for a KGB or MVD functionary and lead to criminal sanctions. Press exposés of security excesses occasionally appear on the front pages of widely circulated newspapers and magazines. The openness of debates in the Congress of People's Deputies, and to a lesser extent, in the USSR's full-time parliament, the Supreme Soviet, also provide a lively, new forum for the airing of such abuses. The scrutiny and criticism of the state's most secret instruments of oppression and control have brought instability and uncertainty to the Soviet security apparat—it is no longer clear what is sanctioned and what is forbidden. This measure of uncertainty has created an opening for political activism and independent organizing.

To be sure, KGB and MVD surveillance has not been curtailed. Nor is there an independent judiciary to protect civil liberties. Most national rights advocates assume that files on their emerging movements are growing thicker. In our travels through the USSR in 1989 and 1990, we found that groups of independent activists are being closely monitored. What is different is the clear absence of fear. Party chief Mikhail Gorbachev's constant exhortations to "democratize" the system and to increase popular participation in political life have helped raise expectations, particularly among the long-quiescent non-Russians.

Well before mass protest changed the face of Hungary, Czechoslovakia, East Germany, and Romania, widespread public ferment first surfaced among the non-Russian peoples of the USSR. It was as early as December 1986 that thousands of Kazakh students took to the streets of Alma-Ata to protest limitations on their national rights. Within a year, they were followed by thousands of Lithuanians, Latvians, and Estonians. By 1988, as many as a half-million demonstrators were regularly taking to the streets of Yerevan in Armenia and Baku in Azerbaijan to press their claims against a stultifying and unresponsive empire.

When he came to power as general secretary in March 1985, Mikhail Gorbachev could not have anticipated that he was ushering in an unprecedented era of national ferment. Few Western analysts could have predicted the important liberalizations that glasnost would bring to culture and politics in the USSR. Gorbachev's maiden speech, after all, revealed little sign of a major policy shift. In it and other early addresses there are time-worn references to "combatting shortcomings," "strengthening discipline," and "inculcating patriotism and internationalism."

There was little evidence of innovation in Gorbachev's pronouncements on ethnic and national issues. Speaking on the occasion of the fortieth anniversary of the "victory of the Soviet people" in World War II, Gorbachev was keen to praise the "mass heroism" of Soviet citizens, "united and inspired by the Great Russian people, whose bravery, endurance, and unbending character were an inspiring example of an unconquerable will to victory." "The blossoming of nations and nationalities," Gorbachev went on, "is organically linked to their wide-ranging drawing together [sblizheniye]." A shift in policy could be found only in Gorbachev's use of the term sblizheniye—"drawing together"— which appeared to be a step away from the Brezhnev doctrine of sliyaniye—the "merger" of nations. Perhaps, this was an indication of the Soviet leader's more relaxed approach to the non-Russians.

By 1986, the tone of Gorbachev's speeches had undergone a remarkable alteration. The USSR's economy was in a state of crisis, he insisted. And there was a need for "radical restructuring." The terms glasnost and perestroika had made their permanent entry into the contemporary political lexicon. But the Soviet leader was notably reticent about offering any sense of a major change in the area of national relations.

Within the republics, 1986 saw the usual denunciations by local Party leaders of "bourgeois nationalists" and exhortations for a "struggle against nationalist and chauvinist sentiments." The first storm clouds of national ferment appeared at a Congress of the USSR Writers Union. There the Georgian writers' delegation stormed out over the issue of "Great Russian nationalism," the idea that it is Russia's destiny to rule over a great empire. And the Ukrainian poet Boris Oliynik (who later became the deputy chairman of the Soviet of Nationalities in the USSR's parliament) castigated "great power chauvinists." Radicalized by the nuclear accident in Chernobyl, he denounced those of his fellow countrymen whom he charged with servility to Brezhnev-style political orthodoxy. In Oliynik's view, self-serving Party officials from his republic had been given pieces of political turf in "their own native land in exchange for speaking broken Russian" to satisfy their Russian masters in the Kremlin.

Inspired by the Chernobyl catastrophe, grass-roots ecological movements began to emerge in late 1986 in the Ukraine, Byelorussia, Armenia, and Lithuania. The pollution of native lands was increasingly becoming a catalyst for the political mobilization of forces eager to break free from the domination of the central authorities. Protests calling for the closing of nuclear power plants in the Ukraine and Lithuania, and the curbing of industrial pollution in Armenia, drew people away from state-controlled organizations and led to the emergence of these small, highly effective independent groups.

In December of 1986, amid growing ferment on ecological and language issues, Mikhail Gorbachev got his first taste of the incendiary power of national upheaval. The event that signaled the first salvo of an ensuing wave of unrest occurred far away from Moscow, in the distant capital of Kazakhstan, Alma-Ata. There on December 17, students and young workers gathered by the thousands in what was then still known as Brezhnev Square. They came to protest the removal of an ethnic Kazakh from the republic's top Party position and his replacement by a Russian. They carried signs with the slogan KAZAKHSTAN FOR THE KAZAKHS and sang patriotic songs. In the evening, some in the crowd dispersed, but thousands remained to stage a sit-down strike in front of the Central Committee building.

Finally, according to eyewitness accounts, the authorities moved—first with water cannon; then with trucks. In the melee, a young girl was crushed by one of the vehicles and a struggle broke out. The police and soldiers moved in and beat students mercilessly with truncheons and sticks. The demonstration at the square had been suppressed, but the authorities went after the students and workers at their university and schools. One Kazakh eyewitness claims that soldiers tore into residence halls and threw students who resisted out of dormitory windows. In all, several thousand protesters were said to have been arrested. Estimates of the toll of dead range from a couple dozen to nearly three hundred. Hundreds were wounded, and hundreds were later expelled from the university and polytechnic institute. To this day, the Soviet authorities have thwarted an open and thorough inquiry and insist that only two died in the demonstrations. But the event had signaled that ethnic unrest was about to reemerge as a major factor in Soviet politics.

In 1987, movements for national rights were given a further stimulus when Mikhail Gorbachev released hundreds of political prisoners—the bulk of them nationalist activists from the non-Russian republics—from the Soviet prisons and forced-labor camps. Many of them returned to their homes and began to rebuild the national rights organizations sundered by the repression of the Brezhnev era. At the same time, even as ecological issues were creating a new opportunity for independent public organization, non-Russian intellectuals were once again raising the issue of granting Ukrainian, Byelorussian, and other non-Russian languages the status of "state language" in their republics.

By the summer of 1987, mass demonstrations were beginning to break out around the USSR. Five thousand Latvians gathered in Riga to commemorate the forced deportation of thousands of their countrymen in 1941. In July, around one thousand Crimean Tatars came to Moscow to protest the forced deportation of their entire nation by Stalin. A similar protest near Tashkent by five thousand Crimean Tatars was broken up by the authorities. In October, several thousand protesters demonstrated in Armenia and several hundred nationally minded Byelorussian youth marched in Minsk.

The year 1987 was a landmark in Soviet history. It marked the rise of independent organizations, dubbed in the Soviet press as the *nyeformaly*—"informals." The vast majority of those groups began forming in the non-Russian republics. The year also saw the rapid emergence of a lively underground press. Although the new periodicals were generally copied on carbon paper and distributed by hand, they were providing a new outlet for nationalist and separatist ideas.

In the atmosphere of greater press openness and with the release of most political prisoners, the climate of fear that had characterized the Brezhnev era was rapidly diminishing. And by early 1988, the USSR witnessed the eruption of mass protests in a number of non-Russian republics. In early 1988, independent activism reached a new benchmark with a demonstration in Yerevan on February 23: Around one million Armenians called for the transfer of the predominantly Armenian region of Nagorno-Karabakh to their republic. By the summer, 40,000 protesters led by the National Self-Determination Association were pressing for outright Armenian independence.

On June 21, 1988, on the eve of the Nineteenth Communist Party Conference, over 50,000 Ukrainians took to the streets of Lvov in unsanctioned protests for national rights. At the same time, Azerbaijanis were organizing mass protests in Baku, and violent ethnic conflict erupted between their countrymen and Armenians. By September 1988, a rapidly growing national movement in the Baltic republics was bringing out as many as 300,000 protesters into the streets of Tallinn, Estonia. When October arrived, it was Byelorussia's turn, as 10,000 nationalists marched for cultural and political autonomy. Demonstrations of as many as 100,000 took place in Tbilisi, Georgia, on November 12 under banners proclaiming LONG LIVE INDEPENDENT GEORGIA and AN END TO RUSSIFICATION!

By the early autumn, a new phase in the movement of the non-Russians had been reached with the creation of the popular fronts. Initially, these movements were self-styled citizens' initiatives to "support perestroika." Some Western experts felt that they were initiated by liberal Communist Party activists eager to bolster Gorbachev in his struggle to purge old-line, Brezhnev-style conservatives. But very early on, it became clear that for the non-Russians who flocked to the popular fronts, reform of the Soviet Union meant national sovereignty if not outright independence. The Estonian Popular Front, the Latvian Popular Front, and Sajudis, the Lithuanian Movement to Support Reform, were the first organizations to hold founding congresses. They soon became powerful organizations around which hundreds of thousands of Baltic citizens would unite.

Simultaneously, popular fronts emerged among the Byelorussians, Ukrainians, Georgians, Azerbaijanis, Uzbeks, Moldavians, Tajiks, and Turkmenians. A similar national organization also was active in Armenia.

In 1989 and 1990, the USSR saw even more remarkable ferment, growing organizational strength of independent groups, and heightened political pressure for national self-determination. A major breakthrough for the movements for national sovereignty was achieved in March 1989 with the defeat of many Communist Party candidates in elections to the USSR's Congress of People's Deputies. In the Baltic States, the popular fronts swept the elections, and supporters of similar groupings were elected in the Ukraine and Armenia. Many town and city councils were taken over by newly elected candidates from democratic and pro-independence groups.

The year 1989 saw the emergence of independent trade unions in Latvia and Lithuania and of militant strike committees in the coal mining regions of the Ukraine and Kazakhstan. General strikes motivated by a rising tide of nationalism became a regular feature on the Soviet landscape in Georgia, Western Ukraine, Azerbaijan, and Armenia.

Violence and tragedy were also part of the nationalist and ethnic ferment. In Georgia, Soviet troops killed peaceful demonstrators. Conflict erupted between Meshkhetian Turks and Uzbeks, Abkhazians and Georgians, and in Kazakhstan. And the death toll mounted in tragic confrontations over territory between Armenians and Azerbaijanis.

In 1990, there was no letup in the bloodletting. January saw the explosion of violence in Baku, Azerbaijan, where anti-Armenian pogroms led to the deaths of thirty, before the violence was stopped largely through the intercession of Azerbaijani democratic activists. Such activists had helped spirit Armenians, Russians, and Jews out of the city. But days after the violence had ceased, Soviet troops entered Baku and proceeded to impose a brutal military rule in which nearly 150 civilians were killed. In the days that followed, the Soviet military moved to repress the Popular Front and other independent groups. In February, more than twenty were killed and five hundred injured in antigovernment riots in Dushanbe, the capital of Tajikistan. In May, blood was shed in Armenia, where dozens were mowed down by the Soviet Army in what dissidents said was an attempt to provoke unrest as a pretext for crushing proindependence forces. And in June 1990, violence in Kirgizia pitted impoverished Uzbeks and Kirgiz in a struggle over land rights.

The Gorbachev Effect

In April 1989, Aleksandr Yakovlev, a Politburo member and perhaps Gorbachev's closest confidant and ally, admitted candidly to a Georgian member of the Congress of People's Deputies, the filmmaker Eldar Shengelaya, "We just never expected national feelings to arise as they have."

Such an honest admission tells us a great deal about the thinking of Mikhail Gorbachev and the team of insiders he has assembled to help restructure the moribund Soviet state and economy. Many of the new members of the Gorbachev team are respected academics, competent technical experts; in short, they are pragmatically oriented technocrats. With a technocratically, rather than an ideologically, oriented team around him, Gorbachev was ill-equipped to understand the depth of feeling that is attached to such ideas as nationalism and cultural heritage. His experience of ethnic aspirations, too, was exceedingly limited. Gorbachev was the first Soviet leader since Lenin who had not served in a multinational setting: He spent his formative political years in Stavropol, where Russians make up about 90 percent of the local population, before making the move to Moscow.

In the past, Communist Party leaders—Stalin, Khrushchev, and Brezhnev, most prominently—had cut their political teeth on the knotty national question. Stalin served as the commissar for national affairs, and, as an ethnic Georgian, he was quite familiar with the depth of nationalist sentiments in his native land. Khrushchev served as first secretary in the Ukraine, before being called up to Moscow. He was well skilled in taming the nationalism of the Ukrainians, having presided over the brutal suppression of broad-based resistance to Western Ukraine's incorporation into the USSR in 1939. There, a substantial guerrilla movement waged a fierce war until 1949 against the Soviets and across the border against the Kremlin's Polish Communist allies. Brezhnev, too, emerged out of the Ukrainian crucible, albeit in the less nationally conscious city of Dnepropetrovsk. Even the short-lived leaders, Yuri Andropov and Konstantin Chernenko, had important experience of national issues. Andropov, as head of the KGB, had supervised the suppression of nationalist dissent throughout the USSR, and Chernenko had been posted in Moldavia.

Gorbachev's inexperience in ethnic and national issues revealed itself in a series of blunders early on in his tenure. While on a highly publicized visit to the Ukraine in June of 1986, the Soviet general secretary made an embarrassing mistake that offended the indigenous people's national sensitivities. In the midst of an impromptu street conversation in the Ukrainian capital, Kiev, and before an audience of millions of Soviet television viewers, Gorbachev confused Russia with the current Soviet Union and offended Ukrainian sensibilities, stating:

> Listen, we coped after the Imperialist war, after the civil war, when the country was in ruins. . . . Nothing was left after that. But we coped. We coped. They predicted Russia would never rise again after the war. But we rose again. . . . For all the people who are striving for good, Russia—er, the Soviet Union, I mean—that is what we call it now, and what it is in fact—for them it is a bulwark.

He compounded this blunder with an early policy mistake. In replacing a corrupt, longtime leader of the Kazakhstan Party apparatus, the Kazakh Dinmukhammed Kunayev, Gorbachev opted for a clever, efficient ethnic Russian, with little experience in Kazakhstan—Gennady Kolbin. The appointment of the technocratic outsider outraged the Kazakh populace, and led to the mass student-led demonstrations in front of the Party headquarters in Alma-Ata. This was Gorbachev's baptism of fire. It was more than three years until the Soviet leader grudgingly conceded his tactical error: He elevated Kolbin to a top post in Moscow and replaced him with Nursultan Nazarbayev, a native Kazakh.

Despite the Gorbachev team's initial surprise at the rise of national sentiments, today they are well aware that the mass protests in the non-Russian republics are not isolated or random manifestations of pent-up discontent. They realize that such protests are part of a profound national awakening that is challenging the imperial basis of the Soviet centralized state. Moreover, this national rebirth is accompanied in most of the USSR's republics by an upsurge in independent cultural activity, by intensely spiritual rediscoveries of national traditions, by a profound revival of religious faith, and by a substantial independent press published outside the purview of the authorities. This national renaissance also brings with it the emergence of mass-based democratic movements that are challenging the monopoly of power enjoyed by the Communist Party. In most instances, those new movements openly seek to engage in Soviet electoral politics. In the winter of 1989, the non-Russian popular fronts and other independent democratic groups scored remarkable electoral successes in elections for the USSR Congress of People's Deputies. In Lithuania, Latvia, and Estonia, popular fronts swept the elections and even in the Ukraine, long regarded as firmly in the hands of Party hard-liners, the population defeated a fair number of high-ranking Party officials. The results would have been even more impressive had local officials not resorted to vote rigging or antidemocratic manipulation of the nomination process.

By the winter of 1990, proindependence movements had flexed their political muscles once again. In the Baltic republics, where popular fronts had their own newspapers and access to state-run television, proindependence forces scored overwhelming victories. In Latvia, they captured over two thirds of all seats. In Estonia, the Popular Front won 49 of the 105 seats in the Supreme Soviet, while the slate backed by the Estonian Communist Party, which had emphasized its independence from the Communist Party of the Soviet Union, captured 29 seats. In Lithuania, Sajudis-backed candidates won approximately 70 percent of the seats to the republic's legislature, paving the way to their declaration of independence from the USSR. In other republics, such as the Ukraine and Byelorussia, proindependence forces made impressive gains despite being denied access to the mass media and being subjected to relentless mass media smear campaigns. In the Ukraine, 60 percent of the 191 candidates of the Rukh-supported Democratic Bloc won, holding a quarter of the seats in the republic's parliament. Ukrainian nationalists also captured the majority of seats in the regional councils of Lvov, Ivano-Frankivsk, and Ternopil, as well as in the city council of the capital city, Kiev. In Byelorussia, the Popular Front, "Adrazhdeniye," came close to capturing control of Minsk, but lost badly in rural areas and in smaller towns. And in the huge Russian Republic, proreform forces did well in the March 1990 elections, capturing overwhelming control of the Moscow and Leningrad legislatures and establishing a slim proreform majority in the republic's legislature, which only weeks later would elect Boris Yeltsin as Russia's president on a prosovereignty plank.

The upsurge in popular assertiveness among the USSR's many nations is unprecedented since the consolidation of Soviet power. A confluence of factors has led to something exciting and exhilarating—a massive outpouring of popular activism, most of it unofficial and informal, on the part of diverse political, cultural, and social interest groups. Most of that activism, however, is not to be found in the heart of the Soviet empire—in

Russia proper, but on its peripheries. It is here that nearly half the Soviet Union's citizens—its hidden nations—live.

What's in a Name?

The rise of national movements springs from something far more deep-rooted than the mere lifting of the most onerous restrictions of the totalitarian state. The call of the people is for something far more profound than, simply, the necessary amelioration of economic injustices. They have suffered through decades of discontentment, and their struggle has been against a complex state structure that has many of its origins deep in the history of the Russian empire.

For decades, the West's limited understanding of the Soviet Union was best demonstrated by the use of the term "USSR" interchangeably with "Russia," and Soviet citizens were frequently called Russians in a fashionable shorthand. In the 1960s and 1970s, even *The New York Times* consistently employed this imprecision. Such conventions persist to this day in many respected American and British periodicals.

For the nearly 50 percent of the Soviet population that was not Russian, this practice relegated them to a netherworld. The non-Russian peoples became, in essence, hidden nations. Terminological imprecision masked an insensitivity to the cultural richness, history, and ethnic variety of the Soviet population. It also made it easier to ignore the decline of the languages and traditions of distinctive peoples with ancient histories and independent identities. Few voices were raised when individual nations withered, or, as was the case with several dozen small ethnic groups, virtually disappeared under the forces of assimilation, totalitarian rigidity, deportation of entire peoples, censorship, and Russian-dominated culture. The profound spiritual crisis of the deracinated non-Russian peoples lurked just below the surface and was only dimly understood by the rest of the world.

In part, this state of affairs, this hidden reality, was reinforced by the extensive restrictions that were placed on Western correspondents based in the USSR. For decades, their dispatches were Moscow-centered in the extreme. So cumbersome and fruitless was any effort to secure permission to travel, that few correspondents tried. Those who were more adventurous, including Andrew Nagorski of *Newsweek* and David Satter of the *Financial Times*, were punished for their enterprising reporting with expulsion. Today travel is easier. Yet, even so, Moscow-based reporters usually visit the non-Russian regions for only two or three days at a time, often to cover some mass protest or breaking political crisis. They therefore have little chance to immerse themselves more deeply in what are immensely rich cultures, traditions, and political movements. To this date, not a single Western correspondent in the USSR is posted anywhere besides Moscow. Although they have been the topic of numerous specialized academic studies, the non-Russians have still not been the subject of even a single book of reportage. Instead, at best they have been relegated to a cursory chapter or two in books on the contemporary USSR.

Such inadequacies in reporting have helped shape Western consciousness. In turn, the attitudes of Western reporters on ethnic politics were shaped by the conceptions of experts and policymakers back home. In the 1970s and 1980s, such Soviet affairs experts were exceedingly skeptical about the potential for mass unrest among the non-Russian peoples. Although a few Western experts—most notably Helene Carrere D'Encausse, Zbigniew Brzezinski, and Richard Pipes—pointed to the latent potential of the non-Russian factor, the majority of the academic community was increasingly convinced that the force of nationalism in the USSR was losing its potency and had been successfully suppressed by state control.

For decades, the West has ignored the true nature of ethnic relations in the Soviet Union. Americans, in particular, have tended to assume that the Soviet Union, while a multinational state, was becoming a great melting pot of nations, merging through intermarriage, a common Russian language, a common Soviet culture, and mass migration. In part, Americans have projected their own domestic arrangements onto a Soviet setting, believing that the Soviet republics are something more or less akin to the states of their own union.

Yet the Soviet Union remains, in large measure, what it was at its inception, an agglomeration of national republics, usually with a dominant indigenous national group, bound to the center by a complex network of economic links and to political associations revolving around the centralized structure of the Communist Party. The formation of the Soviet Union was accomplished with the defeats of a number of non-Communist independent states in the aftermath of World War I. The collapse of the old Russian empire had meant that new, democratic states could proclaim their independence in the Ukraine, Lithuania, Latvia, Estonia, Georgia, Armenia, and Azerbaijan. And in Central Asia, a powerful insurgency, the Basmachi, valiantly challenged Sovietization between 1918 and 1923. To achieve unification of most of these independent regions required not only the military power of the Red Army, but tactical alliances of the Bolsheviks with some strata of the regions' indigenous patriotic groups. As a result, the early years of Soviet power were characterized by policies of "indigenization" designed to develop loyal local non-Russian Communist elites. This structure was designed to allay local fears about Russian domination. Yet even through its early years, the Party never tolerated the independence of the Communist parties of the constituent republics.

Still, buffeted by rising industrial unrest, wearied by a long war, and, in large measure, driven by the necessity to build support in the struggle against the monarchist White Russians, Lenin and the Bolsheviks had paid more than lip service to the national aspirations of the native non-Russian populations.

The Soviet state formed in 1923 was far from ideal. It was the product of a collision between Marxist-Leninist ideology and local demands for autonomy. It has been described by Harvard historian Richard Pipes as "a compromise between doctrine and reality: an attempt to reconcile the Bolshevik striving for absolute unity and centralization of all power in the hands of the party, with the recognition that the empirical fact of nationalism did survive the old order. It was viewed as a temporary solution only, as a transitional stage to a completely centralized and supra-national world-wide soviet state." Pipes notes that although the Bolsheviks destroyed all rival parties, centralized power, and eliminated independent institutions, they also granted non-Russians two important concessions: "constitutional recognition of the multinational structure of the Soviet population" and the establishment of the "national-territorial principle as the base of the state's political administration."

In the light of this very narrow interpretation of federalism, some may be surprised that to this day, the Soviet constitution reflects the notion of a formally voluntary Union: Article 70 of the current Soviet constitution (ratified in 1977) asserts the "free self-determination of nations and the voluntary association of equal Soviet Socialist Republics," and Article 72 states that "each Union Republic shall retain the right freely to secede from the USSR." While the Soviet constitution itself has guaranteed since its first version in 1924 the right of secession from the union, it goes without saying that, in practice, the right was suppressed. The few bold souls who dared try to exercise that right were subjected to brutal repression. One case in point is the Ukrainian dissident leader Levko Lukyanenko. A lawyer by training, Lukyanenko was a thirty-three-year-old firebrand when he decided to test his rights under the law. In 1960, he created the Ukrainian Peasant and Worker Party, and included in its platform a call for a referendum on the secession of the Ukraine from the USSR. The call, made at the height of the Khrushchev era, brought a swift and vicious response. Lukyanenko was sentenced to death by shooting "for treason." The sentence was later commuted to a fifteen-year term of imprisonment. Lukyanenko, today the chairman of the opposition Ukrainian Republican Party and deputy to the Ukrainian Supreme Soviet, has spent twenty-six of the last twenty-nine years in prison, forced labor, and exile—a punishment for invoking a constitutionally protected right. Only on April 3, 1990, under pressure of growing nationalist ferment, did the Supreme Soviet adopt an extremely onerous and drawn-out procedure for the secession of constituent republics from the USSR.

Although the roots of centralized domination were in place in the 1920s, there was some relaxation in the cultural sphere. Millions of formerly illiterate non-Russians were educated in their native languages, and some economic prerogatives remained with the republics, particularly during the period of Lenin's New Economic Policy. The process of *korenizatsiya* ("indigenization") was introduced in 1923 to win the hearts and minds of the non-Russian citizens of the new state and to build a loyal non-Russian Communist cadre. As the years passed, and as a consequence of Stalin's relentless drive toward the fulfillment of the Bolshevik imperative of centralization and concentration of power, the rights of the non-Russians were eroded. By the 1930s, the privileged role of the Russians was openly asserted and celebrated, while a brutal purge of the non-Russian elites was conducted. Though ethnically a Georgian, Stalin revealed himself to be an extreme Russian chauvinist in his policies. For example, he toasted the Nazi surrender thus: "I drink firstly to the health of the Russian nation because it is the leading nation of all nations belonging to the Soviet Union . . . it earned in this war general recognition as the guiding force of the Soviet Union among all the peoples of our country."

After Stalin died and his security chief, Lavrenty Beria, was purged, *Izvestia*, the Soviet government's daily newspaper, proclaimed a continuity in this chauvinistic celebration of the Russians, when it declared in July 1953: "The Russian people rightfully merited recognition as the most outstanding, the directing nation of the USSR." Under Leonid Brezhnev, the ambitious aim of creating a monolithic "Soviet people" reached a modern-day apogee. The Soviet leader raised the Russian ante further when he claimed that "the revolutionary energy, the selflessness, diligence and profound internationalism of the Great Russian people have rightfully won them the sincere respect of all the peoples of our socialist homeland." It was, "above all, the Great Russian people," Brezhnev said, who strengthened and developed the "mighty union of equal peoples."

Mikhail Gorbachev's putative mentor Yuri Andropov, too, was a proponent of this line. In his first major speech as the new Soviet leader in 1983, the former KGB chief offered his "gratitude to the Russian people [without whom] in none of the republics would the present achievements have been conceivable."

Other articles in the Communist press of the 1980s extolled the Russians as "first among equals" and a nation with a "special role" in the development of Soviet society. The Gorbachev years, too, have echoed similar tones. In September 1989, the Communist Party unflinchingly pronounced "Russia . . . the consolidating principle of our nation" and told non-Russians that Russia "made a decisive contribution to the elimination of the backwardness of the outlying national districts."

Decades of such paeans have had a clear effect on the national con-

sciousness of non-Russians. The resentment such glorification fostered is
only today revealing itself with full force. It is quite obvious why the
exalted Russians have been the group most reluctant to rise up and challenge the system.

For seven decades, the Soviets masked the true state of ethnic relations in their domain by projecting two simultaneously false images: one,
of their own polity as a voluntary agglomeration of peoples linked by the
promise and success of "real, existing socialism"; and the other, of the
Soviet Union as the foremost ally of national liberation movements opposed to "Western imperialism." Today, both those images have lost their
luster. Soviet leaders are widely acknowledging the economic failure of
the centrally planned Soviet economy; and Mikhail Gorbachev is shaping
an *entente cordiale* with the Western industrial democracies. Such a
foreign policy objective has meant the abandonment of Soviet "anti-
imperialist" rhetoric for the promise of greater East-West trade.

Still, the outward complexity of the Soviet Union's ethnic mix continues to mask the underlying basis of national relations in the empire.
While, outwardly, the USSR appears as an intricate latticework of over
one hundred separate nations, ethnic relations in the USSR are not hopelessly tangled and inapproachable. The USSR consists of a handful of
larger nations. Indeed, ten ethnic groups make up over 90 percent of the
Soviet population. And the pattern is even more simple, for out of 287
million Soviet citizens, 147 million are Russians, 43 million are Ukrainians, and around 55 million are ethnic Turks. Those three groups alone
account for nearly 85 percent of the Soviet population.

According to the 1989 census, Russians currently represent a little over
half (50.8 percent) of all Soviet citizens. Of those, the vast majority (81.3
percent) live in the territory of the Russian Soviet Federated Socialist
Republic, one of the fifteen constituent republics. Similarly, the hidden
nations now hold, in the majority, their own hidden peoples. In each of
the fifteen republics, with the exception of Kazakhstan, the indigenous
population constitutes the majority, and in an overwhelming number of
republics more than two thirds, of the population. According to the recent
census figures, these proportions are increasing.

For these diverse peoples, Soviet rule has meant a constant, wide-
ranging attack on the integrity of national cultures. Some distortions have
arisen because of the widespread Communist politicization of culture.
Such distortions affect Russians and non-Russians alike. But non-Russians
have borne the heaviest burden of the USSR's policies. The central government has fostered the Russian language as a kind of all-encompassing
cultural cement to hold the union together, and it has glorified aspects of
Russian tradition, particularly its imperial past.

The introduction of such policies led to decades of profound cultural
degradation. Native cultures and traditions faded, and were replaced by

a superficially Russian culture drained of its spirituality and rendered empty and vapid by totalitarianism. Today, however, national pride is reasserting itself and these once hidden nations are at the center of a storm of protest and political mobilization that challenges the fundaments of Soviet rule. In the more open and frank atmosphere of glasnost, they are beginning to challenge the official Soviet doctrine that, with the creation of the Soviet Union, a new fraternity of peoples was created voluntarily out of the aspirations of sovereign nations.

The Soviet Man

In the 1970s, the now officially reviled period of Leonid Brezhnev's rule, a new twist on the idea of nationality was added—the concept of the "Soviet man." It was argued that as the "socialist" Soviet society moved inexorably toward Communism, so too a new type of human being was emerging—internationalist in outlook, Communist in ideals, severed forever from the old order's parochialisms, patriotisms, and nationalisms, which Soviet rule had supplanted. The affirmation of the inevitable, natural movement toward the Communist man created both disturbing and dismaying formulations. Stalin, for example, had laid the groundwork for the Brezhnevite "Soviet man" when he proclaimed and posited an astonishing revolutionary faith in his exotic work *Marxism and Linguistics:*

> After the victory of socialism on a world scale we will have . . . hundreds of national languages from which at first the most enriched single zonal languages will emerge as a result of lengthy economic, political, and cultural cooperation of nations, and subsequently the zonal languages will fuse into one common international language . . . neither German, nor Russian, nor English, but a new language which has absorbed the best elements of the national and zonal languages.

This concept, carrying within it the optimistic aim of creating a new society and new type of citizen, was given further, more elaborate theoretical impetus in the 1970s, long after Stalin's passing, by the Communist Party's hard-line ideological czar, Mikhail Suslov. According to the Ukrainian Party chief Petro Shelest, Suslov's colleague on the Politburo until his purge in 1973, the Kremlin's chief ideologist provided the theoretical underpinnings for the notion of *sliyaniye*—the "merger of nations." In practical terms, that "merger" was not remotely natural. It was conducted with a high degree of coercion and, oftentimes, outright repression. At the center of this approach to "nationalities" was the policy of Russification—the compulsory learning of Russian and the use of the Russian language by the institutions of party and state authority in the non-Russian republics. Russification was particularly advanced in the

Ukraine and Byelorussia, whose languages, while differing from Russian more than Spanish differs from Portuguese, and somewhat less than Spanish from Italian, were the ideal locus of Russificatory efforts. It was Suslov's personal belief and the Kremlin's apparent conclusion that Russian dominance of an increasingly non-Russian USSR would be assured if the Russian bloc were to be joined by the other two Slavic-speaking nations in the empire. Russification, according to this approach, was to be used as an instrument for stability—the creation of a Russian-speaking Slavic majority.

Interestingly, although Russification had also been a mainstay of the Soviet state under Stalin and Khrushchev, Brezhnev and Suslov revived it in the 1970s with an almost missionary zeal. The policy, however, was not a novel construct of Communist totalitarianism. Like many features of statecraft in the Soviet Union, it had antecedents in the prerevolutionary czarist empire. As the eminent British historian of nationalism, the late Hugh Seton-Watson, has written in his *The History of the Nation State*, the leaders of the powerful Russian nation "considered it their task, and indeed their moral duty to impose their nationality on all their subjects— of whatever religion, language or culture. As they saw it, by drawing these people upwards into their own superior culture, they were conferring benefits upon them; while at the same time they were strengthening their state by creating within it a single homogeneous nation."

Such policies came into vogue in the middle of the nineteenth century and were given ideological shape and coherence in the doctrine of "official nationality" formulated under Czar Nicholas I. The doctrine became the ideology of the conservative Alexander III and was carried out as well by his reactionary successor, Nicholas II. The policy included the introduction of czarist decrees (*ukazes*) that banned the use of non-Russian languages in publishing and education.

While the Soviet totalitarian state did not go quite so far as to rigidly restrict non-Russian publishing and education, it created various career incentives for those who were Russian speakers and a "voluntary" policy of Russification was introduced as the counterpart of political centralism. Today, even among some liberal Russians, one still encounters the notion that the introduction of the Russian language and culture had a civilizing effect on the more backward nations, particularly those of the East. Among those who hold to this view are such impeccable anti-Stalinists as the exiled writer and scientist Zhores Medvedev and his brother, the historian and deputy to the Supreme Soviet, Roy Medvedev.

For the canny ideologue Suslov and his superior Brezhnev, the non-Russian nations were not only a source of potential instability and an impediment to the exercise of total central control, they were a potential obstacle to scientific progress and economic growth. After all, the single economic network needed a single language in order for the wheels of commerce to turn easily and efficiently. Unless effectively Russified, the non-Russians also could prove unreliable members of the Red Army. Such Russification made eminent sense for the powerful Soviet military and its requirements for coordinated command and control.

Today, the Soviet authorities are slowly edging away from some of these now discredited tenets. Leading Party figures are beginning to acknowledge that they have created a gigantic muscle-bound, inefficient system of economic, social, cultural, and political institutions. This system has, in turn, led to the current economic crisis. Still, it is equally apparent that the leaders of the Communist Party are not about to orchestrate the dissolution of their superpower state into a series of smaller, weaker geopolitical entities. Mikhail Gorbachev's views on this matter have been made explicit in a series of statements in the summer and fall of 1989. Gorbachev has left no doubt that the USSR, as currently constituted, is indivisible. Moreover, the ruling Communist Party itself must remain a unitary multinational entity, implicitly dominated by the majority Russian population—the bedrock of a strong union. Gorbachev has lashed out at "separatists," warning that their formulas are incendiary and exceedingly dangerous. He and the Party have rejected and unsuccessfully resisted efforts to pry loose the Communist parties of the Baltic republics from the control of the center. By contrast, Gorbachev is willing to hold out the prospect of significant economic and cultural autonomy. The real question—which only the course of events will answer—is whether such cultural and economic concessions when put into practice will placate or only further fuel the great awakening of peoples that is occurring throughout the Soviet Union.

According to Soviet doctrine, the USSR's many nations and "nationalities" are amicable partners in a voluntary union—a union in which there is social justice, ethnic equality, and fraternity among peoples. But the reality has been radically different. Resentments among national groups have been deep-seated. In the 1960s and 1970s, there were sporadic eruptions of interethnic conflicts, frequently in the form of violent street fights and soccer riots.

Ethnic resentments were also reflected in a broad lexicon of ethnic slurs that reflect underlying attitudes. Among Russians, the pejorative for Armenians is *Armyashka* ("little Armenian"); Central Asians and the darker-skinned Caucasian peoples (Georgians, Armenians, and Azerbaijanis) are called *Chernozhopy* ("black asses"); Ukrainians are called *Khokhly*, a slur that connotes stupidity and stubbornness. In turn, Ukrainians and Lithuanians call Russians *Katsapy*, a pejorative of unknown etymology and meaning. Central Asians and the feared and hated Chinese are called *Kosoglazy* ("slant eyes") or *Ploskomordy* ("flat snouts") and even *Zhopomordy* ("ass faces"). Ukrainians, many of whom have pursued military careers as noncommissioned officers, are called *Makaronniki* ("macaronis") for their corporal or sergeant stripes. In Russian, the widely used slur *Zhid* means "yid" or "kike." Such phrases are heard quite frequently in ethnically homogeneous settings. They also are widespread in the Soviet Army, where young men from different ethnic groups are thrown into an ethnically diverse setting for the first time in their lives. In 1988 and 1989, as national self-assertion grew in most of the Soviet republics, many non-Russians claimed that their young men were being killed while on military service, as a result of growing interethnic tensions and Russian resentment.

Insensitivity to other peoples reveals itself in many ways in Soviet society. Only recently have ethnic minorities begun to raise their voices against manifestations of such rudeness. In June 1989, one prominent Uzbek writer was disturbed and justifiably outraged at a recently published Russian handbook on dog breeding that offered Uzbek and other Turkic names as suggestions for the names of canine pets. Among those suggested by the handbook's author as appropriate were Rafik, Alisher, Akbar, Anwar, and Mukhtar. The article reminded its readers that "friendship begins with respect."

Clearly, respect is in short supply in the sphere of intergroup relations. Even the widely used *natsmen*, an acronym meaning "national minority," is a latter-day pejorative. Connoting "colonial" or "wog," it is today applied to the non-Russians indiscriminately in everyday conversation. It reflects an everyday culture in which national tensions are far from resolved, and are percolating very near the surface.

Ever mindful of the power of words to alter perceptions, Soviet doctrine has even coined a new term for the peoples of the USSR: "nationalities." That formulation suggests a new category less fully authentic than that represented by the term "nation." It helps to conveniently hide the fact that the USSR is composed of a series of fully fledged nation states and, as Zbigniew Brzezinski has reminded us, contributes to the obfuscation of Soviet reality.

The Last Great Empire

Just as with culture, governance, and politics, the demographics and geography of national and ethnic life in the USSR may appear to be hopelessly confusing or intricate. But, despite this outward complexity, there are, broadly speaking, national winners and losers in the USSR. For the Soviet Union is the last great empire. Decades after the decolonization of Africa, after the British retreat from India, the French defeat in the Battle of Algiers, and the withdrawal of Portugal from Mozambique and Angola, the Soviet Union is beginning to confront a challenge to its very nature.

Some pundits and policy experts, both in the Soviet Union and in the West, have argued that Gorbachev has made a terrible miscalculation in consenting even to a modest relaxation of central control in the area of national relations. Those critics fail to appreciate the depths of national discontent and the resultant popular mobilization. Moreover, they appear to underestimate the intended focus of Gorbachev's economic reforms. The principal aim of the program is the release of the creative economic powers latent in the Soviet population. For the non-Russians, such an aim cannot be attained without the dissemination of power from the center to the peripheries. Thus, the many ills that confront the Soviet Union cannot be solved unless the Soviet Union's national question is openly discussed and forthrightly resolved. The real question is whether the USSR can survive the resolution of that issue. Apparently, Gorbachev and his team believe that it can. But the factors in the equation keep shifting. And the intensity of the political revival of the hidden nations grows with every passing day.

Even beneath the coercive tranquility of the Brezhnev-Suslov period, an idealized image of ethnic relations could not hope to approach reality. For the recent emergence of nationally conscious, patriotic movements had its roots deep in history, and its antecedents in the 1960s and 1970s. One scholar, Ludmilla Alexeyeva, conducted an extensive study of mass protests in the post-Stalin–pre-Gorbachev era. She found that from the mid-1950s to the mid-1980s, the overwhelming proportion of the dozens of protests, mass demonstrations, strikes, and violent clashes had occurred in the non-Russian republics. Soviet leaders recognized the incendiary nature of national discontent, attempting to deal with it through propaganda, coercion, and repression. The end result was that more than two thirds of all known political prisoners during the Brezhnev era were non-Russians, the majority of them from the Ukraine and the Baltic States. There were published vast numbers of books and pamphlets slandering national rights advocates. Such propaganda tracts bore titles like *Judaism Without Embellishment* and *The Trident and the Star of David* (a text suggesting nefarious links among Western security services, Ukrainian nationalists, and Jewish rights activists). The Russian-dominated media became a principal instrument for combatting nationalism. And the culturally and nationally rootless segment of the working class—the most materially deprived segment—was used as the cement of an idealized "internationalism."

Despite these symptoms of a deep-seated illness within the Soviet imperial system, the majority of Western experts accepted the view that the USSR was an inherently stable entity. But the fact is that, today, even Mikhail Gorbachev acknowledges that no question is more decisive to the success or failure of reform, no issue is more critical to the Soviet Union's future, than that of growing nationalism.

For many in the West, the very challenge of grappling with the unwieldy idea of the USSR as a nation of separate nations, with a multiplicity of diverse interests, has proven unnecessarily complicated. For Western policymakers, nationalism in the USSR has seemed to be at best a secondary factor in understanding Soviet global conduct or the inner workings of the all-powerful Party and state.

In this light, it must be acknowledged that the West has contributed to making "hidden nations" out of the Ukrainians, Azerbaijanis, Armenians, Georgians, Byelorussians, and other non-Russians. And Soviet propaganda has taken advantage of Western propensities to intentionally mask an ethnically and politically complex matrix of interests and aspirations.

As a result of that tendency, the West knows little about what these exceedingly diverse nations want, what is the level of their political culture, what their agenda is, and how they view their future place in the Soviet Union. At times, it seems as if a kind of bias has emerged that sympathizes with the imperial center, and the non-Russian movements are, at best, offhandedly dismissed as backward-looking, opposed to modernization and reform. At worst, they are suspected of antidemocratic tendencies—xenophobic, violent dictatorships in the making.

In recent years, there have been a few pioneering writers and political specialists in the West who warned that the multinational Soviet society was an unnatural and unstable entity that might one day begin to unravel. It was, they maintained, certain to be a source of lasting political instability. Yet theirs was long a minority view, ignored in the rush for cordial relations.

Attention to this issue was more evident during the height of the cold war in the 1950s and 1960s. It was in that period that first Radio Liberation and later Radio Liberty were created by the United States to broadcast uncensored information in the languages of the non-Russian peoples. Yet even then, in the West's approach, the idea of the Soviet Union as colonial empire was subordinated to the dominant, anti-Communist critique.

But by the time of the Nixon-era detente, such concepts as the defense of the national rights of the non-Russian nations came to be regarded as retrograde, a holdover of the cold war, an obstacle to the necessary East-West rapprochement, in short as an unwelcome intrusion into the United States-Soviet relationship. During the Nixon-Ford years, the prerogatives of detente banished the non-Russians to the back burner of policy concerns. And under United States President Jimmy Carter, even the annual commemoration of Captive Nations Day was forgotten. President Carter's noble advocacy of global human rights linked American government interventions almost exclusively to the personal fate of individual dissidents, and not to the fate of nations. During the early years of the Reagan administration, a turnaround occurred in United States policy, most notably at the United Nations, where, under Ambassador Jeane J. Kirk-patrick and her counselor Carl Gershman, the United States began articulating a coherent view of the rights of nations, including the USSR's national minorities, by counterposing the Wilsonian view of national sovereignty with that offered by Leninism. Emphasis, too, was placed on the Baltic States, whose forced incorporation into the USSR is not recognized by the United States government.

The years of Western silence and shortsightedness notwithstanding, the contradictions that issue from national inequity have reappeared. And in the Soviet Union today, there is a new spring of nations, akin to two periods in modern history—the Europe of 1848 and the Russian empire of 1905.

In 1848, European nations rose, after a protracted cultural flowering, to make a quick dash for freedom. Then the names of revolutionary nationalists like Italy's Mazzini and Garibaldi and Hungary's Petofi and Kossuth were inextricably linked with representative governance and democracy. The struggle was waged in an atmosphere of infectious international solidarity. When a Polish rising was crushed by the Prussians in May of that fateful year, thousands of workmen and students gathered in Paris's Place de la Concorde to shout, "Vive la Pologne." After Kossuth was driven into exile and his revolution crushed, tens of thousands of New Yorkers poured out to greet him in a massive, enthusiastic show of support. He was lionized by United States editorialists and hailed by the houses of Congress.

The idea of nationalism and the struggle for independence from empire had been celebrated a generation earlier in the poetry of Byron and Shelley. Greece's struggle for independence from Ottoman rule became a byword for liberal democratic values of the generation of the 1820s. Indeed, it was the famous failed Greek rising against the Turks at Missalonghi that was the first cry of that century's hidden nations submerged by empire. Then came Shelley's revolutionary lament for the internal contradiction of empire: "And empires gleam, like wrecks in a dissolving dream."

While 1848 was, as Lewis B. Namier wrote, "the revolt of the intellectuals," that spring of nations also had its decidedly anti-intellectual aspects. Not all the writings then were scrupulously democratic. Still, the intelligentsia of that age felt, rightly or wrongly, the inexorable pull of the people and a seamless kinship with the nation. That link appears to be palpable as well in the burgeoning national movements of the Soviet Union today. Here, too, journalists and novelists, playwrights and poets, musicians and artists, are the central players in a high drama of protests, strikes, mass rallies, and rising expectations. And the once rarefied issues of language and the recovery of a vanished past occupy the thoughts of many more than the schooled elites.

In a brief essay for the *Times Literary Supplement*, written in 1923, Lewis B. Namier, characterized the state of affairs in the last century:

> About 1848 the nationalities inside the Habsburg Monarchy formed two marked strata: there were the historic nations—the Germans, Magyars, Italians and Poles—with well-developed upper classes, and therefore with cultural continuity and an articulate political life; and the peasant races—the Czechs, Slovaks, Yugo-Slavs, Ukrainians and Roumanians—who, having in previous centuries lost their upper classes, had practically no historic experience. But with the rise of a new middle-class intelligentsia and the entry of the working classes into political life, the subject races recovered conscious national individuality and entered upon a bitter struggle against the master nations.

The condition of Europe from 1848 to 1914 resembles the processes surrounding the recent movement of the peoples of the USSR. Today among the non-Russians there exist the same strata described by Namier. Among the historic nations are the peoples of the Baltic seacoast—the Lithuanians, Estonians, and Latvians—and the Georgians and Armenians of the Caucasus. Each of those nations has preserved in some measure its cultural continuity and its sense of national political tradition, despite the traumas of Communist repression. There is a middle, transitional stratum—consisting of the Ukrainians, the Byelorussians, and the Azerbaijanis. The former two are Slavic nations, whose ruling classes have been Russified, whose cultural elites have become marginalized, and whose cultural continuity had been disrupted by the carnage of Stalinism. Yet in the Gorbachev years, those peoples have made significant progress in rebuilding their sundered national, cultural, and political institutions. Similarly, the Turkic Azerbaijanis, led by the intelligentsia and workers of Baku, have succeeded in building a sophisticated national movement. These three peoples clearly have reached the point where a "new middle-class intelligentsia" and the working class enter political life.

The remaining large non-Russian nations—the Turkic-speaking Uzbeks and Kazakhs are further behind. The processes of political mobilization are occurring, but their educated middle classes and their working classes are proportionately far less extensive than those of the other mobilized non-Russian peoples. Their more atomized peasantry is still the dominant class in terms of population. But they are clearly embarking on the process of political mobilization.

Standing on the sidelines in this process, there is the single, dominant nation—the Russians—which does possess a clearly defined ruling elite. Russian history is lionized in the state-controlled media and in the education system, but as it has been glorified, it also has been altered and fundamentally distorted. The Russians, as the imperial nation nonpareil, have never developed a sense of the limits of their own ethnos; they have lived instead with only a vague notion of where their state and people

begin and end. So the Russians, as a nation, have not yet spoken deci-
sively and they hold a critical hand in determining whether the Soviet
future will be one of evolution or revolution—one of gradual but certain
democratization or of violent repression and bloody resistance.

While the Europe of 1848 resonates in the events in today's USSR, the
experience of 1905 more precisely defines the contours of the struggles of
the hidden nations. That year, the Russian empire was dealt a severe
setback through its defeat in the Russo-Japanese War. The failure of the
Russian Army created a crisis of confidence in the ruling czarist elite and
encouraged revolutionary agitation and unrest. Still, the year-long revolution of 1905 was, above all, a rising of the Russian empire's
peripheries—populated mainly by the non-Russians. Its eventual failure
resulted from a lack of cohesiveness among the dissatisfied middle classes,
discontented workers, and impoverished peasants.

If nationalism in the nineteenth century was heroic and democratic,
nationalism in the twentieth century took a far different turn, a detour.
National socialism and fascism severed the link between nationalism and
democracy. Today, many in the West, particularly Americans, regard
nationalism as an ideology of extremism and backwardness. For them, the
images of nationalism include Mussolini's jackboot and Hitler's gas cham-
ber, and represent an atavism commingled with irrational paganism in the
metaphors of blood and soil. Contemporary perceptions of nationalism,
too, are shaped by the national liberation struggles conducted against
Western European colonies in Asia and Africa and against United States
geopolitical interests in the rice paddies of Southeast Asia. In this latter
variant, nationalism is linked in Western consciousness to economic backwardness and marginality. It is a manifestation of the rage of the perma-
nently disadvantaged, often erupting into the mass murder represented
by Pol Pot's killing fields. The experience of fascism, decolonization,
Vietnam, and Kampuchea has become part of a mythology that hinders
Americans and Europeans in understanding and endorsing the national
awakening in the Soviet Union. As the essayist William Pfaff has noted,
America's historic failure has been its inability to factor the power and
persistence of nationalism around the world into its foreign policy.

Yet ideologies of democracy are finding new strength precisely in the
new redoubts of nationalism around the unraveling Soviet empire. Poland's Solidarity movement was, after all, driven as much by the logic of
Polish patriotism and wounded dignity as by trade union solidarity. In
Hungary, Czechoslovakia, and East Germany, the new democratic upsurge not only springs from a desire to restore a culture debased by
Marxism-Leninism, but is also inspired by the chilling presence of Soviet
troops. Protesters in the streets of Prague, Warsaw, and Budapest were
driven by an anger at the violation of their national sovereignty as well as

by a generalized unhappiness at the failure of the Russian-imposed Communist economic and social model.

The non-Russian peoples of the Soviet Union feel similarly. They have been brutalized and dehumanized by almost three quarters of a century of totalitarianism.

For the non-Russians, Marxism-Leninism is an alien ideology. In most of the non-Russian republics, after all, the Soviet system was imposed by a foreign Red Army, often aided and abetted by a segment of the Russian-dominated urban population. The Communist revolutions of the non-Russian nations are fictions given reality only by the instruments of the Soviet state's propaganda.

The violence that has erupted in several Soviet republics has fueled the notion that the leaders of the national movements of the non-Russian peoples are voices of atavistic tribal instincts. Yet this popular view verges on being a new form of racism that stems from a near total unfamiliarity with the cultural, religious, and political traditions of most of the non-Russian nations. It reflects the belief that it is far simpler for the West to deal with a single, albeit immensely powerful, economic and territorial entity than to have to confront the Balkanization of the Soviet Union with its potential for unstable border disputes. Ironically, this is the same theory that had permeated the arguments of the Boers in South Africa, of the European colonialists in central and west Africa, and of the British in India.

Yet the idea that the non-Russian national movements are anti-democratic and xenophobic does not stand up to scrutiny. This new Western myth-in-the-making is a latter-day version of a Soviet myth, which has long held that in the USSR, nationalism was a phenomenon of a vanishing generation of antidemocratic extremists—the bourgeois nationalist voices of the displaced capitalist order.

Today, Western policymakers are wary of the disintegration of the Soviet Union. In this, they are not so far from the Soviet authorities themselves. Officials in the U.S. State Department and British Foreign Office as well as leading Sovietologists worry that the newfound nationalism of the non-Russian peoples of the USSR poses a fundamental threat to the processes of glasnost and perestroika. This view has been encouraged by Soviet ideologists—foremost among them the Kremlin's most recent ideological czar, Vadim Medvedev. It also has been repeated by visiting Soviet delegations of skilled propagandists; and it has been whispered to Western diplomats visiting the USSR.

Paradoxically, others in Moscow believe that the national awakening of the peoples of the USSR goes hand in hand with glasnost and perestroika. One proponent of this view is the prominent establishment Communist Vitaly Korotich, the fifty-four-year-old editor of the immensely popular weekly magazine *Ogonyok* (circulation: 3.2 million). Korotich, regarded in the West as a beacon of glasnost, is a paid functionary of a magazine published by the Central Committee of the Communist Party. Yet even he puts to rest fears of an ethnic explosion. The national movements, he believes, are essential to propelling the economic growth of the moribund Soviet system.

The late Dr. Andrei Sakharov also became, in his last months, a strong defender of the responsible agendas of the national movements in the Baltic States, Armenia, and the Ukraine. This towering moral figure clearly did not give credence to the theory that the growing popular fronts might help unsettle the process of democratization.

Somewhat different, however, were the views of leading Communist Party hard-liners. In a major interview published in *Pravda* in August 1989, just weeks before he was purged from the top leadership, the former KGB chief and archconservative Viktor Chebrikov expressed the consensus position of the central Party leadership on the national question. While some Western doomsayers predicted that a crackdown on the increasingly radicalized national movements was likely, Chebrikov suggested that the Party was likely to take a balanced approach, emphasizing the immense advantage of its media monopoly, the use of petty bureaucratic restrictions against the national rights and nationalist movements, and only the occasional, highly selective resort to repression.

Chebrikov admitted that the Party had failed in its goal of promoting "internationalism" and in dampening the appeal of nationalism. However, he also was quick to emphasize that international education would have to retain its "class basis"—code words for propaganda that promotes the territorial integrity of a Russian-dominated, Communist Party-led state. Chebrikov did make some bows to the aspirations of the non-Russian nationalities, acknowledging that "national nihilism"—i.e., the negation of one's ethnic heritage—had contributed to a wide-ranging spiritual crisis in the USSR. As if to balance this admission that not all was well among the USSR's peoples, Chebrikov suggested that the Party was warming to the idea that criminal sanctions would be used against radical advocates of separatism and national rights: "The need for laws on . . . increased liability for fueling national dissension has started to become increasingly tangible."

Chebrikov's pronouncements on the national question came at a time of heightened Communist Party anxiety over the growing strength of the non-Russian movements. It was followed in short measure by a series of sharp attacks on the popular fronts in Lithuania, Latvia, and Estonia, which were vaguely accused of collaboration with "Nazi sympathizers" and charged with "secessionist tendencies." There were many disquieting indications in Chebrikov's interpretation of the Kremlin's "new thinking" on nationalities that the Party might restrict the republics to a very narrow set of prerogatives, reserving for the central government "questions of the political system, the defense and security of the country, the pursuit of foreign policy, the coordination of general tasks in the sphere of the economy, science and culture, the place of the individual, and the dynamic, steady development of the country's national economic complex."

Chebrikov's interview in the authoritative Party daily *Pravda* was far more than a casual statement of his personal views. It was a high-level policy statement that reflects an emerging consensus within the top Kremlin leadership. The bottom line, Chebrikov was unequivocally asserting, was that in a multinational state the supremacy of the union law must be paramount. "Without that, the existence of a united state is inconceivable. Decisions made by the central authorities," Chebrikov was telling *Pravda*'s readers, "must remain immutable."

The Communist Party, which for more than a year had postponed a long-anticipated plenum on the nationalities, felt compelled to state its view on the issue again on August 27, 1989, just four days after as many as two and one-half million Lithuanians, Latvians, and Estonians participated in a 370-mile human chain on the occasion of the fiftieth anniversary of the Hitler-Stalin pact. It had been the largest mass demonstration in the history of the USSR. The Baltic national movements had used the occasion as a dramatic reminder of their forcible absorption into the Soviet Union. But for the CPSU Central Committee such sentiments, though massively supported by the Baltic nations, had to be squelched. The committee's wide-ranging statement on the Baltic States carried within it an implicit warning. "The current situation in the Baltic republics," the Party asserted in a front-page statement in *Pravda*, "is the cause of increasing concern." The process of national revival that was occurring throughout the USSR was a positive development, proclaimed the Party hierarchy. "But," the Central Committee declared, "at a certain stage nationalist, extremist groups took advantage of democracy and openness and gradually began to introduce an unhealthy aspect into the development of events." In language reminiscent of the Brezhnev or Stalin era, the Party declared that these nefarious interests isolated the Baltic republics "from the rest of the country," thus disrupting the "long-standing organically formed links with other Soviet nations." In essence, the Baltic movements were accused of having been usurped by "antisocialist" and "anti-Soviet" elements. This atmosphere, the chilling document argued, was "destructive, anti-Soviet, and antinational."

The Party's pronouncement was intended not only for the assertive Balts. It was also a warning to the other non-Russian peoples—a drawing of the line beyond which they must not cross. Several new formulations were enunciated in what seemed to be a watershed document affecting relations of the Soviet hierarchy with its ethnic minorities. The document even went so far as to remind the Lithuanians, Estonians, and Latvians that their sovereignty could be put in jeopardy: "The very viability of the Baltic nations could be called into question." The warning was clear and implied action: If you move toward separatism, you risk losing the limited sovereignty your republics now have.

Was the Kremlin then signaling the beginning of a wide-ranging crackdown against the non-Russians, and the Balts in particular? In late 1989, such a prospect still seemed far from likely. Rather, the August 1989 document may well have been yet another indication that propaganda was replacing repression as the preferred means for dealing with national assertiveness. Yegor Ligachev, perhaps the quintessential Politburo hardliner, revealed as much in a TV interview one month later, when he noted that it was necessary to wage a war of ideas and to convince people not to accept nationalist slogans. Not only was the Central Committee's chilling proclamation a part of just such a propaganda campaign that has been raging in the Soviet media, its hyperbole was calculated to inject the element of fear into the Baltic political landscape. It was designed to send a strong antinationalist signal in the months that led up to elections to the parliaments of the fifteen republics, where popular fronts were to mount formidable challenges to the Communist Party's political control.

It was no accident that General Secretary Gorbachev was in the Crimea on his annual summer holiday when the Party's strong warning was issued. His absence at a time when the Party issued its hard-line pronunciamento may well have been a product of subtle calculation designed to preserve Gorbachev's image as a decentralizing reformer and democratizer. Gorbachev simply cannot afford to alienate the intelligentsia and qualified workers in the non-Russian republics. The very groups that have given shape to the popular fronts, and other informal movements among the non-Russians, are also the strongest potential allies in his efforts to modernize and reform the moribund Communist system. If he alienates this "knowledge class," perestroika is finished. If he cracks down on this stratum's freedom of expression, glasnost is finished, and with it the distinctive cast of his rule.

Gorbachev left himself yet another opening. While *Pravda* adopted a mercilessly hard line, the assessment of the August 23, 1989, protest by millions in the Baltics and the view of the Baltic popular fronts were more nuanced in *Izvestia*, the government daily.

What, then, were Mikhail Gorbachev's own views on the national question? They were expressed in a meeting with Baltic leaders in early September of 1989. There, he adopted a line of conciliation. Still, just months before, on July 1, 1989, Gorbachev took over the Soviet airwaves to deliver a widely publicized major address on the theme of relations among the nationalities. The twenty-minute address came after a tumultuous month of mounting interethnic turmoil and death in Uzbekistan, Kazakhstan, and Georgia. Speaking in measured, somber, even angry, tones, Gorbachev warned of a "tremendous danger" arising from inter-ethnic conflicts. He resolutely denounced those who were sowing inter-ethnic hatred and fanning the flames of separatism and nationalism. He warned that he would take "the most resolute measures, in accordance with the requirements of law and the people's vital interests, against those who provoke interethnic clashes and call for borders to be redrawn and for the expulsion of national minorities." He used the unfortunate violence of the USSR's long, hot summer to heighten anxiety about nationalism among the more than 35 million Soviet citizens who live outside the confines of their own national republics, asking, "What if the interethnic strife spreads and embraces regions were millions of people of other nationalities live alongside people of the indigenous nationality?" And he went on the offensive against the proponents of independence:

> We must not take the road of destroying . . . and abandoning what the fed-eration has already yielded, which can be magnified within its framework. Therefore, calls for economic autarky and spiritual isolation must be deemed profoundly alien to the vital interests of any people and of the entire society. Their implementation would throw us all a long, long way back and bring immense material and moral losses to each nation and every person.

Gorbachev made an impassioned appeal to the intelligentsia, urging it to behave responsibly and in rather demagogic fashion exhorted the Soviet working class to exercise its internationalist obligations.

In September 1989, just days before the Communist Party plenum to examine the question of interethnic relations, Gorbachev delivered yet another somber-toned address to the nation. In it, he didn't scold the leaders of the non-Russian national movements. Instead, he retreated from his cataclysmic scenarios of ethnic strife and concentrated on exco-riating those alarmists who were opposed to his program of restructuring. He spoke of a "multivoiced chorus" in which "we can hear talks of ap-proaching chaos and talk of a threatened coup, even of civil war." Down-playing the idea that the rise of ethnic movements was tearing the USSR apart, Gorbachev told Soviet citizens, "It is a fact that some people would like to create . . . an atmosphere of alarm, a feeling that there is no way out, a feeling of uncertainty." Instead of retrenching, however, the Soviet leader promised to "continue along the road of planned change." Days later, he would strike at some of those very voices of negativism, purging from the Politburo such hard-liners as Ukrainian Party boss Vladimir Shcherbitsky and former KGB chief Viktor Chebrikov.

In 1990, Gorbachev would alternate between intimidation and nego-tiation. After Lithuania's declaration of independence on March 11, the Soviet president would respond with an economic blockade. By June, however, the Soviet president moved away from confrontation, indicating that he was ready to negotiate with the Baltic States and with all the

USSR's constituent republics about independence or sovereignty within a radically decentralized USSR.

Who the real Gorbachev is and how he will respond to the national question cannot yet be predicted. His response will depend on a number of factors, one of which is whether the movements for national rights will take the road of peaceful protest. But it is clear that for the moment the Soviet leader is aware that any attempt to quash with force the national revival will derail his program of economic reform at home and, in the context of the democratic revolution sweeping Eastern Europe, risk making the Soviet Union a politically and economically isolated state. But there can no longer be any doubt that the national question, as it was called by Marx and later Lenin, clearly had become a critical, and perhaps the central, issue in Mikhail Gorbachev's fifth year in office.

The radicalization of the non-Russian peoples is likely to accelerate in the years to come. The Baltic States, the Ukraine, Byelorussia, and Moldavia, in particular, are likely to be drawn more and more into the orbit of the dramatic democratic ideas reemerging on the Western boundaries of the Soviet Union. As Hungary, Poland, and Czechoslovakia become more and more a part of the West—of a unified Europe—they, in turn, will influence the expectations and agendas of the non-Russian peoples whose borders they abut and whose destinies have for centuries been inextricably linked to theirs. The porous borders that some Soviet republics share with Poland and Hungary are likely to see an influx of independent publications and, with them, of democratic ideas. Polish television, too, is likely to have a radicalizing effect on the Western Ukraine, where it can readily be received and understood. And as Romanians shake their decades-long tyranny and struggle to transform their land into a multiparty democracy, they are likely to have a profound effect on their fellow nationals in the Soviet Union—the Moldavians.

The influences of Poland's Solidarity trade union movement on the Western Ukraine already are apparent. In dusty Chervonohrad, a mere eighteen miles from the Polish border, gritty coal miners announced, in July 1989, the establishment of their own Ukrainian Solidarity trade union movement. In Lithuania, too, an independent trade union organization patterned after Solidarity, the Lithuanian Workers Union, has been launched. Estonian and Latvian workers are following this pattern.

Economic changes and political changes in Eastern Europe are proceeding at such a rapid pace as to threaten to bring the West—its free market economy, political pluralism, democracy, and independent institutions—to the very portals of the last remaining empire.

In the face of these new uncertainties, some verities persist, among them the power of Russian nationalism. While Mikhail Gorbachev has paid some lip service to Great Russian patriotism, he has done so more in an effort to preempt his more reactionary Communist Party rivals than out of any deeply felt sense of his own Russianness. Nonetheless, with the collapse of the legitimacy of the Communist ideology and with mounting calls for separatism by non-Russians, Gorbachev may, in the months and years ahead, be forced to rely on Russian nationalism for its potential to maintain the cohesiveness of the Russian-dominated Party and state structures of the Soviet empire.

Yet this recourse to the last remaining source of imperial legitimacy, though very real, remains a depressing option. For Mikhail Gorbachev, the choice is exceedingly stark: to opt for a reliance on the dark, anti-democratic, and backward-looking tradition of what Lenin called in his cautionary polemics "great power Russian chauvinism" or to choose the path of true confederalism, with a necessary loss of power at the Soviet Union's center.

As the 1990s begin, already there are some signs that for Gorbachev the resort to Russian nationalism and repression is an unpalatable option. Although the Party he heads and the deputy prime minister he put in place—the moderate Leonid Abalkin—had offered a decidedly conservative plan for restructuring relations between the Kremlin and the republics, the Supreme Soviet dealt a rebuff on the centralizing approach to the question of the rights of the non-Russian peoples and republics. On November 20, 1989, the Soviet legislature, the Supreme Soviet, rejected by a vote of 211 to 149 a proposal that restricted the rights of the USSR's constituent republics. They did so because the proposed legislation did not go sufficiently far in providing independence from Moscow's central control.

The effort, led by nationalist-minded legislators from the Baltic republics, could not have succeeded without the tacit support of Gorbachev, as it is well known that no more than 20 percent of the membership of the Supreme Soviet is in the hands of radical reformers.

Growing ferment throughout the Soviet bloc clearly contributed to the change of thinking within the Soviet legislative hierarchy. There should be no doubt that the Gorbachev team's decision to reject as inadequate legislation that restricted the sovereignty of the non-Russian republics, was taken out of a desire to preempt a resurgence of non-Russian mass discontent on the Polish, Czechoslovak, Hungarian, Romanian, and East German model. Another contributing factor was the growing radicalization of views within the parliaments of the non-Russian republics and, more dangerously from the Kremlin's point of view, even among the Communist Party organizations in the non-Russian regions.

In the days before the vote on national sovereignty was taken, the legislature of Soviet Georgia unanimously reaffirmed the "holy and inviolable right" to secede from the USSR and asserted its view that Georgia had been annexed to the USSR as a result of "military intervention and occupation." In so voting, the Georgians affirmed the sovereign rights of their republic following action taken by the legislatures of Azerbaijan, Estonia, Latvia, and Lithuania that had proclaimed the right to veto any legislation passed by the central, USSR legislature. In January 1990 the Communist Party of Lithuania, too, had rebuffed Gorbachev's entreaties and voted for complete independence from the Communist Party of the Soviet Union. Only days later, as Soviet troops moved into Azerbaijan, the legislature there warned that it would proclaim the republic's secession from the USSR unless all Soviet occupation forces were removed from its territory.

In the face of secessionist threats in Azerbaijan, the Soviet authorities were forced to acknowledge that a dialogue with the leaders of the local popular front was inevitable. And as the Baltic States of Lithuania and Estonia moved toward independence in March and April of 1990, the Kremlin's response was one of saber-rattling military maneuvers, and the seizure of key buildings—not of outright repression. This unwillingness or inability of Soviet authorities to introduce full-scale police state repression indicates the power of the independent movements among the non-Russians and augurs well for their survival. It suggests that a full-scale crackdown is not in the immediate offing. Rather, the USSR is headed for a protracted period of ideological battle and skillful use of the mass media. When necessary, the Kremlin is signaling a desire for compromise to avert the resort to martial law that would put an end to the crucial experiments of glasnost and perestroika.

The struggle of the USSR's hidden nations is only beginning. Before it is over, the Soviet Union and the world may well be profoundly transformed.

The Rulers and the Ruled: The Economics of Inequality

Citizens of the USSR of different races and nationalities
have equal rights.

Any direct or indirect limitation of the rights of citizens or establishment of direct or indirect privileges on
a racial or national basis . . . is punishable by law.

—Soviet Constitution, Article 36 (1977)

GREAT MOVEMENTS of people arise from fundamental social causes. Certainly, no movements among the non-Russian peoples could have
emerged on the scale they have without first having firm roots in profound
social, economic, cultural, or political inequalities.

Yet the reality of social and economic injustice had been among the
Soviet Union's darkest secrets. It had been buried by the strictly controlled Soviet press and by the USSR's politically manipulated academic
community. However, in the endless flow of Soviet statistics published in
the USSR, there was clear evidence of profound national and even racial
inequities at the core of daily Soviet life. While the state-run Soviet media
kept this reality from broader public awareness and out of public discourse at home, Western Sovietologists, too, began to pay less and less
attention to the profound ethnic and racial inequalities among the peoples
of the USSR. Similar inequities that existed in the United States began to
be widely reported and subjected to extensive and vigorous debate in the
early 1960s, under pressure from the growing civil rights movement. At
precisely the same time, interest in such inequities in the USSR began to
wane among Western scholars, who became ever more interested in
uncovering the sources of Soviet stability. For Western analysts of the
USSR, the economic disparities among the Soviet Union's peoples had

47

ceased to be a matter of inquiry, and in Sovietological circles the issue of ethnicity and nationalism in Soviet life was no longer regarded as important.

Today, gross inequities among the USSR's nations are one of the main causes of national upheaval. Seven decades after the October Revolution, the promotion and safeguarding of the equality of peoples—rights guaranteed by the Soviet constitution—is a goal very far from realization. Not only has the Communist experiment failed to create equality among the nations of the USSR, but, under Mikhail Gorbachev's rule, such inequity has, in some instances, widened. In broad relief, inequities between Russians and non-Russians are significant. Non-Russians, particularly the Turkic peoples of Soviet Central Asia and the smaller nationalities in the autonomous republics of the Russian Soviet Federated Socialist Republic, are at a profound cultural, economic, educational, and social disadvantage. Despite the many economic privations confronting most citizens of the Russian Republic, it still pays to be Russian in Mikhail Gorbachev's USSR.

The upsurge in non-Russian national discontent that has swept the Soviet Union has brought the long-simmering national problems of the Soviet Union into the international news headlines. The Western media and Soviet affairs experts from the United States and Western Europe have rushed off to the USSR to try to account for this unprecedented outburst of unrest in parts of the USSR that had been all but ignored until now. In its early stages, the nationalist upsurge that began in 1987 was interpreted as a series of isolated phenomena. Group enmities were frequently reported as the products of historic animosities and local political misrule. Yet the persistence of these phenomena has confounded Western commentators, who are still searching for a way to explain wave upon wave of non-Russian protests. And they have found few answers offered by any Soviet academics, because the issue of nationalism in the Soviet Union has long been relegated to the domain of linguistics experts and ethnographers.

Some commentators put forth spectacularly wrong judgments on the root causes of growing non-Russian protests and national conflicts in the Soviet Union. They ignored the essential motivation of the mass protests—the imperial nature of the Party-state system and its social and economic injustices. With time, some press commentators began to draw on the analogy of empire in order to explain the manifestations of nationalism erupting with increasing regularity among the peoples of the Soviet Union. British journalists, mindful of the experience of the twilight of their own empire, in particular, began to employ a few vague references to "colonialism" and "exploitation" in their reporting of unrest among the peoples of the Russian-dominated Soviet state. Yet few commentators have gone beyond examining population statistics and demographics to take a look at the economics of ethnicity in the USSR.

Evidence of inequality is easy to find. During a visit to Yugoslavia in March 1988, even Mikhail Gorbachev himself admitted to a group of reporters that the upsurge in national unrest could be attributed to the fact that the Soviet south had "been neglected for a long time" by past Party leaders. Because the Soviet press has been given a bit of breathing space by glasnost, reporters are increasingly explicit in their discussions of the "nationalities question" as a product of economic and social dissatisfaction.

Still, official Soviet explanations have only hinted at the dimension of the problem and have shied away from analyzing in detail the systematic pattern of advantages enjoyed by ethnic Russians—both those who reside in the Russian Republic and those who occupy disproportionately privileged positions in the fourteen non-Russian republics.

One hundred and forty-seven million ethnic Russians today represent approximately half (50.8 percent) of the Soviet population. But they are the beneficiaries of significant advantages in virtually all spheres of life. A recent Soviet statistical handbook, issued in 1987 to commemorate seventy years of Soviet power, provides ample evidence of this pattern of advantage. Similar trends are confirmed on the basis of statistics contained in 1979 and 1989 census data and culled from other statistical handbooks. The patterns of inequality that follow come from such Soviet sources.

The Russian Soviet Federated Socialist Republic (RSFSR) is the USSR's largest republic with a population of 147 million. Russians make up 81.3 percent of the republic's population. Yet, although it accounts for about 50 percent of the Soviet population, in 1986 the fixed assets of the Russian SFSR amounted to 61 percent of the USSR's fixed assets in construction, industry, and agriculture. Per capita, by the beginning of 1987 there were 46.5 percent more such fixed assets invested in the Russian Republic than in the non-Russian republics.

Under Mikhail Gorbachev, recent trends in capital investment continue to promote this disparity. Within the planned economy, over the years there has been a clear effort to allocate an increasing proportion of resources to predominantly Russian regions, frequently at the expense of the non-Russians. In 1986, Gorbachev's first full year in power, new capital investments in the Russian SFSR rose to 62.4 percent of all Soviet capital expenditures—and in absolute terms were 66 percent greater than for the non-Russian republics. This policy is not new and has had a significant cumulative effect over the years.

Some argue that these inequities are largely the consequence of historic differences in the patterns of development of the various republics.

While that may have been a sound argument in the first decades of Soviet rule, today, after two thirds of a century of central economic planning, the resulting socioeconomic landscape must be regarded as explicitly Soviet. Indeed, the economic growth of some of the republics has been deliberately retarded by Soviet rule: In the Ukrainian SSR, for example, central planning has taken away more than it has provided and there is evidence of economic plundering.

In a 1977 study, Zenon L. Melnyk, professor of finance at the University of Cincinnati, demonstrated that some 20 percent of national income was transferred each year from the Ukrainian SSR to other parts of the Soviet Union. He concluded that that level was "unprecedented in international economic relations." Such income transfers are one reason why Ukrainians and other non-Russians are pressing for the principle of *khozraschet,* or economic accountability, by republic. Such cost accounting, they say, would openly demonstrate the disadvantages conferred on non-Russians. Non-Russians are increasingly denouncing the inequities of the pricing, investment, and allocation decisions of the five-year-plan economic system. Non-Russian popular fronts, therefore, are nearly unanimous in their belief that all economic decisions and control over natural resources should be turned over to the republics. They also are convinced that the State Planning Committee (Gosplan) and the Ministry of Finance have structured prices for commodities to the economic disadvantage of the non-Russian republics and are arguing for new policies that link Soviet pricing to the international market and create internal market mechanisms. At the Congress of the Ukrainian Popular Movement, the Rukh, held in Kiev in September 1989, Volodymyr Chernyak, an economist and member of the USSR Congress of People's Deputies, reflected a growing sentiment among the non-Russian movements when, in his economic keynote speech, he raised the slogan "From a free market to a free Ukraine."

We are by now accustomed to the steady flow of TV reports on the economic hardships faced by the residents of Moscow and other Russian centers. There is no question that millions upon millions of Russians live in appalling conditions. The strike in July 1989 by hundreds of thousands of coal miners in the Kuznetsk Basin and in Vorkuta vividly demonstrated the misery of everyday life. Yet such sharp images of incredible indigence ought to convey all the more clearly the even more disastrous economic status of non-Russians. For Soviet statistics indicate that in broad economic terms, ethnic Russians clearly come out on top.

Although prices throughout the USSR have historically been centrally determined and are identical, blue- and white-collar workers in the Russian SFSR earn over 11 percent more than their counterparts in the non-Russian republics. This national wage gap widens even further in the Russians' favor among collective and state farm workers. Not only do

Russians earn more, they are able to purchase more. Retail trade statistics, which measure per capita purchases of foodstuffs, clothing, electronics, automobiles, and other consumer goods, show a 30 percent advantage for residents of the Russian Republic.

The income and privilege gap that favors ethnic Russians is probably even greater than these statistics show. Even in the non-Russian republics, ethnic Russians command a disproportionate share of the better-paying and influential jobs. They also are provided greater opportunities by the state to settle in the urban centers of the non-Russian republics, where they can take advantage of cultural, educational, and social amenities that are less available in the underdeveloped rural regions.

The Urban Advantage

Anyone who has traveled to the Soviet Union is aware of the vast disparities between urban and rural life. Many rural communities feature ramshackle housing without running water, adequate heating, or telephone service. Most villages are far removed from decent public transportation. Most have no cinemas or cultural centers. In short, villagers live in near total isolation. Consequently, leaders of the non-Russian popular fronts have begun to raise the issue of urbanization, questioning why the cities and towns in their republics are so few in number and pressing for the advancement of their predominantly rural peoples. They also are beginning to focus on opportunities and the extent to which their citizens are able to rescue themselves from the poverty of rural life by entering the industrial work force.

"We need a proletariat," Addurakhim Pulatov, a leader of Uzbekistan's popular front, Birlik, insists. His plea is not purely economic. In the context of Soviet society, it has important political implications, as well. In an ideologically ordered society that regards the industrial proletariat as its most progressive force, the absence of an urban working class places more rural Uzbeks and other non-Russians at a distinct economic *and* political disadvantage. The Communist Party continues to emphasize that its policies are guided by the interests of the industrial working class. As it stands now, because the Soviet working class is disproportionately Russian, the policies of the Party are biased in favor of the Russians.

The statistics on urbanization reveal striking disparities among the republics. On the basis of figures from the 1979 census, 69 percent of the residents of the Russian SFSR lived in cities and towns, while 31 percent were residents of rural areas. In no other republic, except tiny Estonia, was there a higher degree of urbanization. Overall, the urbanization rate of the non-Russian regions was 53.6 percent, with the disparities being most pronounced in Tajikistan, Kirgizia, Moldavia, and Uzbekistan, each with a rural population of about 60 percent or more, and Turkmenistan, more than half of whose population is rural. Among the intermediate republics—with urbanization rates of between 50 and 60 percent—were Georgia, Azerbaijan, Kazakhstan, Byelorussia, and Lithuania. Among the more urbanized non-Russian republics were the Ukraine (60.8 percent urban); Armenia (65.4 percent); and Latvia (67.7 percent).

This gap between the Russians and non-Russians was greater still than the statistics for each of the republics indicate: Among families in which all family members come from one nationality (around 85 percent of all family units), the urbanization rate was 90 percent higher among Russian families than their non-Russian counterparts. And conversely, among non-Russians, the rate of those living in the countryside was 220 percent higher than among Russian families. In 1979, around 77.4 million members of all-Russian families were living in urban centers, compared to 37.3 million non-Russians. In the villages, on the collective and state farms, the tables were turned: Non-Russian families outnumbered all-Russian families two to one (56.4 million to 28.2 million).

Even in a totalitarian society, politics and governance are primarily urban phenomena. The urban populations have had and will continue to have the greatest influence on policies and politics within the USSR. All the newspapers, major cultural institutions, industrial centers, and political organizations are based in cities and towns. And the battles over the allocation of resources are fought there. The dominance of the Russian population in most of these urban centers has assured that their voice is the best heard, both within their titular Russian Republic and in most of the major urban centers of the non-Russian republics. And as the old totalitarian order moves through authoritarianism toward a more pluralistic order based on power sharing, the influence of the urban masses will likely be further enhanced.

Many other significant indicators of material well-being reflect inequality for non-Russians. In housing, for example, between 1971 and 1986 the number of new housing units built in the Russian Republic was 43 percent greater than in the non-Russian republics. Even the amount of rubles spent to construct each housing unit was greater for Russians. The results of such long-term planning can be seen in one clear indicator of housing— square footage per capita. On average, there are about 15 square meters of housing space (around 150 square feet) for every man, woman, or child in the USSR. This statistic, which of course tells us nothing of the dilapidated state of such housing, is about one third the average in the United States. It is, however, further evidence of a major Soviet housing crisis. Yet this difficult housing situation is far worse in the Central Asian regions of the USSR. There, the housing situation is catastrophic. In Kazakhstan, there are 13 square meters of housing per capita; in Kirgizia, 11.3 square meters; in Uzbekistan, 11.0 square meters; in Azerbaijan, 10.5; in Turk-

menistan, 10.2; and in Tajikistan, 8.7. Yet even such bleak housing statistics minimize the cramped conditions under which most Soviet citizens
live, as they include in their calculations the areas occupied by kitchens,
bathrooms, closet space, and internal hallways. Such statistics also include the "shared" spaces of the USSR's numerous multifamily, communal apartments.

These statistics would be even worse if many of the non-Russians had
not taken matters into their own hands. According to the last available
detailed statistics, published in 1986, there were 17.4 million square
meters of housing built with private funds. About three quarters of this
private housing was built in the non-Russian regions. Ukrainians, for
example, built 300 percent more such housing per capita than their Russian counterparts. Lithuanians built 400 percent more such housing than
their Russian neighbors. And among Uzbeks and Azerbaijanis, the per
capita amount of privately financed housing was 500 percent greater than
among Russians. These statistics reveal two important facts: First, housing conditions are so appalling that they compel the non-Russians to build
more shelter for themselves; and, second, non-Russians are more inclined
to take initiative than the more economically passive citizens of the Russian Republic.

Discrepancies in health care between Russians and non-Russians are
equally substantial. Infant mortality rates within the non-Russian republics are some 60 percent higher than in the Russian SFSR. The statistics
for infant mortality in the Russian SFSR show that in 1986, there were
19.3 deaths per 1,000 births of children up to the age of one. By contrast,
the comparable infant mortality figures for Uzbekistan (46.2, per 1,000
births), Tajikistan (46.7), Turkmenistan (58.2), Kirgizia (38.2), Azerbaijan
(30.5), and Kazakhstan (29.0) were all significantly and sometimes drastically higher. The infant mortality rates for Georgia and Armenia were
higher, too, in 1986. More significant, while infant mortality has shown an
improvement of more than 17 percent in the RSFSR between 1970 and
the mid-1980s, over the same period, infant mortality climbed in Uzbekistan by 50 percent, in Turkmenistan by 25 percent, and in Kazakhstan by
8 percent.

One important reason for these appalling discrepancies is the unavail-
ability of adequate health care. Per capita, today there are 19 percent
more nurses and other medical personnel in the Russian SFSR than in the
non-Russian republics, with the largest gaps evident among the Soviet
Central Asians.

The state of the environment also contributes to these disparities.
Many non-Russians today complain about the cavalier attitude of central
planners to the question of pollution in the non-Russian areas. Ukrainian
activists in the Rukh, for example, note that although their republic makes
up 3 percent of the territory of the USSR, fully 40 percent of all nuclear

power plants are located there. Kazakhs complain that their republic has been turned into a nuclear weapons testing site, in close proximity to an important urban center—Semipalatinsk, a region with a majority Kazakh population. And Uzbeks point to the disaster that has befallen the Aral Sea. The sea is an evaporating sewer, poisoned with the toxins of insecticides that are used to promote the production of cotton—a commodity that is today produced almost exclusively in Uzbekistan, against the will of the population there.

Such ecological catastrophes endanger the health of the indigenous population. Environmentalists and popular front leaders say that these circumstances and the ensuing dangers are the result of policies enacted and decisions taken by the Moscow-based and Russian-dominated central state ministries and by the enormous, detached bureaucracy of the Gosplan.

Alarming as the above disparities between Russians and non-Russians are, by far the most pronounced inequities are to be found between the Soviet north and the impoverished Soviet south, which is populated predominantly by the Muslim nationalities—the vast majority of them Turkic. The gaps between the white European peoples and the Asian, dark-skinned peoples are glaring. The USSR faces its own racial dilemmas. A Tass press agency report from September 16, 1989, admitted that in Azerbaijan "half the able-bodied population does not take part in social production."

In that same month, *Izvestia* revealed the alarming degree of poverty among the non-Russian peoples of the Soviet south. Calculating poverty in the Soviet Union is a difficult matter. A purely statistical approach cannot do justice to the harshness of daily life and the drab misery in which most Soviet citizens find themselves. Poverty, clearly, is not only a matter of income. After all, the inability of relatively well-paid Soviet coal miners to secure adequate housing, with water and gas heating, or to purchase such necessities as soap and detergent, was among the sparks that ignited the massive wave of strikes in the Ukraine, the Kuzbas, and Kazakhstan in July 1989.

Still the USSR calculates the poverty line to stand at 78 rubles per month per capita. On the basis of that calculation in 1988, the USSR State Committee for Statistics determined that 41 million persons had incomes below 78 rubles per month (about 14.5 percent of the population). The patterns of poverty revealed by *Izvestia* once again highlighted the Russian–non-Russian dichotomy. In the Russian SFSR, the percentage of those living below the poverty line stood at 6.3 percent (about 9 million residents). That meant that in the non-Russian republics the proportion of people living below the official poverty line was nearly 25 percent (32 million residents of the non-Russian regions). The level of poverty in the Muslim, Turkic regions of Soviet Central Asia is truly disturbing, standing at 36.6 percent in Tajikistan, 44.7 percent in Uzbekistan, and 58.6 percent in Turkmenistan.

In urban centers like Uzbekistan's capital, Tashkent, the indigenous population is crowded into tiny, dilapidated one-room dwellings, often without benefit of running water. In Baku, Azerbaijan, a huge, jerry-built shantytown holds 200,000 Azerbaijanis. In a pathetic effort to hide the sprawling eyesore, the authorities have erected a wall around it. And in a vast dismal countryside in Uzbekistan, children whose families desperately need the income, use sticks to break up the harsh, chemically poisoned soil so that cotton can be grown and exported for hard currency.

In the Kazakh town of Novy Uzen, which was rocked by ethnic violence in the summer of 1989, of 56,000 inhabitants, 21,200 had jobs and the official number of unemployed stood at 1,500. Tuberculosis is widespread, with approximately 2,500 cases reported in the city and the incidence of new cases steadily growing. There is no local newspaper or cultural facility. Telephone lines are restricted to government and Party offices and to members of the *nomenklatura*.

Unemployment is rapidly growing in the Soviet south. In October 1989, an article in the Communist Party daily, *Pravda*, revealed that more than three million people had lost their jobs during the current five-year plan as a result of economic restructuring. According to Soviet experts, the article revealed, unemployment is expected to increase fivefold as economic perestroika takes hold. *Pravda* also noted that for the last year for which statistics were available (1986), the highest unemployment rates were to be found in the non-Russian republics: 28 percent in Azerbaijan; 26 percent in Tajikistan; 23 percent in Uzbekistan; 19 percent in Turkmenistan; 18 percent in earthquake-ravaged Armenia; and 16 percent in Kirgizia. It is no wonder that such intense poverty and rampant unemployment create the social basis for ethnic violence.

Even among those lucky enough to find work, the gap between Russians and non-Russians is also apparent. By 1979, 31 percent of all workers in the Russian SFSR were employed in what was defined as "mental work" and 69 percent were engaged in what was defined as primarily "physical work." Among the non-Russian republics, 27.4 percent of workers were engaged in intellectual labor and 72.6 in physical labor. Yet throughout the 1970s, Soviet planners continued to create greater opportunities for intellectual labor in the Russian SFSR. There, between 1970 and 1979, 483,000 new jobs were created in the intellectual sphere and only 459,000 involving physical labor. In the non-Russian republics, the trend was entirely different. There, 422,000 intellectual jobs were created and 601,000 jobs involving physical work appeared. The gap, therefore, had widened under Leonid Brezhnev. There is as yet no evidence that there will be any significant departure from this pattern under Mikhail Gorbachev.

The Politics of Culture

While social and economic disparities between Russians and non-Russians are astounding, Russian dominance in the fields of culture and education is even more overwhelming. Of the 2.2 billion books printed in the USSR in 1986, 86 percent were in Russian and only 14 percent in the non-Russian languages. That meant that there were nearly 14 books in Russian for every Russian man, woman, and child, and only 2.4 books per capita in the native languages of the non-Russians. According to national rights activists, such figures are not a reflection of consumer demand but a statistical expression of the long-term policy of Russification.

Similar gaps are seen in newspapers, magazines, films, and television productions. A look at the yearly accounting of books and periodicals for 1987 reveals a culture decidedly out of balance. In the Soviet Central Asian republics, for example, the state of book publishing is nothing short of disastrous. In Tajikistan, there were only 1.9 books, pamphlets, and brochures published for every resident of the republic. Upon closer examination, even that statistic understates the reality. For in Tajikistan itself, a republic with a current population of 5.1 million, there were only 361 books or pamphlets published in Tajik and 469 published in Russian. In that same year (1987), the Turkmen SSR (population 3.5 million) published 302 books and pamphlets in the native language versus 426 in Russian. Such an imbalance is particularly shocking given that in each of these republics well over 80 percent of the population is non-Russian. In Kazakhstan, where the number of Russians is about equal to the number of indigenous Kazakhs, there are nearly three times as many titles published in Russian as in Kazakh.

In the realm of culture, however, there are even more dangerous imbalances. The Ukraine has traditionally been the target of the most relentless assimilatory and Russificatory policies and its culture has clearly paid the highest price. Today, only 81 percent of Ukrainians consider Ukrainian their mother tongue. After the Byelorussians, this is the lowest proportion among the fifteen nations with their own titular republics. The reason why Ukrainians might be drawn to Russian culture can be understood if one considers some striking statistics pointing to this radical shift: For in this nation of more than forty-four million citizens, there are just over one hundred magazines published in Ukrainian. In the Russian SFSR alone, Russians have fourteen times as many periodicals to choose from in their native language as do the Ukrainians.

In book publishing, the Ukrainians are equally far behind. In their own republic, the Ukrainian SSR, the books published in Russian outnumber those published in Ukrainian by almost four to one. Compared to book publishing in the neighboring countries of Eastern Europe, the Ukrainian SSR (population fifty-two million) lags far behind the less populous states of Poland, Czechoslovakia, and Hungary. Poland, for example, publishes five times as many books as the Ukraine each year; Czechoslovakia issues four times as many; and Hungary, with a population of about one fifth that of the Ukraine, produces six times more titles with a print run that is 60 percent greater.

This lack of variety constricts Ukrainian readers, forcing them to seek out the Russian-language press. The non-Russian intelligentsia is thus increasingly drawn into the habit of reading, writing, and thinking in Russian. And consequently, it sends its children to Russian-language schools. Such trends create a growing gap between educated non-Russians and non-Russian workers and peasants. The native culture in this situation seems like something second-rate, inferior—linked to the less intelligent and badly educated workers and rural inhabitants.

Cultural monotony cripples the magazine world. The USSR publishes around 5,000 different periodicals. Of those, 4,245 appear in Russian and only 774 in non-Russian languages. That is nearly a six-to-one advantage.

The restrictions and limits on non-Russian publications are all the more astonishing when one takes into account how little variety there is in the Soviet press in general. In the USSR in 1987, there were but ten weekly magazines published in Russian. And there was just one Ukrainian-language weekly magazine. There were no other weekly magazines published anywhere else in the USSR in any of the non-Russian languages! Even in the period of glasnost, the Soviet authorities prefer to cling to the concept of "gigantism." It is comforting to the Party ideologues to know that each day 25 or 50 million readers are reading precisely the same periodical. Such centralization simplifies censorship and makes the tasks of the Party propaganda apparat all the more simple.

The statistics on newspaper publication reveal a similar pattern. There are nearly 5,000 newspapers published in the Soviet Union. Of those, more than 90 percent appear in Russian. Variety is a problem in the newspaper industry, too. The Russian SFSR, for example, produces only 97 different daily newspapers for a population of 147 million. Meanwhile, Uzbekistan, a non-Russian republic with around 20 million inhabitants, has only 4 daily newspapers.

When it comes to books on commercial, agricultural, and industrial topics, the gaps between Russians and non-Russians are even more astonishing. In 1987, there were more than 2,500 different titles on transportation topics published in Russian, while only 90 appeared in the non-Russian languages. Titles dealing with machine building show the following breakdown for the same year: thirty times as many in Russian as in the non-Russian languages. Among industrial construction texts, there were one hundred times more titles issued in Russian than in the non-Russian languages. And over 4,000 Russian-language books on agricultural topics were published in the USSR in 1987, while 1,000 appeared in non-Russian languages—an apparent concession to the overwhelmingly non-Russian rural population.

Films, too, tend to be dominated by Russian-language products. In the Ukraine, one writer asked, "Why do film studios have to request funding for each film from Moscow?" The screenplays, he lamented, then have to be translated into Russian at great delay and cost. He complained that Kiev's once renowned Dovzhenko Film Studio and its counterpart in Odessa had been almost completely Russified. The Ukrainian cinema, he concluded, "is a fiction." To that writer's indictments could be added the fact that in the Ukraine as in other non-Russian republics, the most popular films—recent imports such as Francis Ford Coppola's *The Cotton Club* or *The Conversation*—are available usually only in Russian versions. As a rule, no provision is made for dubbing these objects of intense public interest into the native non-Russian languages.

Only the Georgian republic has its own developed film industry. It has produced, among others, Tengiz Abuladze's celebrated condemnation of totalitarianism and Stalinism—*Repentance*. The national identity of the studio also has meant that filmmakers in the Georgian capital of Tbilisi are aiding that country's popular front and other dissident groups. Indeed, the building of the Georgian Cinematographers Union was, throughout most of 1989, the nerve center of the country's burgeoning national rights movement.

Russian dominance is apparent, as well, in education and popular culture. The enforced acculturation of children into the Russian-dominated Soviet culture is achieved through schooling and through television. In most of the non-Russian republics, there are often three television channels. Two are usually Russophone. The last, while devoted to local affairs, is frequently filled with Russian-language programs.

The pattern of Russian dominance begins in grade school, permeates all stages of the educational system, and is reinforced by the mass media. Graduate students, whether Russian or non-Russian, are required to write their advanced-degree dissertations in Russian, another technique for promoting Russification of the non-Russian peoples. Sometimes, the requirement can be quite absurd. In Moscow, we met a young Ukrainian screenwriter who was studying at Moscow University's prestigious film school. He had begun writing a screenplay about life in a small Western Ukrainian town. Although one of his themes was the gradual encroachment of Russian language and culture onto a formerly pure Ukrainian setting, he was for a long time prevented by teachers and school officials from writing any part of the script in Ukrainian. "The whole point would have been lost on a viewer. The rule rendered my subject nonsensical. How can you accurately convey the sense of place, the local color, and the underlying conflict without using the Ukrainian language," said the young man. At last, the authorities relented, agreeing to pass him provided that he wrote a Russian-language synopsis. But his success is one of a handful of exceptions. Ironically, had he been a student in the Ukraine, there, too, he would have been compelled to write his dissertation screenplay in Russian.

The Russian advantage carries over into the sciences. Over two thirds of all scientists and scientific workers in the USSR are to be found in the Russian Republic. In secondary education, Russians enjoy further advantages. Adjusted for population, the Russian SFSR has 20 percent more secondary school students than Georgia, 30 percent more than Azerbaijan, 20 percent more than the Ukrainian SSR, 30 percent more than Uzbekistan, 12 percent more than Lithuania, 75 percent more than Tajikistan and Turkmenistan, 25 percent more than Armenia, and 30 percent more than Estonia. Indeed, there is not a single republic that does better than the vast Russian Republic in secondary or higher education. Overall, there are roughly 20 percent more students in the RSFSR than in the almost equally populous non-Russian republics.

The gap in higher education is even greater: The Russian SFSR has more than one third more college and technical school students per capita than the non-Russian republics. Indeed, the proportion of college and technical school students in the Russian Republic population exceeds that of the fourteen other republics in proportions that range from 10 to 70 percent.

Government statistics confirm the superiority of the Russians and their language. Although "bilingualism" has become the Soviet buzzword in nationalities policy, only 3 percent of all Russians have bothered to learn to speak a language of one of the non-Russian nationalities, despite the fact that some 20 percent of all Russians live in the non-Russian republics. By contrast, nearly half of the non-Russians speak Russian. "Bilingualism" clearly is one area in which the educational advantage of the Russians does not appear to yield concrete results.

With all the intense pressure to assimilate, particularly among Ukrainians and Byelorussians, it is astonishing that so many non-Russians continue to cling to their mother tongue. By 1989, more than 95 percent of all Uzbeks, Kazakhs, Georgians, Lithuanians, Tajiks, Turkmenians, Kirgizians, Latvians, and Estonians regarded their own language as their mother tongue. Among the 6.5 million Tatars (who do not have a titular republic of their own), the rate of identification with their own language was 85 percent; among Armenians, many of whom live outside their republic, it stood at 91.6 percent; among Ukrainians, it was only 81 percent; and among Byelorussians, it was at a USSR low—70.9 percent.

With growing ferment among the non-Russians, new concessions are today being made in the areas of education and language. Undoubtedly, the above figures will climb in the years ahead as a result of changes in the constitutions of the non-Russian republics, many of which voted in 1989 to make the indigenous languages the official state languages in their republics. Some republics went even further, and enacted laws that will define and enforce the constitutional changes.

In no realm of their personal and professional lives do the non-Russians enjoy a significant advantage. The statistics are grim. Even in an area as innocuous as leisure time, the Russians come out well ahead. In the 1980s, on a yearly basis, and adjusted for population, 33 percent more citizens of the Russian SFSR were able to take vacations in state-run resorts than were their counterparts from the non-Russian republics.

A Matter of Respect

The economic policies of perestroika seek to increase the accountability of the individual workplace. Consequently, they also contribute to a debate on the distribution of new capital investment, on pricing, and on the inequities in fixed investment.

While the economic concerns of the rising wave of nationalisms in the Soviet Union may not be readily apparent to the many Western correspondents, and to not a few Sovietologists, all aspects of the Russian versus non-Russian dichotomy are being investigated thoroughly by the popular fronts. And while these organizations are giving voice to some decades-old concerns, they are also using economic disparities in their arguments for independence, autonomy, or sovereignty within a true confederation.

While some may still argue that inequality is, in the end, a matter of perception and that many of the people are better off now than they were before Soviet rule, the Soviets themselves have begun to publish and discuss the incriminating statistics of inequality. In a society whose one firm ideological pillar has been its profession of social equity, it was clearly a matter of time before the non-Russians began to take them at their word.

At a time when the USSR is turning to greater decentralization in the sphere of economic life, centralized cultural, educational, and publishing policies make absolutely no sense. Over the years, Soviet authorities have justified existing cultural imbalances by claiming that they need to publish, educate, and develop a mass culture in a language that is understood by most everyone. But the need for standardization and dissemination of information could easily be overcome; the polyglot culture of the European Economic Community seems to be solving the problem through multilanguage editions, the promotion of multilingualism in the educational system, and the use of translators and interpreters. These measures have, perhaps, added some cost and increased paperwork. But they also have maintained intact the spiritual essence of peoples, and so have encouraged them to be productive and creative. In the successful societies and economies of the emerging European Community, linguistic diversity has not proved an obstacle to cooperation.

Non-Russian dissidents attribute the broad range of imbalances to the true nature of the Soviet state—a continuation by other means of the centuries-old Russian empire. The policies of centralization and Russification, given explicit expression during the Brezhnev years, have become a source of great discontent within the cultural and political elites of the non-Russian republics.

Dissent by non-Russians, even those non-Russians who are loyal to the system and are an integral part of its political establishment, is the natural outcome of a system that has stacked the deck in favor of Russians and Russian speakers. The uniformity and cultural inequity that such centralism breeds have resulted in pent-up discontents. Those, as recent years show, have great potential for fueling mass unrest and political activism.

The average non-Russians are not yet fully aware of all the statistical disadvantages they confront. For decades, their opportunity to travel within the USSR was severely circumscribed, by both regulations and economics. The heavily controlled Soviet press did not address these sensitive issues. Now, the openness engendered by glasnost has allowed some of the issues of equality to permeate the Soviet media and for the first time to be depicted forthrightly in the print media and on Soviet television.

It is true that most people form their worldview on the basis of what they observe directly in daily life. In all too many republics, workers may be unaware of the life-styles and living conditions of their counterparts in adjoining neighborhoods, not to say in other republics. But increasingly in a more open USSR, the indigenous non-Russian populations, particularly in urban settings, are becoming more and more aware of the gap that separates their countrymen from the living standards of average Russians within their own republics and without. Non-Russians are certainly aware of the limited variety to be found in their cultures. The potent slogans of economic reform and glasnost are, for the non-Russians, appropriate banners under which to rally. They are urging a recutting of the economic pie in the hope of a more equitable arrangement. Even if they win, they're not necessarily bound for the good life.

The ordinary Russian citizen's life is hardly idyllic, and his position is hardly privileged. It is, however, the life of a citizen tied to an empire. Although the British and French working class may each have benefited from the expansion of their nation's empire in the nineteenth century, such direct material benefits were rather modest. At a time when the British Empire was at its height, Friedrich Engels was describing the immense poverty of working-class Manchester. Today, working-class Vologda or Sverdlovsk is hardly the locus of privilege. As Mikhail Heller has recently written about the Russians: "They live impoverished, poor, hungry lives. In the Smolensk region, in the heart of Russia, sixty-five years after the Revolution, it is impossible in the winter to travel from one village to another. But that is because the Russians have to feed the Afghans and build roads in Nigeria and Kampuchea." The USSR also has to maintain a vast security system and a world-class military-industrial complex.

In this setting of economic decline, the non-Russian peoples are increasingly looking for a more equitable share of the economic pie. In this regard, self-perceptions are decisive. And increasingly the voices of the popular fronts are accusing the Kremlin of gross inequities that have proved ruinous to local economies. More significant, even the central press is beginning to acknowledge the verity of these complaints. In a November 2, 1989, issue of *Pravda*, K. T. Turysonov, a secretary of the extremely conservative All-Union Central Council of Trade Unions, put it this way:

> Nowadays, there is recurrent talk that social justice is not observed in the distribution of consumption funds. . . . Prices and wages in our country are deformed. This has its effect. . . . Sometime in the mid-1960s, our economists put forward the thesis that the equalization of the economic level of the republics had been achieved. Economic strategy was elaborated on the basis of this premise. In actual fact, there had been no economic equalization. For example, vast regions of the RSFSR to the East of the center, and parts of Kazakhstan and the Ukraine, possessing tremendous natural resources and having become the nation's pantry, are at the same time regions that have been done out of their fair share socially.

It is clear that no set of statistics can fully measure quality of life. A number of the non-Russian cultures have preserved traditions and styles of conduct, work habits, and other features that create a more pleasant life-style and a sense of community. Certainly, the average visitor coming to a city like Kiev in the Ukraine or Tbilisi in Georgia is struck by their relative prosperity, by the dignity with which shopkeepers maintain their places of work, and with the greater variety of available goods. But these often are the by-products of industrious national cultures. Still, it is clear that when the Soviet state intervenes as it does massively, it usually does so against the interests of non-Russian cultures.

It is for this reason that most of the popular fronts are united in their belief that the non-Russian republics would fare better under self-governance. With greater control over the allocation of their own resources and a decisive say in the setting of prices for natural resources and finished products, non-Russians would inevitably better their lot.

These increasingly powerful movements certainly oppose the trend toward centralization that occurred under Brezhnev and that persisted in the first years of Mikhail Gorbachev's rule. Paradoxically, under Brezhnev, 53 percent of all industrial output was controlled exclusively by the central, All-Union ministries. Under Gorbachev—his rhetoric of decentralization notwithstanding—this all-Union control grew from 57 percent in 1986 to 61 percent in 1987. In 1987, a further 33 percent of industrial output was produced under the shared jurisdiction of central and republic ministries, which de facto meant central control. Indeed, by 1987, as nationalist and separatist sentiments were mounting, only 6 percent of all Soviet industrial output was under the jurisdiction of localities and republics.

According to the draft program on economic power sharing issued in 1989 with the concurrence of the Politburo of the CPSU, the proportion of local and republic control over industrial production would rise dramatically in all the republics: from just 4 percent to over one quarter of such output in the Russian SFSR; from 5 percent to over 40 percent in the Ukrainian SSR; from 7 percent to about one half in the Byelorussian SSR; and from around 10 percent to between one half and three quarters in the Caucasian republics, the Baltic States, Soviet Central Asia, and Moldavia. Yet that formula for the devolution of economic power—though a step forward when compared to the centralized system now in place—was rejected in late 1989 by the USSR's Supreme Soviet as too conservative. This legislative rejection may well have been evidence of Mikhail Gorbachev's growing understanding that the centrally controlled state apparat is at the root of the USSR's economic crisis. It, likewise, was a sign of the mounting demands and growing strength of non-Russian movements pressing for sovereignty. The most important legislative changes that promote the devolution of central control have been passed for the Baltic States. These are meeting with immense bureaucratic barriers and administrative hostility from the central authorities in Moscow, the most clear-cut of which was the economic blockade of Lithuania in 1990.

Still, despite some signs of concessions, Soviet propaganda has responded to the upsurge in national assertiveness by promoting new myths of the interrelatedness of the USSR's economy. That theme is used to sow uncertainty and fear among non-Russians and to raise the alarm among Russians and thus to mobilize support for the unity of the land of the Soviets. This propaganda line contrasts markedly, however, with growing Soviet admissions that the non-Russians have been given a raw deal economically.

In the United States in the early 1960s, few of the marchers in the civil rights movement were armed with economic statistics contrasting black living standards with those of their more privileged white counterparts. In the United States, civil rights protests were animated by an anger at the outward manifestations of racism and discrimination. So too in the Soviet Union, it is the perception by increasing numbers of non-Russians that they are second-rate citizens in their own union of putatively equal and sovereign republics that has motivated much protest and political action. Many of the economic arguments are likely to come, as they eventually did in the American struggle for civil rights. And they are likely to come in large measure because the popular fronts are beginning to press for self-financing and workplace decentralization as the first economic steps in the movement for autonomy and independence.

In a time of economic difficulty and resultant economic austerities, the fight for the reallocation of limited resources is also a fight over the distribution of hardships. It therefore may awaken resentment among the more privileged strata, who are disproportionately Russian. After all, the Soviet Union finds itself in a period of economic stagnation, mounting shortages of consumer goods, growing inflation, rising unemployment, and declining living standards. The struggle over resources when the economic pie is not growing will lead to heightened resentment by the economic have-nots. By contrast, the more highly skilled, ethnically Russian, urban haves are likely to view growing regional and national economic and cultural assertiveness as a direct challenge to their interests, particularly in the non-Russian republics, where some twenty-five million Russians still live. And Russian fears are helping to fuel rather base, racist, and chauvinistic instincts. Increasingly anxious Russians also are forming the bedrock of movements resistant to any form of change, including that advocated by Mikhail Gorbachev. Russian anxieties are also fueling a countervailing Russian turn inward. Such a Russian rejection of the burdens of empire is associated with the election in May 1990 of Boris Yeltsin to the presidency of the Russian Republic.

Rising Russian Resentments: A Front Against Perestroika?

Yeltsin's victory notwithstanding, a pattern of Russian conservatism and resistance already has occurred in the Baltic republics, where Russians are creating interfront organizations in a struggle to protect their privileged status and the supremacy of their language. In many instances, these antiperestroika fronts are being given material support by the discredited segments of the Party apparat and by the declining, once moribund state- and Party-controlled trade unions of the All-Union Central Council of Trade Unions. That dinosaur of the old order appears to be engaged in a campaign to revive its flagging fortunes by appealing to Russian imperialist nationalism and by advancing conservative slogans masked by demagogic populist appeals.

Clearly, the struggle is over much more than living standards or culture. It is a struggle for political power and national dignity. The non-Russians are pressing on a variety of fronts—economic, cultural,

educational, and political. But the net effect of their challenge is to widen
the fissures in the last remaining empire and to pose a profound challenge
to the integrity of the Soviet state. At the same time, because that challenge is being led for the most part by non-Russians who come from the
most talented and best educated segments of their societies, their movements are likewise the main forces for the kind of economic and political
reform Mikhail Gorbachev has professed to support. For the Soviet
leader, the challenge is coopting some of these forces on behalf of his own
agenda for decentralization and economic change. It's a high-wire tightrope act. And with every eruption of nationalist mass protests, it's a
high-wire act being performed on thin rope.

The implications of economic inequity are certain to play an ever growing role in Soviet political life. As the Communist leadership moves reluctantly toward a policy of local accountability, questions will be raised
about the base from which the non-Russian republics are forced to start
their self-sufficient economic activities.

The very idea of economic self-sufficiency for the republics that make
up the USSR is being greeted with greatest enthusiasm by the non-
Russians. By contrast, it's generating a degree of trepidation among many
leaders and citizens of the Russian SFSR. In October 1989, the then
chairman of the Council of Ministers of the Russian Republic, Aleksandr
V. Vlasov, denounced what he called the growing tendency toward
"autarky" in economic life. Speaking at a session of the Supreme Soviet of
the Russian SFSR, Vlasov, who also serves as a nonvoting, candidate
member of the Politburo of the Communist Party of the Soviet Union,
expressed worry over what economic self-financing would mean to the
giant republic:

> Almost two-thirds of the republic's territory is in the far northern zone or
> equivalent regions. Gigantic reserves of natural resources, which are of great
> importance for bringing into circulation throughout the whole country, are
> concentrated here. However, the severity of natural and climatic conditions
> and the remoteness from developed regions causes a significant increase in the
> cost of building and operating enterprises and facilities of the social sphere in
> that zone. . . . The intensive development of new regions is unthinkable with-
> out concentrating the efforts of all the union republics.

He expressed the growing worry of Russians that the Russian SFSR
could confront severe economic difficulties if left to its own devices.
Vlasov noted that even within the republic, great climatic and environmental variations make "the standardized leveling approach to territorial
self-financing in the context of the Russian Federation . . . totally unacceptable."

He went on to issue a wide-ranging attack on greater economic self-
determination for the republics that make up the USSR, saying that it

"can lead to a disruption of the objective processes of the socialization of production, the all-Union division of labor and specialization, and co-production within it." Terming this process an "unfortunate" reality, Vlasov charged that an "inclination toward regional isolation" was mounting and with it "a manifestation of regional egoism and an aspiration to escape one's obligations to the country and the republic." He expressed the view that the Russian SFSR's government is "resolutely against the transformation of our state into a union of national states."

But Vlasov's warnings did not carry the day. In late May 1990, he was defeated in his bid for the presidency of the Russian Republic by Boris Yeltsin. In a stunning victory, Yeltsin was elected to the Russian presidency by a bare majority on May 29 on what amounted to a Russian patriotic platform. Yeltsin immediately proclaimed his intention to fight for Russia's political and economic sovereignty. By June, the Russian parliament had proclaimed this sovereignty, plunging the USSR into the murky seas of the proper division of power between the republics and the center.

Indeed, all the republics have something to fear in the rigors of the free market; while economic accountability may well be beneficial in the long run, in the short run it can create as many problems as it solves. As the economic debate mounts, the true basis of economic relations may reveal the Russians, though, to be the most uneasy, since they face the danger that their beneficial economic arrangement with the other Soviet republics may be coming to an end.

Party and State: Russian Predominance

What has created the immense social, economic, and cultural disparities among the republics? A glance at the Soviet power structure offers some possible explanations why the non-Russians tend to lag behind in almost all indices. Power in the Soviet Union, above all, has been and in large measure continues to be exercised through the Communist Party, 60 percent of which is made up of Russians. The proportion of Russians increases as you move up the power structure to its very pinnacle—the ruling Politburo and the Party's executive arm, the Secretariat. By January 1990—nearly five years into Mikhail Gorbachev's tenure—of the twelve voting members in the Politburo, only three were non-Russians (Eduard Shevardnadze, a Georgian; Nikolai Slyunkov, a Byelorussian; and Volodymyr Ivashko, a Ukrainian), and only one member of the Politburo (Ivashko) represented a non-Russian republic (the Ukraine). In part, this state of affairs reflects Mikhail Gorbachev's decision to make leadership appointments on the basis of individual abilities. While this is a decided improvement over the formalistic past practice according to which as many as seven of the top Party leaders of the republics were given positions on the Politburo, the de facto acknowledgment that the republics had nothing to offer the central leadership is a comment on both the caliber of the Party apparat in the republics and of how the interests of the peripheries are regarded in Moscow. The non-Russian prospect looks even more bleak if the seven nonvoting candidate members of the Politburo are anything to go by; only one of them (the Latvian, Boris Pugo) is non-Russian. Within the Secretariat, which runs the Party's day-to-day affairs, of the twelve secretaries only three are non-Russians.

In the Central Committee, the principal policy-making body between Communist Party congresses, the situation is remarkably similar. As Radio Liberty's Ann Sheehy, who specializes in Soviet nationalities issues, has written: "Owing to the large number of personnel changes that have occurred since the present Central Committee was elected, the non-Russian republics are less represented than at any time in the recent past." In the Central Committee, which in September 1989 was charged with the ratification of potentially far-reaching policies on ethnic and national issues, only about 15 percent of full (voting) members come from the Party organizations of the non-Russian republics. Indeed, but half of the current Communist Party first secretaries from the fourteen non-Russian republics even have a place in the Central Committee as full members. They include the first secretaries from the Ukraine, Byelorussia, Moldavia, Kazakhstan, Kirgizia, Tajikistan, and Turkmenistan.

Although the Communist parties of the non-Russian republics are facing a profound crisis of authority and confidence, this underrepresentation, nonetheless, has elicited a great deal of unease among the non-Russians, including within the opposition popular fronts. If the Communist Party retains its place as the leading force in Soviet society and its vast prerogatives in the control of education, culture, and the media, this representation gap is certain to be a source of significant tension, especially within the indigenous Communist Party organizations. And at a time of growing national assertiveness, the Party organizations in the non-Russian republics are likely to drift further from the control of a center in which they have so little voice.

Of course, there is another, countervailing factor at work here—the principle of democratic centralism. Although each republic is allowed to maintain its own Communist Party structures, they are all subordinated to the rule of the central organization, the Communist Party of the Soviet Union. The tensions and discontents occasioned by such subordination already have come to a head in Lithuania. There, in October and November of 1989, the Communist Party of Lithuania began to assert, against great central pressure, its intention to withdraw from the CPSU. And in December 1989, the Communist Party of Lithuania seceded from the CPSU and reconstituted itself as an independent, sovereign political entity. The move, motivated by the Lithuanian Party's desperate desire to maintain some measure of public support in a republic increasingly swept up by the forces of democratic change and nationalism, strikes at the heart of the imperial structure of the Communist state. Its effect, however, is to make the CPSU an even more ethnically Russian entity.

In the ministries, which run the central Soviet economic complex, and where fundamental decisions concerning the allocation of resources are made, the level of non-Russian representation and participation is even lower than in the Communist Party. When on June 10, 1989, Soviet Prime Minister Nikolai Ryzhkov announced a proposed new Presidium of the Council of Ministers of the USSR, consisting of the three first deputy chairmen and ten deputy chairmen, there was not a single non-Russian. The twelve men and one woman nominated for these top spots hold the key positions in a Soviet system that increasingly is moving to greater reliance on governmental and not Communist Party structures. The responsibilities of these key government leaders are enormous. Most of them chair the critical committees and bureaus that determine the allocation of key resources and set the agenda for the still highly centralized and planned Soviet economic projects. Included in this roster are the chairmen of the State Planning Committee (Gosplan), the State Commission for Food and Purchases, the State Commission for Military-Industrial Questions, the State Committee for Science and Technology, the bureau that supervises the Fuel and Energy Complex of the USSR, the State Commission for Economic Reform, and the State Committee for Material and Technical Supply (Gossnab), the vital agency that seeks to guarantee access by enterprises to needed supplies and equipment.

In 1990, as President Gorbachev began shifting power from the Communist Party to the presidency, he created a presidential council, a consultative body with extensive executive functions. Here, too, the predominance of ethnic Russians is apparent. They represent eleven of the sixteen members of the council, and include but one Ukrainian and one representative of the Turkic Muslim population.

The rapid growth of national consciousness and assertiveness means that this state of affairs can no longer be ignored by the now more open Soviet media. More and more voices are raising the question of how responsive a Moscow-centered, ethnically Russian elite can be to what for them are distant, detached, parochial concerns. In an August 24, 1989, interview published in the daily *Komsomolskaya Pravda*, economist Professor E. Bagramov reflected growing popular concern about the unrepresentative nature of the higher decision-making bodies of the Soviet system when he forthrightly observed: "The Politburo . . . is selected . . . not on national grounds but according to political and professional qualities. But bearing in mind that this question has major internal repercussions in the republics and that it meets with different interpretations abroad . . . I think a future party congress must choose a Politburo composition that will more fully reflect the CPSU's multinational structure."

Under the czars, the Russian empire's development was a decidedly unequal affair. Indeed, it was to destroy this inequitable "prison of nations" that the Bolsheviks claimed to have launched their revolution. Yet, in the last years of his life, even Lenin, who had ruthlessly crushed independent Ukrainian, Georgian, Azerbaijani, and Armenian states, grew increasingly concerned with the reemergence of Russian chauvinism under the new Soviet order. Hoping to correct a potential imbalance, he urged the preferential treatment of the non-Russian nationalities to close the gap in their level of development.

Lenin's views on power sharing, advanced in the last year before his debilitating stroke and eventual death in 1924, were quite explicit. While the new USSR constitution was being discussed, Lenin had written the following note to his colleagues on the Politburo: "We must *absolutely* insist that in the Union TsIK [then the Soviet legislature], the *presidency* shall go in turn to a Russian, Ukrainian, Georgian, and so forth. *Absolutely!* Your Lenin" (Lenin's italics).

For decades, this instruction not only has been ignored, it has positively been traduced in the upper reaches of state power. Indeed, Lenin's formula for power sharing in a multinational state, as advanced in his famous "Theses on Autonomisation," bears almost no resemblance to the USSR of today. In that essay, dictated in December 1922—a little over a year before his death—the father of the Soviet system lashed out at what he saw as the growing danger of "the Great Russian chauvinist." Lenin worried that he and his colleagues had not structured the delicate multinational balance of the USSR with sufficient care to create "a real safeguard against the truly Russian bully." Lenin also was careful to note that the advantaged nations, the "great" nations, as he called them (including the Russians), must observe not only a "formal equality of nations" but must take affirmative steps leading to "an inequality of the oppressor nation, the great nation, that must make up for the [advantage] which obtains in actual practice."

Although he insisted on the unity of the "union of socialist republics," Lenin made clear that the unity was not to hamper the national development of the non-Russians, whose national language rights, he insisted, must be subject to the "strictest" protections. He even speculated that it might prove necessary to retain the "union of Soviet socialist republics only for military and diplomatic affairs, and in all other respects restore full independence to the individual People's Commissariats." Such a decision, he felt, should be made by the non-Russian republics *alone*.

As Mikhail Gorbachev attempts to revive Leninist traditions of internal

Party debate, he may also be contributing unwittingly to the upsurge in non-Russian demands. During the 1920s, Lenin listened to the nationally conscious Communist leaders from the non-Russian republics who pressed for the expansion of education in native languages, argued for increased economic resources to overcome centuries of czarist exploitation, and demanded some local autonomy in decision making. This trend was known as "national Communism." It ultimately was uprooted by Stalin's "Great Terror" of the 1930s.

Today, of course, the very term "Great Russian chauvinism" has been effectively banished from the Soviet political lexicon. It is a modern-day Soviet taboo, as is any discussion of a turn toward a confederal arrangement.

Still, nearly seventy years after the Soviet founder's musings on the question of national rights, the selfsame issues that troubled Lenin in his declining years have once again risen to the surface of Soviet politics.

Interestingly, although Mikhail Gorbachev consistently has tried to cast himself in Lenin's mold, thus far, he has shied away from quoting from this explosive analysis that underlies Lenin's view of relations among the various peoples of the USSR.

Still, the trends that led Lenin to issue warnings in 1922 have, indeed, become a permanent feature of the Soviet power structure. Russian dominance in the Party and state apparatus is unquestioned. Today's ethnic Russian dominance in the upper rungs of the Party-state establishment without doubt has had a dramatic effect on the distribution of material and cultural resources in a state that touts its egalitarianism. This dominance offers evidence of something approaching a classic imperial arrangement: with most of the non-Russian republics playing the role of pliant colonies—cash cows for a centrally determined pattern of resource allocation *and* redistribution.

Of course, this economic inequity does not affect all the non-Russian nations equally. Indeed, the Baltic States enjoy a higher standard of living than the Russian SFSR. Yet this can be attributed in part to their advantages of geography (i.e., proximity to the West), their later incorporation into the USSR (which meant that traditions of private ownership and the work habits of an entrepreneurial culture are still a part of local consciousness), and their already having attained a higher standard of living than their Soviet counterparts at the time of their forcible incorporation in 1940.

For even in the Russian SFSR, the gap between Russians and other indigenous peoples is profound. Increasingly, glasnost has led to exposés of the alarming poverty that afflicts the smallest of the USSR's one hundred national groups. Those helpless peoples live in the autonomous republics or autonomous *oblasts*—territorial units that in principle are intended to preserve the identity and interests of indigenous peoples. Yet even these self-styled minority preserves have increasingly come to be Russian-dominated centers where indigenous cultures are in decay and economic exploitation is rampant.

This is not to say that a degree of economic progress was not achieved—albeit at great cost to human life and accompanied by the merciless destruction of tradition and culture, one should add—in the period of Soviet industrialization and collectivization. Still, even if one accepts the paternalistic benevolence of Soviet intentions, ought not a nation have the right to assess its own best interests once it has reached a certain level of progress and an appropriate level of education? Indeed, if it is the stated purpose of Communism to eliminate the inequities among nations and to reduce the gap between town and country, then seventy years is a sufficient period in which to assess whether the experiment in equality has been a success. In the light of a broadening debate over the allocation of wealth and resources in the Soviet economic system, it is equally appropriate to ask whether trends toward economic equality are growing.

Regrettably, the evidence is that they are not. Poverty is on the rise in the Soviet south, the environmental crisis is accelerating, and capital investments in the non-Russian republics declined in the early Gorbachev years.

There is no question, however, that today the inequities integral to the Soviet system are provoking independent activism and a plurality of interest groups. These, in their turn, are the rudimentary building blocks of a civil society that is emerging in the non-Russian republics and, more hesitantly in the Russian Republic itself. The course this competition of interests takes will be decisive to the future of the Soviet Union and to the cause of democracy in this, the world's last empire.

Ukraine:
The Pivotal Nation

Nobody listens to a people that loses its word.
—François Mitterrand

I T IS Europe's secret nation. With a population of fifty-two million, a territory about the size of France or Texas, and a history of dogged resistance to foreign rule, the Ukraine dimly exists on the fringes of Western consciousness. As the Czech writer Milan Kundera has written: "Over the past five decades forty million Ukrainians have been quietly vanishing from the world without the world paying heed."

The word "Ukrainian," in Russian and Ukrainian, is derived from *okraina*—meaning "the borderland" or "the frontier." It is here in antiquity that the easternmost of the European Slavic peoples settled and shaped its nation. Because it is a borderland between East and West, the Ukraine's evolution was convulsed by a series of invasions and occupations by Tatars, Mongol hordes, the medieval Lithuanian principality, by Poland, Russia, and the Nazis. Yet the Ukraine is far more than a borderland. Here the rich and highly developed medieval culture of the ancient *Rus'* emerged, bringing with it Christianity and monotheism to a series of warlike tribes that had roamed the Ukrainian steppe, engaging in a cult of sun worship. Russians, Byelorussians, and Ukrainians regard the Ukraine's capital city—Kiev—as the cradle of their Orthodox Christian civilization. Kiev had enjoyed a precarious history of intermittent autonomy alternating with Russian or Polish rule. In the seventeenth century, the city was home to the Ukrainian Cossack *hetman*, and the de facto capital of the independent Cossack state. By the eighteenth century the Ukraine had developed an advanced culture that was producing many of the czarist court's leading government functionaries, writers, theologians, and musicians. Under Russian imperial rule, the city's distinctive Ukrainian identity was undermined, as the czars flooded Kiev with Russian merchants, soldiers, and administrators, displacing the indigenous elite.

Ukrainian history is filled with dualities and ironies. The Ukrainians were a separate, distinct people, yet they were constantly told that they are merely an appendage of the Russian empire, inextricably linked through a common faith and a similar language. These two contradictory views created a divided consciousness that tugged at the loyalty of the Ukraine's educated elite. Equally significant was the Ukraine's dual status of frontier outpost and wellspring of religion and civilization. And no less significant to Ukrainian identity was the fact that its lands were frequently partitioned, with the result that the Catholic Western Ukraine is more clearly linked to the traditions and values of the European West, while the Orthodox East has, for centuries, been influenced by the frequently violent and aggressive rule of the Russian empire. Thus, even as Ukrainians struggle with their place in the Soviet empire today, they must also settle the question of their own national unity.

Over the centuries, the Ukraine has been a much contested prize. It is an exceedingly rich land, with vast mineral resources, a moderate climate, access to the Mediterranean sea lanes, and a rich soil. It is here that the humus-rich black earth—the *chernozem*—is found. And it is from this bountiful soil that the Ukraine derived its famous reputation as the breadbasket of Europe.

But its greatest resource is its people, at once stubborn and warm, tough and friendly. They have determinedly clung to their traditions and kept the ways of their ancestors. Yet centuries of foreign domination have left a deep mark on Ukrainian national consciousness, producing an incomplete culture that is bottom-heavy in its emphasis on folk tradition, yet has very few great writers, sculptors, and artists in its pantheon.

Here are the facts. Of all the non-Russian nations of the USSR, the Ukrainians are by far the most numerous. Some 44 million strong, Ukrainians constitute around 16 percent of the Soviet Union's population. Their republic, the Ukrainian SSR (in which about 38 million Ukrainians live), has a population of 52 million, 21 percent of whom are Russians, 1 percent Byelorussians, and 1 percent Jews.

The economic, strategic, and geopolitical weight of the Ukraine made it the jewel in the crown of the Russian and, later, the Soviet, empire. The eminent British historian Norman Davies has explained the Ukrainian contribution to the Russian empire in this way: "There is Moscow and the Ukraine—all the rest is window dressing." The size and location of this republic and the size of its population also have made the Ukraine the decisive factor in the future of the struggle of the non-Russian peoples for sovereignty. There are, for example, more than twice as many Ukrainians as there are Lithuanians, Estonians, Latvians, Georgians, Armenians, and Azerbaijanis combined.

As important as the Ukraine is economically and geopolitically to the future of the Soviet Union, its significance stems as well from its persistent resistance to foreign domination.

A History of Unrest

Over the centuries, the Ukrainian national identity has withstood the fierce onslaughts of the Tatars, Turks, Russians, Poles, and Nazis. The leading exponents of Ukrainian culture, men like the nineteenth-century poet Taras Shevchenko, died in exile far from their native soil and society. In the late nineteenth century, scores of prominent and nationally conscious Ukrainian scholars escaped the czars and lived in exile in Vienna and Geneva. Thousands later fled the Communist takeover, and tens of thousands from the intelligentsia—some 80 percent of the Ukraine's writers and artists—fell victim to Stalin's terror.

The attempt to behead the Ukrainian nation, by destroying its small, talented, and politically dangerous intelligentsia, was a practice that was inherited from the czars by the commissars of the new Soviet order. Under Stalin, the physical eradication of the Ukrainian intelligentsia was accompanied by an equally monstrous phenomenon: the replacement of writers, thinkers, and artists by the totalitarian equivalent of intellectuals. These substitute intellectuals produced trite and hackneyed works. While many refused to bend in the ensuing maelstrom of Stalin's terror of the 1930s and were broken, others bent to suit the demands of the totalitarian state. Talented writers like the revolutionary Ukrainian poet Pavlo Tychyna surrendered their creative integrity to the rigors of Stalinist aesthetics. Other writers, like the heretical Ukrainian national Communist Mykola Khvylovy, perished in 1932 at their own hands as their revolutionary ideals crumbled before their very eyes and Stalin's march against Ukrainian patriotism revealed the Kremlin dictator's true hand.

Some talented writers, artists, and filmmakers of lesser courage bent like reeds or broke in the prevailing storm of Stalinism. Others, like the filmmaker and novelist Oleksander Dovzhenko—best known for his pathfinding 1930 film *Zemlya (Earth)*—were virtually prevented from making films, and kept quiet records of the ensuing years of pain in intimate memoirs that only today, as a result of glasnost, are beginning to see the light of day.

Not only was the flower of Ukrainian culture destroyed, in the face of

Stalin's rigid censorship and Brezhnev's Russification, so too was its distinctive tradition, and, with it, the principal source of national identity—the Ukrainian language. In many Ukrainian cities (as in the coal mining center Donetsk), there is not a single Ukrainian-language school. And the Ukrainian university system also has been largely Russified. Even dissertations on Ukrainian literature were required to be written in Russian. The state's attempts to construct difficulties for Ukrainian speakers were manifold. Today, for example, there is still not a single factory in the Ukraine, or for that matter anywhere else in the USSR, that produces typewriters with a Ukrainian script.

The effects of this stultifying cultural environment are reflected in the fact that nearly one in five Ukrainians regards Russian as his native language. According to leaders of the independent Ukrainian Language Society, today less than half the Ukrainian population speaks Ukrainian on a regular basis. Outside Western Ukraine, where the language is dominant in both urban and rural areas, in the central and eastern parts of the Ukraine, Ukrainian is heard mainly in the villages and on collective farms. It is spoken by a distinct minority in the larger cities.

In daily discourse, as a language of commerce, in the work of the Ukrainian government, in higher education, and in science, the Russian language has replaced the native Ukrainian. The alarming state of the Ukrainian language has reached crisis proportions in the view of activist Ukrainians, particularly those in the Ukrainian Writers Union—a center of the Ukrainian Popular Movement, the Rukh.

Today, the Ukrainian republic's Sovietized flag flies atop Kiev's administrative and government buildings. It resembles the Soviet flag, a huge red field with a golden yellow hammer and sickle confined to a near corner. Crowded out of this Soviet pattern, occupying a precarious place on the margins, is a hint of sky blue—a remnant from the blue and yellow colors that symbolized the independent state that emerged from under the rubble of the czarist empire in 1918. That state, created by Western-oriented leaders, maintained a precarious control over Ukrainian territory in the face of invading promonarchist Russian forces and the overwhelming numbers of the Red Army, until it finally fell in 1921.

Like the blue stripe, crowded out of the flag, Ukrainian nationalism was marginalized but not banished. Despite intense repression, it manifested itself variously through nearly seventy years of Soviet rule. A Ukrainian form of national Communism emerged in the 1920s, with Party leaders seeking greater autonomy, resisting the centralizing tendencies of the Russian-dominated central Party apparatus, and promoting a blossoming of Ukrainian culture. These phenomena alarmed Stalin and by 1930 the first show trials of Ukrainian artists and intellectuals began. Stalin's forced famine of 1932–33, likewise, claimed from four million to seven million victims, who starved as a result of a brutal policy of forced grain confiscations and collectivization. The tenacity of resistance to collectivization was not to be found in Russia proper. It demonstrated a significant historical difference between Ukrainians and Russians: Communal land ownership, the norm in Russian areas freed from serfdom in the nineteenth century, had been virtually nonexistent in the Ukraine. The principal aim of the forced famine was to break the back of the Ukrainian peasantry, who were the traditional bedrock of the national movement. In the words of the eminent Russian writer Lev Kopelev, Stalin's "destruction of the peasantry" amounted to no less than "pulling out the living roots of national historical existence."

During World War II, the Ukrainians were dealt a further blow. With its population caught in a vise between two totalitarian empires, the Ukraine lost nearly six million people, four million of them civilians, including nearly one million Ukrainian Jews. In Kiev, where one in five citizens died during the 788 days of Nazi occupation, monuments to the war dead abound. They memorialize only Hitler's victims, not Stalin's.

In the postwar period, Ukrainian nationalists continued an armed struggle against Communist rule in substantial number until 1949. The long-standing resistance waged in Western Ukraine during and after World War II would not have been possible without the support of large segments of the Ukrainian population. Their intense opposition to Soviet rule, collectivization, and the suppression of the Ukrainian Catholic Church was met with mass deportations to Siberia and Soviet Central Asia of more than half a million Ukrainians during and after the war. The Ukrainians had fought on bravely and resisted for so long because they mistakenly believed it was only a matter of time before the Western democracies would be forced into inevitable war with Soviet totalitarianism.

But Ukrainian quiescence was short-lived. The 1960s and 1970s saw the emergence of a new Ukrainian democratic dissident movement. Artists, writers, and scholars joined in testing the limits of official tolerance to independent thought. An extensive underground literature, called *samvydav* (Ukrainian for "self-published"), emerged, urging greater cultural freedom, resisting the Soviet policy of Russification, and reclaiming a history suppressed by decades of Communist censorship and distortion. Yet, even this largely cultural expression of national identity proved too much for the Soviet authorities. And a generation of the Ukraine's most talented writers and artists soon found themselves behind bars or the barbed wire of the Soviet gulag.

Resistance to centralization and domination by Moscow also manifested itself within the Ukrainian Communist elite. Discontented Ukrainian officials began publicly denouncing the extensive recentralization of economic power that occurred in Brezhnev's early years. Although he had been a Communist Party official in the Ukrainian city of Dnepropetrovsk, when he assumed the reins of power in Moscow, Brezhnev alienated rather than allied himself with the Ukrainian Communist elite by keeping a tight rein on them and "trampling" on their ambitions. The Ukrainian apparatchiks did not take this well, but they were in no position to correct the imbalance. As historian Bohdan Krawchenko described it, the Kremlin "succeeded in making that elite 'more Ukrainian than Soviet.' " In 1972, Moscow's fear of Ukrainian separatism and a possible emergence of a Titolike "national Communism" had evolved into an extensive purge of the Ukrainian Party and cultural elite. First to go was the Ukrainian Party's First Secretary Petro Shelest. Soon thousands of other high-ranking Party, government, press, educational, and cultural workers were purged. Russification was stepped up and Moscow's central control once again firmly established.

Shelest was a crusty, plain-spoken tyrant. But in a style reminiscent of Khrushchev, he tried to reach out to the people. And he did so by defending Ukrainian culture against Russian domination and by reclaiming the Ukraine's colorful past. In a book prosaically entitled, *The Ukraine, Our Soviet Land*, he proposed a heretical rendering of Ukrainian history, reaching back to the Cossack age to paint a picture of an independent Ukrainian state guided by protosocialist principles. It was a telling of history that coincided with his Communist beliefs. Yet because it glorified the anti-Russian Cossacks, the book was a heresy that sealed his fate.

The Shelest era, 1963 to 1972, did indeed prove worrisome for the Kremlin. For under Shelest, Ukrainian Party leaders were increasingly outspoken in their calls for national rights and economic self-determination. And they were joined by writers, artists, and filmmakers who were producing bold new texts that celebrated Ukrainian culture and "separateness." These cultural figures began to speak in increasingly bold tones and to become more and more politicized. They were joined, too, by scholars and educators who reinterpreted the past from a distinctly Ukrainian perspective. In 1972, Shelest, who had imprisoned many Ukrainian nationalists, was himself judged a cryptonationalist and purged from the Soviet Politburo and later from the post of first secretary of the Communist Party of the Ukraine.

The scale of the Shelest purge was immense. Thousands of Party officials were stripped of power. Additional thousands of figures in the cultural establishment were removed from their posts. The iron hand of Brezhnev's centralized rule reasserted itself in Kiev and the Ukraine. The purge also ensured that only the most backward, pro-Stalinist cadre remained in the Communist Party, a condition that has plagued Mikhail Gorbachev in his efforts to bring significant reforms to this vital part of the Soviet economy.

In the late 1970s, reeling from more than a decade of severe and sustained repression of the Ukrainian cultural establishment and of the alternative second culture alike, Ukrainian opposition acquired a decidedly more radical tone. Clandestine nonviolent activity supplanted the open, dissident activity of the 1960s and early 1970s. A document written by the Ukrainian Patriotic Movement made explicit the change in orientation and the radicalization of the Ukrainian opposition. It argued: "The spiritual and cultural climate here in the Ukraine and in the USSR has become a horror for all civilized people. . . . The USSR has become a military-police state with wide-ranging imperialist intentions. . . . For more than sixty years the so-called government in the Ukraine has been implementing this policy of national genocide." These anonymous and embittered dissidents declared their desire "to secede from the USSR, and lead our nation out of Communist imprisonment."

While the Patriotic Movement had only a handful of members, it represented the views of significant numbers of Ukrainians. Indeed, Ukrainian dissent has never been confined to the intelligentsia or to small dissident groups. In 1979, for example, tens of thousands of Ukrainians took part in a demonstration in the city of Lvov at the funeral of a popular Ukrainian composer, Volodymyr Ivasyuk. Ivasyuk, a kind of Ukrainian John Lennon, was murdered under suspicious circumstances that implied KGB involvement. His funeral became the occasion for a demonstration of pent-up national dissatisfactions at which Ukrainian dissidents delivered impromptu speeches to the thousands of participants.

Another major form of Ukrainian discontent has been worker opposition. Soviet rule has seen a profound transformation in the social structure of Ukrainians. In 1939, only 29 percent of Ukrainians were of the working class and 13 percent were white-collar workers; 58 percent were collective farmers. By the 1970s, 47 percent were industrial workers, 16 percent white-collars, and 37 percent collective farmers. This movement of Ukrainians from the farms and villages into factories and cities carried with it a concomitant improvement in education and standards of living and for many years was an important safety valve for potential discontent. By the 1970s, a second generation of urbanized Ukrainians was emerging. That generation was far less likely to be satisfied with its living standards and more likely to be filled with rising expectations. As one consequence of this trend, in recent years there has been an upturn in mass unrest and independent trade union activism by Ukrainian workers. Dozens of strikes are known to have occurred in the Ukraine since the 1960s. In the years before the massive strikes by Ukrainian coal miners in the summer of 1989, worker unrest was manifesting itself in Kiev, Kharkov, Odessa, Sevastopol, Priluki, Kerch, and Dnepropetrovsk. Industrial unrest has ranged from citywide work stoppages to strikes of small work brigades involving a handful of workers. Such strikes have focused predominantly on "quality of life" issues such as housing, work conditions, and wages. Yet some also contain elements of resentment against Russian rule.

Surprisingly, in the vast majority of these cases, the Soviet response was to act quickly to improve conditions and satisfy immediate demands. Only subsequently were strike leaders rounded up, arrested, and incarcerated in psychiatric prisons. Under Mikhail Gorbachev, strike movements have operated with much more freedom and are making more and more political demands.

The system of totalitarian repression combined with widespread national oppression kept the abiding force of Ukrainian national identity hidden for more than six decades. It was this double burden that had made of the Ukrainians a quintessential hidden nation.

After Chernobyl

In the aftermath of the Chernobyl nuclear accident of April 26, 1986, the secret nature of the Ukrainian people and politics was further underscored. *The New York Times, The Washington Post,* and the three major United States television networks chose to ignore the national dimension of the catastrophe. Were a nuclear accident to occur in, say, Northern Ireland, it would be unthinkable for the press to disregard the implications for nationalism and separatism.

The Soviet authorities exploited the Ukraine's rich and colorful traditions not only to calm the fears of neighboring republics and states, but to convey an image of cheerful normalcy for a region in the midst of a vast crisis. Only five days after the Number 2 reactor at Chernobyl had exploded spewing dangerous radiation clouds into the air, and with radiation levels dangerously high in nearby Kiev, Soviet television broadcast scenes of May Day celebrations, including smiling Ukrainian folk dancers, twirling and jumping in the acrobatic tradition that had its ancient roots in the *steppe* (the vast Ukrainian plains) of the Cossacks. Viewers could see the sunny faces of Kiev's cheerful Ukrainian children dressed in traditional, intricately embroidered costumes. Marchers carried flowing red banners in honor of the socialist holiday. For the children of top Party officials it was a different story. They were quickly evacuated from the city as the radiation clouds approached.

On that grim May Day, the Ukraine's national culture, once again, was being exploited for political ends. Despite the outward scenes of normalcy and good cheer, in their homes and in the city's streets, most of the citizens of Kiev were angry and sullen. The city was in a growing state of unease. Their government was still not telling them about that which they had learned of only through Western radio broadcasts and word of mouth.

With the Kievans aware that the danger had not passed, a growing sense
of panic and impotence was filling Kiev's streets. But the formally independent Ukrainian government did not act on its own. It could only wait,
as in all crises, for the word to arrive from Moscow.

These days, by first light the vast roundabout at the river end of Kiev's
Khreshchatyk Avenue, gleams in the reddish dawn. On Leninist Komsomol Place, the steps leading up to a modern building have been moist-
ened as if by a dew. As the first sun refracts from the cement and concrete
of this massive, white edifice that houses the Kiev branch of the Central
Museum of V. I. Lenin, a solitary worker daily sprays the sidewalks with
a shower of water.

Years after the nuclear accident, that small act performed in the early
dawn hours is repeated throughout Kiev—a haunting reminder that the
Ukrainian capital is but an hour's drive from Chernobyl. Kiev, after all, is
the only city, and the Ukraine the only country, to have been irradiated
in peacetime.

The invisible wounds that Chernobyl has inflicted on the residents of
Kiev weigh heavily upon the consciousness of the city's residents. But
horrible as the wounds are, they are but the tip of an iceberg of the
ecological catastrophe that has befallen this once bountiful land.

The Ukrainian environment is a vast, poisoned wasteland. According
to Dr. David Marples, a leading Canadian expert on the Ukraine's ecology, the Eastern Ukrainian industrial cities of Dneprodzerzhinsk, Mari-
upol, Cherkassy, and Zaporozhye, are suffering from contamination owing
to the release of phenols, hydrogen sulfides, and ammonia into the atmosphere. In Dneprodzerzhinsk, a heavily industrialized city of 279,000,
there are alarming rates of fatalities among infants. Up to one quarter of
school-age children there are said to suffer from pathological illnesses.

An outdated and aging industrial infrastructure dumps pollutants into
the Ukraine's rivers—one, the winding Dniester, is virtually ruined and
another, the Dnieper, Ukraine's longest river, is disastrously contaminated. A Ukrainian chemical plant has been operating without a unit for
the biochemical cleansing of water. In Southern Ukraine, once verdant
fields are in danger of disappearing—the result of salinization. In the
industrial city of Zaporozhye, industrial pollution stands at one hundred
times acceptable levels, and is doubling every three years.

Four years after the Chernobyl nuclear accident spewed radiation onto
the picturesque Ukrainian landscape, many still-populated Ukrainian villages are unfit for humans. In the town of Narodichi, less than forty miles
from the power plant, thirty mutant farm animals were born in 1989. On
various farms near the reactor, pigs with deformed skulls and calves
without heads continue to be born. In a region ranging from thirty-one to
fifty-six miles from the reactor, more than half of all children are suffering
from thyroid gland diseases. Moreover, the number of cancer cases near

the nuclear plant has doubled, according to the officially published *Moscow News*. Yet the Ukrainian population is still sold milk and eggs that are not tested for radiation.

For Ukrainians, the Chernobyl disaster was more than an ecological catastrophe. It was additional evidence of a centralized political system that denies Ukrainians a say in how their own nation is run. Today, as a result of decisions made in far-off Moscow, the Ukraine, which makes up 3 percent of the vast Soviet territory, has the most nuclear power plants in the USSR and produces 40 percent of the country's nuclear power. "The concentration of all this nuclear power in an area with one of the USSR's highest population densities is sheer madness," observes Dr. Yuri Shcherbak, a leader of the Ukraine's Green World Society and non-Communist member of the Soviet parliament. "We used to be silent and indifferent. Some of us believed, others didn't but were afraid to speak. Chernobyl taught us that silence is impossible," he says.

The men and women of the Green World Society are trying to change all that. They meet each week in a building that is part of the complex of the former czarist Mariyinsky Palace, built in 1755 for Empress Elizabeth, the youngest daughter of Peter the Great. Now the building is headquarters for the Ukrainian Committee for the Defense of Peace, an official organization accessible to the ecologists through the intervention of its chairman, the outspoken novelist Oles Honchar.

Chernobyl was for the Ukraine and the Ukrainians a terrible catastrophe and an important impetus to political action. It led to a steady upswing in environmental activism that helped this gold-domed metropolis awaken from decades of silence.

In a cluttered two-room apartment on Kiev's less than fashionable and decidedly proletarian left bank, we pay a call on two friends—a couple in their early thirties, active in the arts. Oleh and his radiant, blond-haired wife Halyna are cheerful as they reminisce about our last meeting with them in a windswept and rainy Washington several years back. The talk is open and frank. The two are excited at the resurgence of national awareness among the young Ukrainians. They also are delighted at the more open atmosphere. The discussion alternates between an appreciation for the newfound openness that Gorbachev has initiated, and a perceptible fear that any day now the Party line will change and their freedoms will once again be taken away.

The conversation has a subtext that is typically Soviet. There is a degree of cynicism, coupled with a shame about ordinary life. And there is an omnipresent regret: "See how we live." Their quarters, cramped and stifling, are neatly appointed with a shoddily made credenza, a flimsy dining table, a low-lying couch covered with layers of intricate Ukrainian embroideries—*vyshyvky*. Their bedroom, barely usable, is cluttered with a new set of furniture that they are hoarding for a day when they will be able to swap their way into a slightly larger apartment—the payoff for their more privileged access to Western goods and currency.

There are, indeed, traces of the capitalist world here: a Sharp compact disk player, a JVC color television, a boom box. Their music collection heavily emphasizes Western jazz; and they have recently developed a taste for "New Age" music. The couple dreams of a time when travel between East and West will be unfettered by the barricades of the police state or by the worthless ruble. They share a dream of teaching folk music and folk-dancing in Canada to make a bit of money to improve their lot back home. "We've heard that soon, they'll pass a law making it possible for Soviet citizens to spend a year in the West, to earn hard currency," Oleh tells us, his eyes gleaming with delight at what strikes us as unlikely news.

Yet despite the self-deprecation and the endless stream of complaints about daily life and its oftentimes humiliating difficulties, Oleh and Halyna seem inextricably bound to their homeland. When it comes to matters of the heart, of deep-seated emotions, the Ukraine and its ancient tradition beckon. Oleh turns on the double cassette tape player and adjusts the volume knob to very low, so that the neighbors won't hear through the porous walls. It is a tape that also comes from the West, an album of Ukrainian nationalist songs and anti-Soviet military ballads.

These are sensible young Ukrainians. The appeal the music holds is of something forbidden, of something clearly anti-Soviet and yet heroic, noble, and pure. For this Ukrainian couple, the openness that they find on the pages of Moscow's *Ogonyok* or the *Literaturnaya Gazeta* has not made its way into the secretive Ukrainian press, which has been held in an iron grip for seventeen years by Brezhnev holdover, the seventy-two-year-old Vladimir Shcherbitsky. Shcherbitsky has since been purged by Mikhail Gorbachev, but the new Ukrainian Party boss, Volodymyr Ivashko, also appears to have a steely demeanor.

After a heavy dinner of *borshch*, potato and sauerkraut dumplings (called *varennyky* in Ukrainian), and plenty of vodka, Oleh brings out yesterday's newspaper—*Vechirny Kiev*. On its back page is a startling sight—an ominous, gloomy map of the Ukraine. Large chunks of the map are covered with dark crosshatches, other regions are covered in a lighter gray, and the distinct minority of the map is depicted in lighter tones. It is a map of warning. The dark regions represent the areas in which mushrooms and fruits are dangerously contaminated and must not be gathered and eaten under any circumstances. In the gray areas, all such gathered foods are to be subjected to checks for radiation. Only the light-toned areas are free of contamination. More than three years after the Chernobyl disaster, the authorities are at last admitting that much of the Ukrainian countryside is contaminated by dangerous radiation. There is visible anger in Oleh's usually easygoing voice: "I've given up thinking about myself. But my nine-year-old son; he's been eating radioactive food for three years now. Do you know what it feels like when a father can't even protect his own child?"

In Golden-Domed Kiev

Today in Kiev, the capital of the Ukrainian Soviet Socialist Republic, there are few outward traces of a Ukrainian presence. In the shops and offices that line the city's vast boulevards, Russian signs predominate. In the workplaces, Russian-language slogans urge workers on to greater productivity, discipline, and, latterly, the struggle for perestroika. Seven times more copies of Kiev's Russian-language daily are printed than of its Ukrainian counterpart.

Yet, the city's Ukrainian roots run deep. And Kiev has a long and splendid history. The seat of an ancient state, the city's golden cupolas and medieval monasteries are remnants of its glorious past as the center of an imposing empire that comprised most of the territories of today's Ukraine. In 988, the grand prince of Kiev, Vladimir, (Volodymyr in Ukrainian) accepted Christianity from Constantinople and baptized the nation known as Rus. Ukrainians, Byelorussians, and Russians alike trace the origins of their Christianity to that act. And in 1988, the Soviet government, too, joined in the commemoration of this holy event—*in Moscow*. It was an exercise many Ukrainians say was intended to obscure their history and to deny them their traditions.

The beautiful city of Kiev—from its once elegant boulevard, Khreshchatyk, to the Podil, the city's low-lying Old Town—has been touched with Soviet vulgarity. Everywhere there are signs of an intruder. Classical revival architecture is cheapened by its proximity to coarse, poorly built Stalin-era architectural monstrosities, housing the city's numerous ministries, research institutes, and government offices. In the summer of 1989, the facade of the city's post office crumbled, taking with it several lives. At the base of Khreshchatyk, where the boulevard becomes Red Army Street, stands a huge monument to Lenin.

Despite these encumbrances, the Khreshchatyk's tradition shines through. In midsummer there are dozens of cafés, dispensing pastries, cakes, and apple turnovers. Children with their grandparents politely queue up for the purchase of bottles of Pepsi Cola or Fanta. Along the bustling thoroughfare, parents take their children for a small treat: The USSR's once ubiquitous vanilla ice cream is available here in Kiev at a time when it was nowhere to be found in Moscow. Khreshchatyk clearly has seen better times. Still, the people walk with a bit of a spring in their step and their countenances somehow seem more cheerful. The shops are more cleanly kept; the meager shop window displays, more artfully ar-

ranged than in the Russian north. There is none of the oppressive air of
Moscow. Now a boulevard in the Soviet style, there are enough traces of
the past. Even the street's name is redolent of history. Khreshchatyk is
derived from the Ukrainian word for "baptism." Legend has it that the
boulevard courses over a long-gone stream in which the Ukraine's first
Christians were baptized in 988.

Through the centuries, Kiev's Russians and Ukrainians built splendid
monuments to the glory of Christ. The city became a great center of
ecclesiastic and later academic learning, with strong intellectual links to
Constantinople and Mount Athos. Far from the obsessive power struggles, intrigues, and narrow-mindedness of Moscow, the imperial Russian
capital, Kiev's Ukrainian identity and remoteness had inoculated its centers of learning and made of them impressive sanctuaries for free inquiry.

The rulers of the city built impressive cathedrals with huge, glistening
cupolas. Basilicas and monasteries rose along the riverbank of the winding
Dnieper, the broad mother of rivers down which a milliennium ago had
come the Scandinavian warriors—the Varangians, with names like Askold,
Dir, Helgi (Oleh in Ukrainian), and Ingvar (Ihor in Ukrainian). As the
centuries passed, more and more gold cupolas peered through the deep
green trees that populate the city's gentle, insistent hills.

Today's Kiev still bears the traces of this past. But hidden under garish
facades of Stalinist architecture, and buried under acres of pavement, are
the last remnants of dozens of magnificent churches and monasteries
eradicated forever by the horror that was the 1930s. It was then that the
Communist planners—inspired by the ideals of a new socialist industrial
order—had pitilessly bulldozed the comforts and glories of the past. The
ancient and traditional architecture of Kiev was denounced as "meander-
ing in the past." It was, said the commissars, a "peculiar" architecture
inspired by "Ukrainian peasant homesteads," "the Jesuitic style of the
Baroque," and "the Russian empire style."

All this was unacceptable, too nationally specific, too Ukrainian, for the
new internationalist order. After all, said Stalin's zealous aesthetic partners, "Kiev was the site and citadel for various counterrevolutionary nationalistic groups. . . . It was not by chance that the manifestation of class
ideology was especially striking in Kiev's architecture." And so a great
master plan was born, a plan that would transform the central plazas and
expanses of the city, by eradicating the evidence of the old, defeated
order. The instructions were given, the architectural plans drawn, and
the dismantling of the past began. A few brave souls tried to save the
architecture. At a time of relentless repressions, this handful of daring
men and women risked their lives in raising a faint voice of protest. Their
voices were ignored. The structures, the commissars adjudged, were
"insignificant."

Among those "insignificant" monuments were such works as the

Church of St. Basil, built in 1183 as one of the last Byzantine churches of medieval Kiev, and later rebuilt in the late seventeenth century to repair the damage caused by heavy artillery fire in the struggles between Ukrainians and the Russian imperial troops; and the Collegiate Church of the Madonna of Pyrohoscha, built in 1132, the first brick structure in Kiev. In all, over thirty houses of worship and monasterial complexes were destroyed, and with them countless belfries, convents, refectories, and cemeteries—the bulk from the seventeenth and eighteenth centuries, priceless rarities of baroque and rococo style. The golden altar gates—the *ikonostasis*—the friezes, frescoes, mosaics, elaborate porticoes, and articulated golden domes were scavenged, and taken for the collections of Leningrad's Hermitage, Moscow's Tretyakov Gallery, and other museums in Russia.

So enthusiastic were the architects of the new order that they had planned even to tear down St. Sophia, the most revered of all ancient Rus's churches. Such zeal, however, proved even too fanatical for Stalin, who overruled the Ukrainian commissar Pavel Postyshev.

A walk through the remnants of one of old Kiev's vanished glories—the former Mykhaylivsky Monastyr, the Monastery of St. Michael of the Golden Domes—can still bring a chill. The complex, built by the Grand Prince Svyatoslav II from 1108 to 1113, and renovated and enlarged in the seventeenth-century baroque style, included a massive church—the second largest in the city—a belfry, a monastery, a narthex, and tombs. St. Michael's occupied one of the most scenic parts of the city, a rise on the right bank. Below it streamed the mighty Dnieper. And the brisk winds that whistled through its courtyards must have added a note of solemnity and gravity of those who toiled and prayed there—to the faithful, a majesterial reminder of the power of a nature and world created by God.

Now all this is gone. The demolition was completed within a year, commencing in the spring of 1935—the entire process captured by photographers for the proud Party commissars. Part of the complex today is taken over by a massive building that houses the agencies of the Kiev *rayon* (regional) government. Originally, the structure was home to the Central Committee of the Communist Party of the Ukraine. It stands today as a looming, artless edifice with a monumental, sculpted flag and immense columns that wind in an arc facing toward the city's center, overlooking the ground where once stood St. Michael's.

But the grand design, like much of totalitarianism's grandiose human project, was never fully realized. And so today, there are large, empty patches of land. The wounds of those times weigh heavily on Kiev and the Ukraine. And not only on the city's architecture. They can be found too in the numerous killing fields that dot the Ukrainian landscape. Still, the horrors of the past are today assisting in the rebirth of national dignity. The repressed memory of the dark, bloodstained time of Stalin, Pavel

Postyshev, and Lazar Kaganovich is helping to mobilize tens of thousands of average Ukrainian citizens, like the people of the village of Bykivnia.

The Poisoned Land

Located near Kiev, Bykivnia's forest has long held a dark secret. Under its soil, carpeted with thick grass and red mushrooms, lay buried the corpses of thousands upon thousands of men, women, and children. For many years, a wooden fence kept the area undisturbed. But over the years, the fence fell down and vandals began digging up the soil to extract gold from the teeth of the thousands of skeletons.

A few years ago, the authorities placed a plaque here. IN ETERNAL MEMORY TO THE VICTIMS OF THE GERMAN FASCIST OCCUPATION, the inscription said. Later, the villagers learned of plans to build a railway station on the site of the mass graveyard. The sacrilege galvanized the old, grizzled villagers. The elderly men and women, silent for fifty years, began to protest the perversion of the truth. They told everyone who would listen the true story of Bykivnia, of how beginning in 1936 Stalin's secret police, the dreaded NKVD, would drive into the area then cordoned off by barbed wire and there dump truckload after truckload of bodies—the victims of unspeakable horrors. In the summer of 1989, under pressure from the Memorial, an anti-Stalinist organization from Kiev, the Communist authorities of the Ukraine were forced to acknowledge the inconvenient truth: In Bykivnia's forest were the remains of 200,000 or 300,000 victims of Communist repression—Bykivnia held the largest mass grave of the Stalinist terror.

Today, the men and women of Bykivnia are walking a bit more proudly. They have paid their debt to the memory of the victims of Stalin. But for them as for most Ukrainian villagers, life remains grim and hard. Over the last three decades, millions of peasants have streamed out of the villages into the ill-prepared and overcrowded cities of the Ukraine. In recent years, the migration from village to town has numbered over two hundred thousand per year. And in the last two decades, 1,502 villages have been completely depopulated and stand now as eerie ghost towns. The village—long the treasure trove of Ukrainian culture, the conservative bearer of its tradition, and the firm bastion of its language—is fast disappearing. In the villages that remain, and where 33 percent of the Ukrainian population still lives, there are fewer amenities than in the grimy coal mining towns of the Ukraine's Donets Basin. More than one third of the Ukraine's villages have no medical facilities whatever. For those that do, 70 percent are in truth medical stations situated in what the Kiev writer and environmental activist Serhiy Plachynda calls "derelict flop houses." One third of the isolated villages of the Ukrainian countryside have no cultural facilities, not even a place to put up a film projector for the screening of a twenty- or thirty-year-old film. A mere one in twenty of the Ukraine's villages are linked to gas mains. In the midst of such deprivation, it is no wonder that there is a flight to the already crowded cities and towns.

A visit to the village of Muzhyliv in Western Ukraine underscores the desperate state of rural life. The village, now a state farm, has been reduced to a grim latticework of muddy tracks and modest three-room houses. In the 1930s, it was a thriving village of private landholdings; the center of a robust community of highly motivated young landholders, many of them drawn to the cause of Ukrainian independence. Because the village was a hotbed of proindependence sentiment, Stalin's postwar Ukrainian satrap, Lazar Kaganovich, orchestrated the forced exile of hundreds of thousands of Ukrainians to remote, barren areas of Kazakhstan and Uzbekistan, where they were stripped of their native churches and schools, denied the use of their language, and compelled to grow cotton on chemically polluted tracts of land.

For those who remained, life also was not easy as the village's infrastructure began to collapse under the weight of collectivized agriculture. Today, most of the young men and couples have left the farm for urban life, and the knowledge of private, independent farming has all but vanished. Here there is little enthusiasm for any talk of privatizing the land. "We've gotten used to the way things are," says Maria, a sixty-year-old retired collective farmer. "What could I possibly do with the land on my own, without the men. Things might get worse if we were left each to fend for ourselves."

According to Serhiy Plachynda, not only is the village in decline, "the Ukraine is rapidly losing its land. At present," the environmentalist says, "there are eighteen million hectares of eroded lands and another two million are so oversaturated by chemicals that no efforts are being made to recultivate." The country's imposing, even majestic rivers, the Dnieper and Dniester, are extremely polluted by chemicals and nuclear contamination. That pollution has direct consequences for the health of the rural population, since around 90 percent of the republic's villages have no water mains. The water supplies that reach the villages are therefore frequently toxic. According to leaders of the Ukrainian Popular Movement, the Rukh: "The water pollution in . . . the Ingulets irrigation system exceeds the permitted norm by a factor of 27 and in the Danube-Dnieper irrigation system, by a factor of 50." Rampant industrial mining of uranium has placed the Ukraine first in the world in oncological illnesses and cancers.

In November 1988, parents in the historic city of Chernivtsy, near the Romanian border, panicked when scores of children ranging in age from six months to fourteen years began to lose thick clumps of hair and to

suffer hallucinations. While the origins of the mysterious disease are still
not fully known, the illnesses were traced to poisoning from thallium—a
bluish-white metallic chemical used in rat poison and in the manufacture
of antiknock compounds for engines. As the crisis in Chernivtsy was
mounting, a massive chemical explosion in Uman, a city southwest of
Kiev, reminded Ukrainians that factories increasingly are exposing the
local residents to great dangers.

The sense among Ukrainians of unfolding ecological, economic, cultural, and spiritual crisis has not led to passive consent. Instead, in recent
years it has led to a remarkable reawakening in many parts of the Ukraine.

The Voices of a People

Now, the blue and yellow Ukrainian flag, flown in the brief period of
Ukrainian independence (1918–21), is staging a stunning comeback. It is
turning up throughout the country in the growing wave of marches and
protest demonstrations that are sweeping the Ukraine. It has flown at the
head of mass marches and meetings in Kiev, Lvov, Chernivtsy, Ivano-
Frankivsk, and Ternopil. And in April 1990, it was raised atop the city hall
of Lvov, the consequence of a stunning electoral triumph by nationalist
candidates.

The most spectacular manifestations of nationalist ferment are the demonstrations in Western Ukraine that now routinely attract as many as
200,000 participants. Equally impressive has been the rapid rise of the
Ukrainian Popular Movement for Restructuring, which held its founding
conference in Kiev in September 1989. Know as the Rukh—Ukrainian for
"movement"—the organization unites over 280,000 members, including
around two dozen members of the USSR's Congress of People's Deputies.
But perhaps most threatening to the center of power in Moscow has been
the rapid rise of an independent workers' movement led, above all, by the
miners of the Donbass and the coal mining region of Lvov Oblast.

The Ukrainian national revival of the last few years has helped recover
some of the "blank spots" of history, as they are euphemistically referred
to, of the Stalin era. On March 5, 1989, over five thousand citizens of Kiev
gathered for a public meeting of the Ukrainian Memorial organization.
For four hours, they stood in rapt attention as scores of speakers addressed them in a commemoration of the crimes of Stalin and his heirs.

For Laryssa Krushelnytska, an elegant woman in her late fifties, memory of the Great Terror cuts through to the heart of her being. Her entire
family—father Ivan, then a twenty-nine-year-old poet, his father, and six
others in the family were carted off to the NKVD's prisons and death
camps. Her voice crackling with emotion, on the verge of tears, she
explains how her father was "shot in a dark basement" of Kiev's "beau-

tiful" October Palace. "The mass shootings began with my father on December thirteenth, 1934. Before they were over, we had lost our leading writers, artists, scholars, and scientists." All of them, she reminds the crowd, "ended up dead." Hidden by a prominent Red Cross activist, Laryssa Krushelnytska, then a toddler, was saved. "On behalf of my suffering family, I pray that you and your children will not have to go through the horrors I and my family went through," she tells the assembled.

Through the day, the crowd hears other frightening accounts of the enormities committed under the banner of Communism. A secretary of the Ukrainian Writers Union, his entire family also wiped out by Stalin's henchmen, moves the crowd with a stirring call to revive memory and memorialize the Ukrainian holocaust: "If we were to reveal to the world how much blood has been shed, there would be a huge flood. And the anguished cries of those tortured and mutilated souls would be as loud as the rumblings of the tragic Armenian earthquake."

Ukrainian consciousness was deeply affected by these and similar tragedies. Indeed, the carnage through which the Ukrainian nation has passed in this century is second only to the nightmare of European Jewry. In all, 4 to 7 million Ukrainians perished as a result of Stalin's forced famine of the early 1930s. Another 1.5 million fell victim to the Stalinist terror and the gulag archipelago. A further 6 million Ukrainians died in World War II. All in all, nearly 12 million lives were snuffed out in less than two decades.

At the Memorial rally, a softspoken man breaks through to the crowd of thousands, quoting from the Ukrainian national poet, Taras Shevchenko, and reminding them of human dignity, of how special and valuable is the idea of the Ukrainian nation.

He is the well-known dissident Evhen Sverstyuk, an officially sanctioned poet and literary critic until he fell out of favor with the authorities in the mid-1960s. Now sixty-one, Sverstyuk's delicate features and elegance belie the twelve years he has spent in prison and remote Siberian exile. Sverstyuk lives in a cramped, musty three-room flat that he shares with his wife and elderly mother.

For Sverstyuk, the revival of independent political life in his homeland is nothing short of a miracle. Still, he worries about the profound wounds decades of totalitarianism have inflicted on Ukrainian culture. Under totalitarianism, Sverstyuk argues, the thought processes of intellectuals are necessarily incomplete; the consequences of thinking things through to the end are simply too dangerous. Such a system of oppression, he argues, has created a profound crisis for the Ukrainian intelligentsia—the fear to speak the full truth. That crisis is most acute for intellectuals who remained part of the cultural establishment in the years before Gorbachev's liberalization. "The conventional view," Sverstyuk observes, "is

that, deep inside, intellectuals living under totalitarianism have worked
out their ideas about the failings of the system fully and have remedies for
societal ills. But the contrary is the case. Their views of their own predicament and that of their nation have never been fully worked out, either
beneath the surface or in the open."

To underscore this point, Sverstyuk notes that even today, in a period
of cultural and political liberalization, few official writers are emerging
with books and articles that they had kept locked away in their desks
during the Brezhnev period. "You'd have thought there'd be dozens of
such works, just waiting for the right moment to be published. But it
simply isn't the case. There are no such hidden works," says the writer.
"That's because the inner consciousness of most writers was never able to
fully develop."

In Sverstyuk's judgment, even Mikhail Gorbachev is a prisoner of totalitarianism who senses that Soviet society cannot press forward under the
current system, but has not yet reconciled himself with the full implications of his views. According to the Ukrainian writer, only democratic
dissidents—the political prisoners of the 1970s and early 1980s—have developed a comprehensive view of their nation's predicament. This is one
reason why, today, they are receiving the most enthusiastic receptions at
public rallies.

On several occasions in our travels in the Ukraine and throughout the
Soviet Union, we have observed this process at first hand. We have
watched speaker after speaker mount podium upon podium and have
listened to a steady stream of rhetoric. We have heard the speeches of
officially sanctioned members of local writers unions. We have watched
with surprise as local Party functionaries, eager to restructure, avow their
now officially approved anti-Stalinism and anti-Brezhnevism. But consistently, the most enthusiastic reactions from the crowds greet the interventions of speakers like Sverstyuk and Yuri Badzio, the former *zeks*
(Russian slang for "prisoners"), who now are emerging as the conscience
of their nation.

Despite his newfound public popularity and four years of Gorbachev-
styled glasnost, Sverstyuk still is without a telephone. The authorities fear
that this articulate polyglot, who has translated Rudyard Kipling, Gilbert
K. Chesterton, and François Villon into his native Ukrainian, would be a
valuable source for Western reporters, now regularly beating a path to
Kiev to take in the process of national renewal and political ferment.

After his release from exile in 1984, the KGB routinely visited the
writer's neighbors, asking them for information on the comings and goings
of this "criminal." At first, they found willing allies. But as the neighbors
came to learn the true story of the man next door, they began to warn him
of the regular and intense surveillance. These days, the atmosphere is

somewhat more relaxed and there are just too many people and groups to keep track of.

The writer is formally retired. Upon his release from imprisonment, he worked as a carpenter for a couple years. "I took advantage of a trade learned in the prison camp and made furniture," Sverstyuk jokes. Yet, he allows, even in the worst periods of repression, authentic human discourse was possible. "In a microclimate things are fine," Sverstyuk says, speaking of the family and a small circle of friends. The difficulties arose when one tried to write openly. Growing up in postwar Volhynia in Western Ukraine, the young Sverstyuk was aware of the fallacies of the Stalinist doctrine, but kept his beliefs to himself. Later, under Khrushchev's thaw, Sverstyuk emerged as a literate and respected Ukrainian voice for liberal values. A crackdown followed and he and his brave colleagues ended up in the permafrost-covered forced labor colonies of Mordovia and Perm, a period that, he insists, had a liberating effect on him and his compatriots.

Twelve years of imprisonment and decades of repression have left deep marks on Sverstyuk. His careers as writer and psychologist, long in ruins, are only now beginning to reemerge. Colleagues from the democratic movement died while in prison or were crippled and maimed for life. Still, Sverstyuk, a man today suffused by Christian charity, cannot bring himself to denounce others, including the many once close friends who caved in or sold out. The upsurge in independent activism has been a form of vindication for him, with his works now appearing in the officially sanctioned literary journals, and his popularity is growing as well in the underground *samizdat* press. Still impossible to publish in the censored official press are Sverstyuk's careful dissections of totalitarianism, his thoughtful essays on the place of women in Ukrainian society, his powerful essays on the poetry of the brilliant Ukrainian poet Vasyl Stus, who died in 1985 in a labor camp in the Perm region, and whose body was returned for burial to Kiev only in December 1989.

Today, Sverstyuk is a man with an abiding belief in God, a self-styled Christian Democrat who is active in the Memorial movement, a supporter of the Ukrainian Popular Movement, and the chairman of the Ukrainian Association of Independent Creative Intelligentsia. "Many of us see no point in being invited back into the organizations that expelled us for our political thinking. It is totalitarian to think that there should only be one organization for writers, or artists. We are creating an example of pluralism, to show that the state does not have a complete monopoly on organized life."

Even the leading lights of the official Ukrainian Writers Union are beginning to speak out for their nation's freedom. Ivan Drach, a poet, screenwriter, and essayist, is now the elected head of the Ukrainian

Popular Movement for Restructuring—the Rukh. As Rukh chairman, Drach has become one of the leading spokesmen for the national revival that is sweeping the Ukraine. He is a lightning rod—attracting the venom of the Party's crude progaganda attacks.

Once an enfant terrible of Ukrainian letters, today Drach is a balding, plumpish man in his early fifties with the remnants of a once thick head of hair radiating in cascades from a large bald pate. One dissident writer, who regarded this former conformist with suspicion, now is certain of Drach's political conversion to patriotic activism. "He has been seized with a visible passion. Even his poetry has been energized and elevated. He is a man transformed." These days, he receives streams of visitors in his ornate office on the top floor of the stately four-story building that was home to a rich local industrialist in the days before the Bolshevik Red Army captured Kiev, and now houses the Writers Union.

In the space of a few months, Drach has traveled on a long political odyssey. In March 1990, in the wake of the Rukh's impressive election showing (nearly two thirds of their candidates were elected and now consititute more than a quarter of the Ukrainian Supreme Soviet), Drach resigned from the Communist Party. He is busy creating a new proindependence force, the Ukrainian Democratic Party, which will be part of the Rukh coalition.

Drach's transformation was coincident with the growth of a national rights movement. Spurred on at first by a small, isolated band of brave dissidents, many of whom served terms of imprisonment ranging from three to twenty-five years, the Ukraine's modern-day intellectuals have taken up the verbal sword. And they are struggling to restore Ukrainian culture, to protect and revive a poisoned environment, and to press for Ukrainian autonomy—or as many would have it, for complete independence.

The huge room in which Drach works contains a porcelain statue, a modest desk, and an imposing conference table; once empty, it is now cluttered by the thousands of letters that flood in weekly to the Writers Union from supporters of the popular front from around the country. In the antechamber, a dozen or so Ukrainians wait for a brief appointment with Rukh activists. A few are here to seek advice on how to handle an unfair job dismissal, others have come to offer support in building new chapters for the movement, still others want to know how to help the electoral campaigns of Rukh supporters. In this beehive of political activism, Drach reveals the ambitions of his movement. "We want to safeguard Ukrainian culture, to repair the damaged environment, and to create the conditions for open expression."

In the months since these solitary writers boldly published a draft for a Ukrainian Popular Movement for Restructuring in their 110,000-circulation weekly, *Literaturna Ukraina*, the Ukraine has witnessed a near miraculous rise of a mass movement in every way as serious and determined as those in the Baltic States, Armenia, or Georgia. In 1989, demonstrations of as many as 200,000 were held in the Western Ukrainian city of Lvov. The protest wave has stretched from the Polish border in the west to the southeastern industrial town of Dnepropetrovsk. The discontents among the Ukraine's citizens have spilled over into the coal mines of the Donets Basin in the republic's eastern reaches. And in January of 1990, over 300,000 Ukrainians linked hands in a three-hundred-mile "human chain" that linked Kiev and Lvov in commemoration of the 1918 proclamation of a Ukrainian state.

At the inaugural congress of the Rukh in September 1989, about a thousand delegates from around the country gathered. Here are hardened veterans of the gulag archipelago, sturdy and remarkable men like sixty-two-year-old Levko Lukyanenko, a lawyer who has spent twenty-six out of the past twenty-nine years in Soviet prisons and concentration camps and served as head of the Ukrainian Helsinki Union; the tough leaders of the coal miners strikes of July and August 1989; patriotic Communist Party members elected by a wave of popular discontent in March 1989 elections to the USSR's Congress of People's Deputies; ecological activists outraged by the collapse of their once unspoiled environment; and cultural activists from the Ukrainian Language Society concerned about the decline of their mother tongue.

Despite the changing atmosphere in Moscow, the Rukh faces daunting problems; not least among them is their lack of access to the Party-controlled press. Still, one sign that the movement is emerging as a serious political force was the presence of six leaders of Poland's Solidarity at the Rukh's founding congress. They included Adam Michnik, editor in chief of Poland's largest daily newspaper, the pro-Solidarity *Gazeta Wyborcza;* Bogdan Borusewicz, chairman of Solidarity for the Gdansk region; and Zbigniew Janas, a recently elected member of the Polish Senate, who headed the Polish trade union at Warsaw's sprawling Ursus tractor factory. Michnik, a close adviser to Solidarity and one of the architects of the political opening in Poland, electrified the Rukh delegates with a strong condemnation of Russian imperialism and colonialism. "You as Ukrainians and we as Poles know the face of Great Russian chauvinism," he said. "We know how much harm it has brought to the Russians themselves. No nation can be happy if it degrades and oppresses other nations.

"Poland is with you! Solidarity is with you!" Michnik said to thunderous applause. "Long live a democratic and free Ukraine!" Michnik's well-received remarks were not the fanciful ravings of a revolutionary run amok. They were the eloquent formulation of a new, emerging Soviet bloc realpolitik, in which democratic movements throughout Eastern Europe and the USSR provide each other mutual support. It is an expression of confidence in the possibility of a new, decentralized, and democratic landscape that seems each day more likely to replace the postwar Soviet empire.

Although it is clear that the Ukrainian language and Ukrainian identity are staging a large-scale comeback, they have quite a long way to come before Ukrainians can win the cultural and political struggle. In the Dnieper Hotel's cavernous and pedestrian restaurant, we meet with four newfound friends, two couples in their mid-thirties. As is typical through-out the Soviet Union, the central hall this evening is given over to a wedding party. Although the couple, we learn, is Ukrainian, the music and the endless banter of the five-man band are entirely Russian. The rich customs of the Ukrainian wedding have been replaced with the trite and superficial rituals of urban conformity.

The wedding reception has all the atmospherics of a Las Vegas floor show. Intricate religious traditions, too, have been supplanted by rituals much like those of the famous Las Vegas chapels where you can be married in a minute. The brief state wedding ceremonies are conducted in antiseptic Halls of Weddings. In such an empty environment, the gaiety surrounding this new couple seems forced. In its mechanical brev-ity, the moment of matrimonial expectation brushes quickly against the melancholy reality of dead-end jobs, a decades-long wait for a new apart-ment, and endless shortages of consumer goods. Divorces are rampant and, in a society with housing shortages, lead to contradictory living arrangements. Once the church was the center of such important transi-tional moments in a Ukrainian's life, imparting a solemnity to vows taken by husbands and wives; today, the state controls even the most sacred aspects of their personal lives.

In Lvov

If Kiev is the political center of the Ukrainian national revival, and the battleground of an unfolding struggle between the Ukrainian and Russian cultures, the Ukraine's heart is in Lvov, an ancient Western Ukrainian city with a rich history and a great sense of local pride. If Kiev contains the influences of ancient Constantinople's Orthodoxy, Lvov, a Catholic city, is decidedly Central European, eclectic in its architecture, Western in its manners and tone. Traditionally a multinational city, populated at the turn of the century in roughly equal proportions by Ukrainians, Jews, and Poles, today Lvov is overwhelmingly Ukrainian. Still, the roots of this multinational metropolis are everywhere evident. The city's most ancient structures were built by Armenian builders in the thirteenth century. A street—the Virmenska (the Ukrainian word for "Armenian")—cuts through the cobbled streets of the old town, near the famous Market Square. Farther on, a statue of Adam Mickiewicz, the Polish national poet, stands as another reminder of the city's ethnically diverse past.

The city's architectural splendors range from the structures of the ancient Rus of the late thirteenth century to the Gothic traditions of the fourteenth through sixteenth centuries. There are the Church of the Bernardines and the Boims Family Chapel, designed by Italian architects who invested the city with the flavor of the Italian Renaissance. There are, too, such splendid baroque structures as the seventeenth-century Church and Convent of the Order of the Barefoot Carmelite Nuns, until recently given over to the use of the Komsomol; and the ornate, rococo St. George's Cathedral, once the province of the still-outlawed Ukrainian Catholic Uniate Church. Today, St. George's is the property of the Russian Orthodox Church, a legacy of Stalin's anti-Ukrainian policies. And there is the looming, glorious Dominican Church, with its Latin motto: "Soli Deo, Honor et Gloria." The church now houses Lvov's Museum of the History of Religion and Atheism.

There are, as well, other reminders of the Central European influences on this city in the remnants of the art nouveau style that captured popular tastes at the turn of the century. And there are the vestiges of the city's entrepreneurial past, including the former offices of the Land Credit Association, with its Empire-style facades and bas-reliefs that depict mythological scenes and angels. It is now Number 1, Leninskiy Prospekt. There is, too, the former five-story home of the Dnister Insurance Society, closed down by the Soviet authorities in 1939. It once employed 1,200 agents and insured 250,000 Ukrainians. Gone, too, is a vast network of consumer cooperatives with exotic names like the Narodna Torhovlya (People's Exchange) and the Maslosoyuz (the Butter Union). Missing, as well, is the network of stores and savings and loans organized by the Prosvita (Enlightenment) Society, which brought literacy, volunteerism, and economic betterment to prewar Galicia.

Lvov is inextricably linked to the history of Europe. It is here that Poles, Jews, and Ukrainians coexisted for hundreds of years. Today, however, the dynamism of its past is a distant memory. The city's center is suffocating under mounting air pollution. The streets are soot-laden. The once splendid parks feature walkways with gaping holes. Architectural landmarks are dilapidated. The city's central park, named for the patriotic nineteenth-century writer Ivan Franko, is being "repaired." The site of the statue of Franko—where in the summer of 1988, fifty thousand demonstrators gathered—is crisscrossed with scaffolding.

The old city reflects the aesthetic lines of a highly stylized and developed culture. But it is all that is left of a once noble place now savaged by the dead-end culture of totalitarianism. Still, while the newer, postwar

Soviet buildings in Lvov are as elsewhere awkward intrusions, at least the
city's rulers have shied away from the monumentalism that dominates and
distorts so many other Soviet cities.

Since the summer of 1988, when mass demonstrations swept Lvov,
signaling a Ukrainian patriotic awakening, the city has seen a growing
divergence among the generations. Among Lvov's senior citizens, one is
apt to encounter sad eyes, uncertainty, and nervousness—all telltale signs
that glasnost has a long way to go before it removes the fears built by the
experience of decades of terror and repression. Lvov, sadly, has a broken
generation who as young boys and girls had witnessed first the Soviet
invasion of September 1939; then, in 1941, had seen the NKVD slaughter
thousands of prisoners in Lvov's jails; and had lived their early years
under the horrors of the Nazi occupation. As teenagers, Lvov's older
citizens went to the now Sovietized schools in which everything they
learned from their parents was supplanted by a new, Communist creed.

The lessons of the past made these men and women, now in their
sixties and beyond, a part of a fearful, lost generation of Ukrainians. But
the fears of the past generations are disappearing for young Ukrainians,
for those who have emerged into adult life in a time of political liberalization. Typical of this new generation is Ihor Hryniw, a research scientist
in his early thirties. The child of prominent Ukrainian academics with
high Communist Party connections, Hryniw is clearly uncomfortable with
the language of Marxism-Leninism. His ground-floor flat is larger than
most, with high, molded ceilings. It is a throwback to the old, elegant
prewar Lvov. He is an avid collector of Ukrainian folk art.

Although he has adopted the tidy habits and elegant manners of prewar Lvov, Hryniw is hardly living in the past. The youth movement he
has led, the five-hundred-member Lev (Lion) Society is at the center of
the city's political awakening, actively participating in electoral campaigns
against the Party hard-liners, working to restore the neglected landmarks
of his hometown. Taking its name from Lvov (the City of Lions), the Lev
Society has organized thousands of Ukrainians in protests calling for pollution controls to protect the decaying historic center of the city and has
sent cultural expeditions down the Dniester River in Western Ukraine to
uncover and restore abandoned village churches. Another of their mis-
sions is to save from extinction an arcane form of black pottery, and
members are learning the techniques of molding and firing from elderly
village craftsmen. A splendid collection of the black jugs, bowls, and cups
clutters Ihor's stylish old china cabinet. "In a society in which the state
and Communist Party claimed to initiate everything, we have revived
genuine private sector volunteer activities for the first time since Communism was installed," Hryniw proudly notes.

In March 1990, Hryniw, along with his father, was elected to the
Ukrainian parliament on a slate backed by the Rukh. He will now use his

parliamentary tribune to advance a cause he believes is inevitable—the Ukraine's sovereignty.

Andriy Panchyshyn is yet another young activist, a kind of Bob Dylan of the new Ukraine. Panchyshyn has been performing to packed audiences throughout the country. As part of the Ne Zhurys ("Don't Worry") ensemble, the folksinger has performed at dozens of factories and mines before thousands of gritty and worn, but enthusiastic, workers. There is a sharp edge and a clear political subtext in his ironic and sardonic ballads. He sings of Stalin's anti-Ukrainian satrap, Lazar Kaganovich; laments the persistent lies that emanate from a local Lvov radio station nicknamed the Liar; and pokes merciless fun at a bumbling, unnecessary KGB. One of his bitter, sardonic songs is in the form of a classified ad for the Ukrainian language, offering up the "lost, mother tongue" for sale to the highest bidder.

The songs have proved tremendously popular among young people. These days, young workers and students clamor to get tickets to Panchyshyn's latest concert. And the concerts are increasingly turning into large political rallies, with the blue-and-yellow flags of the independent Ukraine unfurled, and the cheerful crowds emotionally singing the long-banned national anthem, which begins: "The Ukraine has not perished."

Among the young people of Lvov, the past lives as a golden age. Satirical musical ensembles abound, and even modern cabarets like those of the Ne Zhurys group hearken back to the past. They're named for a popular 1930s Lvov jazz band.

The turn to the past is called Lvov retro. And it signals a return to this bygone era. Young women dress in the long skirts of the 1930s. Young men wear leather coats, trilby hats (*kapelyukhy*), and reed-thin ties in the fashion of that era. The ambience of the prewar city is making a strong comeback. In nightclub cabarets, ensembles perform the dance hall numbers of the Depression era. Crooners belt out the love songs of the 1920s and 1930s. The nightclub performers strive for near total authenticity. "Alo-eh, alo-eh," they sing, re-creating the aloe facial cream jingles of Lvov's bygone radio days. One student in his mid-twenties explains the popularity and abiding fascination of this subculture: "It's quite simple really. It's the last period before Communism. It's a way of retreating from our current Red nightmare."

The Ivanyuks live in a cramped fifth-floor walk-up apartment on the city's southwestern outskirts, a bleak residential area with no shops and an omnipresent acrid smell of gasoline and burning low-grade coal. Still, the apartment's cheery interior reflects a mother, Iryna, who cares about her two sons, Rostyk, age twenty-one, and Yura, age sixteen. There are numerous embroideries (*vyshyvky*) and weavings (*tkanyna*); a hand-woven *kilim* rug from Bukovina hangs on the living room wall. All around, there are carved wooden crosses and icons.

Yet underneath the tidy surface, there simmer the many tensions of family life. Deep into the night, well past 1:00 A.M., as the drinks flow freely at a reception in honor of American visitors, the father—invited to meet with "foreigners" by his ex-wife of ten years—enters into a state of mild but certain inebriation. His hollow, sad brown eyes survey the guests who have assembled in his former household. He feels his authority questioned, senses the imprecise pressure of his twenty-one-year-old son's judgment and alienation. In the presence of visitors from the West, the estranged father erupts into an extraordinary soliloquy. It is a litany of deep moral crisis, a confession of infidelity, family betrayal, near constant womanizing, and broken family life. "I've tried to be a good father. I've tried to help you all. I admit to my weaknesses. These are failings I deeply regret. But most couples I know, the Romanenkos, the Pronyuks, they have other relationships, too. After all, open marriages are part of the modern world." The explanation, accompanied by a short, nervous laugh, intensifies the anxiety in the air. Rostyk, the twenty-one-year-old son, averts his glance, and then, unable to stand this public confession and entreaty, briskly exits.

In a Western setting, such family dramas are, without doubt, also quite common. Yet, consider the father's specifically Soviet predicament. Although he has been divorced for over a decade, he lives with his mother as he has another five to ten years to wait for his own flat. Ironically, his mother lives directly under the apartment of his ex-wife and sons. For ten years, therefore, the father has heard the comings and goings of his sons through the porous ceiling, seen them growing up as they dart down the stairs. For ten years, he has heard the sounds of the joys and sorrows of a family from which he has been cut off. Into the deep night, the father continues to repeat his by now pathetic equivocations. He pleads for Rostyk's forgiveness, all the while flirting with another neighbor, a twenty-four-year-old unmarried mother.

These are some of the cultural and economic contradictions that confront Ukrainians. With totalitarianism has come the collapse of civility, the destruction of tradition, the erosion of family ties; in short, the renting of the complex fabric that unites us with the past. A profound spiritual and moral crisis is shaking the Ukrainian people. As Evhen Sverstyuk noted: "The collapse of external beauty echoes the collapse of morality occasioned by totalitarianism. It is seen in the monstrous perversity of totalitarian art and architecture." Within the cardboard walls of the Ivanyuks' sad home, there is the internal correlative of the external collapse of the Communist idea.

The discontents that have accumulated within urban Ukraine extend well beyond the dead-end economy and lack of mobility, the crumbling housing, and the fact that hot water is available, as in this household, only six hours a day. They extend to the heart of their national essence—their sense of Ukrainianness. "I'm a student at the local polytechnic," Marianna notes. "I'm studying for my exams right now. My friends and I resent having to take courses in Marxism-Leninism as a condition of our graduation." Her voice rising in anger, she talks of participating in the first demonstrations that rocked Lvov. "We're sick and tired of this nonsense, of the spouting of endless lies. We want something different. We want to be free. The Ukraine would be better off without *them*. Everyone believes we'd be better off on our own." A gold cross dangles from Marianna's neck, an outward sign that she stands with most Western Ukrainians apart from the atheist system that has been imposed on her land.

Because of such mounting indignation, in the last year Lvov has been overtaken by a national awakening of unexpected proportions; demonstrations with crowds ranging from ten thousand to a quarter of a million are a common occurrence. At the center of this political and cultural renaissance is a fifty-year-old grandmother, whose charismatic and fiery speeches have made her a favorite at these demonstrations. A veteran of Soviet forced labor camps, Iryna Kalynets and her fifty-one-year-old husband, Ihor, a boyishly handsome, highly regarded poet whose last book was officially published in 1966 and who like his wife spent nine years in prison and Siberian exile, are an omnipresent force in Lvov's unofficial cultural and political life.

In a modest two-room flat in the southern end of town, the Kalynets household is a beehive of activity. In one room, Mrs. Kalynets meets with the leaders of the Myloserdia (Compassion) Society, a group of about one thousand women who are fighting to revive long-suppressed spiritual and religious traditions of the Ukrainian nation. The group has staged a series of outdoor prayer meetings. The most spectacular, held on January 22, 1989—Ukrainian independence day—was attended by more than ten thousand participants. It led to Iryna Kalynets's arrest and imprisonment for ten days on charges of leading an unsanctioned meeting.

Everyone seems to come to Iryna Kalynets to hammer out tactics and to seek moral support. Her moral fervor and evident charisma, her cool intensity, and her decisiveness have won a broad local following. She knows how to get things done. Iryna Kalynets believes that Ukrainian society has been Communized and drained of its sense of morality. Her stated aim is to help in generating the spiritual rebirth of her nation. Together with a small band of courageous dissidents, she is convinced that she has given the impetus to what is now a mass movement. When they held their first protest meeting in the summer of 1987, around 150 people came. Through that year the crowds grew slowly but steadily. A year later, tens of thousands were attending meetings, open-air masses, and commemorations. "It is a great river rising over the riverbanks," she says, relishing the words.

Her husband agrees, but cautions that the authorities still fear diversity and think in totalitarian fashion. Such Communist hostility clearly has backfired. Pressure from the authorities has helped the movement to spread and has mobilized the people. In the view of this nationalist couple, the Communist authorities are caught between a rock and a hard place. If there is no national rebirth, the USSR will face economic ruin. "In the end," says a confident Iryna Kalynets, "the authorities will have to deal with us."

Although for many, Iryna Kalynets is a folk hero, from the KGB's point of view, she is a dangerous foe. When Mikhail Gorbachev came to Lvov in the winter of 1989, Kalynets was kidnapped by three men and held in an unmarked car for six hours—until the Soviet leader cleared town. Yet even this thuggish act has a positive dimension: "In the past, they would have put me in jail for five or ten years. Things are changing. *They* are becoming weaker in the face of mass activism."

Mrs. Kalynets's optimism appears to be justified. In March 1990, she was elected overwhelmingly as a deputy to the Ukrainian Supreme Soviet.

The Growing Rukh

All across the Ukraine, the intense patriotism most evident in Lvov is gaining new converts. It is even beginning to make some headway in the remote, Russified redoubts of Dnepropetrovsk and Donetsk. The city of Donetsk and the surrounding region form the heart of the Ukraine's coal mining industry. In July of 1989, the region was gripped by a massive coal miners' strike, involving over 250,000 workers. Although, initially, the strike committees were suspicious of all overtures from the nationally conscious Rukh, and sought to limit its demands exclusively to workplace issues, by September the miners were sending representatives to the Rukh Congress. There they voiced opposition to the leading role of the Communist Party and began organizing themselves for upcoming local elections. In the late fall, in advance of elections to the Ukrainian Supreme Soviet, some coal miners were working out the contours of a broad coalition that would unite them with Ukrainian nationalists and national rights activists and the less nationally conscious proponents of radical economic reform.

More important, they had come into contact with the nationally conscious miners of the Galician-Volynian coal mining region, who had created their own independent trade union, called Solidarity, after the union movement in neighboring Poland. Now more and more miners from the Donbass, Ukrainians and Russians alike, are warming to the idea of an economically sovereign Ukraine.

What the future holds for the Ukraine is impossible to predict. But a number of factors augur well for the rapid growth of national identity and separatist sentiment. Geography is one important factor. The Ukraine's proximity to Hungary, Poland, and the other rapidly democratizing Eastern bloc states is contributing to the Ukrainians' growing self-confidence and determination to succeed in their struggle for free institutions and self-determination. Radical economic reforms in Eastern Europe place the more nationally conscious Western Ukrainian territories in an advantageous position to benefit from any consequent improvement in the economies of their neighbors. And because those territories, along with the Baltic States, were the last absorbed into the Soviet Union, traditions of private entrepreneurship are not entirely absent. Equally significant, the porous borders between Poland and the Ukraine are likely to contribute to political liberalization. Already tens of thousands of copies of Ukrainian books and periodicals are being printed by the Polish Ukrainian minority and smuggled into the Ukrainian SSR. They are contributing to a process that occurred in post-martial-law Poland, the breaking of the state's monopoly on information.

There already have been some modest political victories for the Ukrainian Rukh. The movement has succeeded in contributing to the forced retirement of the Party first secretary, the Brezhnev holdover Vladimir Shcherbitsky; has compelled the authorities to enact a sweeping law that guarantees the status of Ukrainian as the republic's state language and primary language in work and education; has succeeded in amending retrograde electoral laws; and has mounted a serious challenge to Communist Party preeminence in republic-wide elections in March 1990. A number of prominent voices for Ukrainian independence, including such former political prisoners as journalist Vyacheslav Chornovil, Rukh secretary Mykhaylo Horyn, and activist Stepan Khmara, were all nominated as candidates for the Ukrainian parliament by large workplaces in Western Ukraine. And in March 1990, they and other national rights activists, like Iryna Kalynets and Ihor Hryniw, were swept into parliamentary office by large majorities.

Thus far, repression, vulgar press attacks, and police brutality have not frightened the new generation of Ukrainian activists, who have even taken their peaceful protests to the militia stations to seek the punishment of those guilty of violence against women and children taking part in demonstrations. Still, the Ukrainians face an uphill struggle. Moscow is not likely to satisfy the people's demands for full autonomy, much less independence. And the Ukrainians are not as unified as their neighbors, the Poles. Western Ukrainians, who are Eastern Rite Catholics, form the bedrock of Ukrainian nationalism. In central Ukraine, traditionally part of the Orthodox Church, the national movement is gaining strength. But in the regions farther to the east, support for outright Ukrainian independence is still weak. Many Russians live there and most Ukrainians are Russian speakers who have lost their links to their Ukrainian roots.

If the Ukraine were ever to secede from what Soviet propaganda has long styled the "Union of fraternal republics," the USSR would practically cease to exist. What goes on in this backwater matters a great deal to the future of the Soviet Union, a place many Ukrainians resentfully view as the world's last empire. The Ukraine's Polish neighbors, including prominent Solidarity leaders, are aware that the Ukrainians have a chance to change the political balance in Eastern Europe. That is why Adam Michnik, editor of the daily Solidarity newspaper, traveled to Kiev to address the Ukrainian Rukh Congress, and why to thunderous applause he called for "a democratic, just, free Ukraine!"

Western experts agree about the Ukraine's strategic importance. Former U.S. National Security Adviser Zbigniew Brzezinski thinks the Ukraine holds the key to the very survival of the Russian-dominated Communist empire. Mikhail Gorbachev certainly appears to agree. That's one reason he spent five days in the Ukraine in the winter of 1989, warning against "nationalist extremism" while trying to convince the Ukraine's workers and peasants that their economic success is inconceivable outside the USSR.

Today in cities and towns around the Ukraine, the banned blue-and-yellow flag of the Ukrainian state and the ancient Ukrainian symbol, the trident, are reappearing in ever increasing numbers. They are but two of the most visible signs that more and more Ukrainians believe their nation should break away from the Soviet Union and once again become a fully sovereign state. Larger numbers favor a radical rearrangement of the Soviet Union into a decentralized, democratic confederation of economically and politically autonomous republics. Many outside the hard-line Communist Party apparat now believe that the Ukraine needs to take control of its economy and natural resources, to restore the status of the Ukrainian language, and to revive the spiritual traditions of the people. And there is near universal agreement that the current imperial status quo will not hold.

As the momentum of the struggle for national rights increases, so too does the pragmatism of its leaders. The activists of the Rukh recognize that to succeed they must incorporate demands for Ukrainian self-determination into a framework that makes economic sense for Russified Ukrainian miners and steelworkers, whose main concerns are their paycheck, the availability of consumer goods, housing, and food. Many dissident Ukrainians have stepped back from calling for outright Ukrainian independence, and now favor an independent Ukrainian republic within a highly decentralized confederation. The current Rukh leadership reflects this effort at consensus building and includes such former Communist Party members as the writer Ivan Drach, who serves as president, and the former prisoner of conscience, Mykhaylo Horyn, who heads the organization's day-to-day executive arm, the secretariat.

The Ukrainian national movement is also fighting for the rights of Jews and Poles living on Ukrainian territory. The Rukh, which has its own minority rights commission, and the Shevchenko Ukrainian Language Society have organized meetings and demonstrations to call for the opening of Yiddish, Hebrew, and Polish language schools, and have actively lobbied for the revival of Jewish organized life in the Ukraine, serving as a catalyst for the creation of the independent Sholom Aleichem Society. And the Lvov chapter of the Rukh has been pressing the government to restore closed synagogues in that city.

The process of the consolidation of propatriotic Ukrainian forces is proceeding along two tracks. On one track, there is the radicalization of members of the Soviet Ukrainian Communist Party and the Ukrainian cultural establishment. On the other, there is the evolution of radical democratic separatists—who for the first time face the responsibility of real political activity—toward a model of Ukrainian sovereignty that encompasses a broad-based confederation. A middle ground is being shaped. All this augurs well for the new movement and suggests that it is likely to follow the trail blazed by Solidarity in Poland and the democratic opposition of Hungary. Such a middle ground also augurs well for the continued cohesiveness of the Ukrainian national movement.

Ukrainian activists from the Rukh, ecological groups, the Ukrainian Helsinki Union, and other patriotic organizations scored impressive gains in elections to local city councils and the Ukrainian Parliament in March 1990. Together with reform-minded Communists and activists from strike committees from the Donbass, they may, with time, be able to wrest control of this vast republic from the hands of Party hard-liners.

Already they are making important inroads. On some key issues, they command as much as 40 percent of the votes in the Ukrainian Supreme Soviet. And within a month of taking their parliamentary seats, Rukh reformers were able to force Volodymyr Ivashko to resign from his post as Ukrainian Communist Party chief as a condition of election to the republic's presidency. In such localities as Kiev, Lvov, Ternopil, and Ivano-Frankivsk, the Rukh-led coalition has captured city and regional councils. Only now is the Rukh's struggle with the Party beginning in earnest. Several of these local councils have had restrictions placed on their access to television, on the right to control government revenues, and on the right to take over regional government newspapers, which, it turns out, are not owned by local councils but by the Party apparat.

In Lvov's town center, in the plaza that the Communists renamed Lenin Square, townsfolk congregate. Some have come to place wreaths and others to light candles on a small clump of soil decorated with national flags and banners. For most of 1989 and 1990, the citizens of this city have persistently come here to signal their allegiance to their homeland, to demand its sovereignty. Here one day soon the authorities will permit the building of a monument to the Ukrainian national poet—Taras Shevchenko. The nineteenth-century bard whose fiery epics and lyrical poems evoked the struggle of his countrymen a century and a half ago is a fitting symbol for the spiritual and national renaissance that is overtaking his homeland. The humble patch of land, too, symbolizes the success of the Ukrainians, who are now reclaiming their own territory—one step at a time.

The Baltic States:
Renaissance in the West

> The Soviet Union turned to secret diplomacy and ac-
> cepted the imperialistic principle of the assigning of
> spheres of influence to powerful States. . . . The Soviet
> German treaties decided the fate of other States, turned
> independent States into military protectorates and then
> forcibly incorporated them into the USSR.
>
> —From a draft statement by the Commission of the Con-
> gress of People's Deputies of the USSR to examine the
> Hitler-Stalin treaty of 1939. July 20, 1989

For ESTONIANS, the date February 24 is charged with significance. It is
the day on which they celebrate the national independence they first
gained in 1918. The commemoration was banned for many years, as was
the flag of independent Estonia. But on that same day in 1989, for the first
time in over forty years, their blue, black, and white national flag was
raised on the Pikk Hermann tower in Tallinn. The red flag of the Estonian
SSR, which was taken down, has not since—and will never again—be
seen flying from the ancient tower on Toompea Hill in the center of the
city.

A ceremony such as the one that took place that February, attended by
officials of Estonia's Communist Party as well as prominent members of
the Estonian Popular Front, would have been unimaginable one year
before. Then, mere possession of the flag of free Estonia, a symbol that
was banned for its anti-Soviet associations, was liable to provoke arrest;
and the thought of hoisting it atop the Pikk Hermann had been just a
dream. But many incredible things had taken place in that year of mira-
cles.

On August 23, 1987, a group of courageous Estonians organized a
meeting in Tallinn. The occasion was the anniversary of the signing of the
Molotov-Ribbentrop pact of 1939, which contained secret protocols for

dividing Eastern Europe between Stalin and Hitler into spheres of influence. The people of the three Baltic States—Estonia, Latvia, and Lithuania—consider that pact to have been the pretext for the incorporation of their territories into the Soviet Union. Thus, it has come to symbolize oppression and the destruction of the liberty, democracy, and national culture experienced by the Baltic peoples over the past fifty years. Public commemorations of the event were strictly forbidden, needless to say. Although the organizers expected only a hundred or so brave souls to turn out to support them, two thousand gathered in Tallinn's Hirve Park to register their resentment against the pact that had brought independent Estonia into the Soviet Union.

On February 24, 1989, when the flag of a free Estonia was raised, Hirve Park was filled with tens of thousands of people looking up to the looming Pikk Hermann. As all eyes fixed on the blue, white, and black flag, the words of Estonian Popular Front leader Edgar Savisaar rang out: "We raise this flag as a fighting flag and we declare that under it we shall have next autumn a new Estonian parliament, a parliament elected in accordance with the will of the people and in the hands of the right men. . . . We are building a new Estonia."

Throughout the Baltic States, the recent democratic revolution has been accompanied by the rise of songs and national symbols. The Lithuanians decreed the yellow, green, and red Lithuanian flag as both their national and state flag some weeks prior to the Estonian decision. The Estonians—whose flag was adopted only as the national symbol at first— believed that the Lithuanians' decision was a poor one. They considered it a mistake to adopt the precious national flag with all its connotations of national independence and guaranteed national rights when no such guarantees could be given under the Soviet system. The fact is, the Baltics are still dominated by the Soviets.

The Lithuanians held their independence day commemoration on February 16, 1989, just over a week before the Estonians. It was for them, as it was for the Estonians, the first time in some fifty years the day was officially celebrated. It was declared a national holiday and hundreds of thousands of people took to the streets to participate in the planned events. The main ceremonies were held in Lithuania's two major cities: Kaunas, the capital of the independent state between the wars; and Vilnius, the present-day capital, which was located within the boundaries of Poland at that time. Each event of the official commemorations would have been a pretext for arrests and harassment in the old days. But in 1989, officials and ordinary people alike took part without incident or obstruction.

On that day, each city was festooned in the yellow, green, and red colors of the Lithuanian flag. A mass was celebrated in Vilnius's baroque cathedral, which had just been handed back to the Catholic Church two weeks earlier after having served as a state-run art gallery for years. Hundreds of people gathered to watch the unveiling of a plaque on the building in Pilies Street, the main thoroughfare of old Vilnius, where the declaration of independence was signed in 1918. (The street was called Gorky Street until shortly before the event, but reverted to its old name, following a pattern throughout the non-Russian republics, where, increasingly, the names of towns, streets, and districts are reverting to their original form.) The event proceeded with the recitation of verses by a renowned Lithuanian poet, and an exhortation for further struggle for the Lithuanian cause by an elderly participant in the 1918 events. Among the crowds, young people held their banners, some emblazoned with such slogans as RED ARMY GO HOME or STOP COMMUNISM IN LITHUANIA; others carried the ubiquitous flag. The ceremony concluded with a once banned song, the Lithuanian national anthem.

All through the afternoon, loudspeakers in Vilnius's main square relayed the proceedings of a historical conference on the struggle for independence to the people milling around, waiting for the rally planned for the evening. The rally was the culminating event of the day, attended by over two hundred thousand people. The proceedings began with a dramatic swearing of an oath: "Let there be the kind of Lithuania that her people want. Our goal—a free Lithuania. Our destiny—Lithuania. May God and all people of goodwill in the world help us." All the flags paraded around the town during the day—the Lithuanian tricolor; the Estonian blue, white, and black; the Latvian deep red and white; and an occasional Byelorussian and Ukrainian flag, brought by Lithuania's neighbors as an act of homage and solidarity—formed a sea of colored cloth around the speakers' platform. Leaders from Sajudis spoke first, followed by greetings from a representative of the Lithuanians in Canada, of the Latvians and Estonians, and the minority Russians in the republic. Only the speaker from the Lithuanian Communist Party was given a lukewarm reception, the rest were welcomed with roars of "Freedom, freedom!"

The moving force behind these events in Lithuania was the Lithuanian Movement in Support of Restructuring, better known as Sajudis, Lithuanian for "movement." In 1989, the Communist Party was their guest at this gathering. Sajudis, like the other popular fronts in each of the Baltic States, led the way to a national renaissance.

By the beginning of 1989, each of the Baltic States had its own mass movement with a membership of hundreds of thousands: Sajudis in Lithuania, the Latvian Popular Front, and the Estonian Popular Front, or Rahvarinne. It is believed in some circles that the idea for popular fronts originated in Moscow and that they were modeled upon the popular fronts that existed in Eastern Europe just after the Second World War; those were used essentially as a ruse by the new, illegitimate Communist power bloc to co-opt and mold a disgruntled population. But the explosion of enthusiasm and national activity within and around the mass-based popular fronts of the late 1980s dispelled illusions that Moscow could be dictating the agenda and swept aside concerns of possible manipulation.

The popular fronts were not the only organizations to flourish in this period. Each of the Baltic States now has a vibrant, evolving independent society made up of many political, cultural, ecological, or other issue-oriented groups. There are numerous independent publications, some published officially, some still unofficial. The people's religious lives are rapidly reviving. And there is a resurgence of activity among different minority groups within each Baltic republic. Some of the more radical groups in existence before the fronts were formed have been given a new lease on life and have carved out an area for themselves either in cooperation with the mass movement or else independent of it and the Communist Party. Even the Lithuanian, Latvian, and Estonian Communist Parties themselves have been forced to respond to the new situation: Many Party members now have a double allegiance, belonging to both the popular front and the Party. In Lithuania, at the end of 1989, this process had advanced so far that the Communist Party determined that the only way it could regain the loss of prestige and influence was to break away entirely from the Communist Party of the Soviet Union. By an overwhelming majority, its leading members voted to constitute an independent Lithuanian Communist Party, and to join in the general national movement to separate from Moscow and to restore an independent Lithuanian state. The Estonian and Latvian Communists soon followed the Lithuanian example.

Anyone who takes a look at the three tiny states on the western periphery of the Soviet colossus might well wonder why the Baltic States have been so much in the news, and why they are important. They occupy an area that covers less than 0.8 percent of the USSR's total territory, and the population of the three indigenous ethnic groups amounts to less than 2 percent of the Soviet population. Nonetheless, the three Baltic States are important as the vanguard and guidepost for what is to happen in the other Soviet republics and, perhaps, in the rest of the Soviet Union. The last to be annexed into the Soviet Union, the three peoples are also among the least Russified and have retained a high degree of continuity in their language and culture. But their fierce resistance against Soviet control is more than a struggle for cultural freedom—it is also a struggle for economic freedom and political independence.

Under perestroika, the Baltic States are seeking to break away from centralized economic control in order to create a free trade zone and an independent economy based on a high degree of private and cooperative enterprise. With their measured approach to reestablishing autonomy, they are creating a model for the other national republics. These three republics have the best memory of independence and of the operation of a democratic, multiparty system and free market economy. Their proximity to Western Europe and links with a lively émigré community in the West have provided them with moral and material support through the years of repression. Their intelligent, deliberate path to reform and independence stands as an example to other Soviet nations.

From Uzbekistan to Azerbaijan to the Ukraine, the leaders of the newly emerging democratic movements have recognized the important role the Baltic States play as a model for organization and political thinking. But that was not always so. Until a couple of years ago, the Baltics were considered to be the most prosperous part of the Soviet Union; but in a climate of repression and intense censorship, little was known about their struggle for independence among the other nations of the USSR. Most Soviet citizens still believed the myth that had been created to strengthen control over the newly acquired states: The Baltic republics, the story went, had been part of the Soviet family at the end of the First World War, and the intervening years of independent statehood—between 1920 and 1940—were merely an anomaly. Soviet historiography perpetuated the notion that the only desire of the proletariats of Lithuania, Latvia, and Estonia was to reunite with the Soviet state, a goal that finally was achieved in 1940, the argument went, when Soviet power was restored.

For almost fifty years, the people of these three republics existed in a twilight zone. No democratic state would condone their annexation by the Soviet Union, but neither would any foreign power support their desire for independence. When tens of thousands of people were deported to Siberia in the nightmarish exodus that followed the consolidation of power, there was no murmur of protest from the West. The United States never recognized the Baltics' incorporation into the USSR, but did little over the years to provide diplomatic backup to its routine assertions of Baltic sovereignty, trotted out once a year for the Captive Nations Day commemoration. Lithuania, Latvia, and Estonia seemed continually to have slipped out of the minds of the two superpowers whenever they had real exchanges, and remained hidden nations lodged on the periphery of consciousness of the Western world. They were equally remote and unknown to the other peoples of the vast Soviet empire, as well.

The Baltic nations have returned again and again to the secret 1939 Hitler-Stalin pact as the root cause of their situation throughout the postwar period: They have campaigned energetically to expose the illegal nature of the act that brought the Red Army into their territories. They have argued that if the protocols could be proved to have been against international law, and perhaps even Soviet law, then the legal basis for their remaining within the USSR would be weakened. In August 1989, a remarkable event was staged by the people of the Baltic States in protest of the continuing injustice of their incorporation within the Soviet Union.

Two million people joined hands in a human chain, which stretched through the three capital cities—from Tallinn to Riga to Vilnius—to denounce the Hitler-Stalin pact. Television coverage showed miles upon miles of people: grandparents, teenagers dressed in parkas and blue jeans, families with young children, holding hands, some dressed in their national costumes, many carrying their national flag, and all standing peacefully in united opposition to the politics that had brought their countries into the Soviet Union.

Perhaps in anticipation of the mass demonstration, and under pressure from the articulate and vocal Baltic deputies, the USSR's Supreme Soviet established a twenty-six-member commission during that same summer to investigate the Molotov-Ribbentrop agreement of 1939 and its secret protocols. The commission was diverse and included respected scholars, ranging from the liberal historian Yuri Afanasyev to the Kremlin's old propaganda hand, Valentin Falin. It was headed by Aleksandr Yakovlev, Gorbachev's chief ideologist and most trusted Politburo ally. It also included eleven Baltic members. On July 20, 1989, the commission and its working group submitted their conclusions. These documents charged that the Hitler-Stalin treaty did indeed have a secret protocol that had violated the "sovereignty and independence of a number of third states." The documents also concluded that the secret protocols were an aberration and in no way reflected the will of the Soviet people, who, moreover, had been misled by Stalin's sudden change of policy toward Nazi Germany, revising in one stroke of the pen the Soviet's "relentless struggle against fascism." The commission's findings were not widely publicized at the time but even where they were, they were generally accompanied by the new line from the Soviet government, which went as follows: Even if the Molotov-Ribbentrop pact had been a violation of Leninist norms, the incorporation of Latvia, Lithuania, and Estonia into the Soviet Union was accomplished through the voluntary actions of their parliaments. Such reasoning severed any connection with the treaty itself.

Despite this setback, and its untenable leap of logic, the Baltic republics intensified their struggle, step by step, using all legal and peaceful means at hand to regain their sovereignty and independence.

Estonia

Estonia, with its population of 1.5 million, has been at the forefront of the Baltic drive for more autonomy. The republic is the smallest of the three Baltic States, covering a mere 17,413 square miles, but is nonetheless larger than Denmark, Belgium, and Switzerland. It stretches about 150 miles from north to south and 210 miles from west to east. And the Estonians themselves number just over one million, making them the smallest ethnic group in the USSR to have its own republic. But these courageous people have built a reputation far greater than their number: Estonia is the mouse that roared, the David that challenged Goliath.

The Estonians were the first to establish a popular front, in April 1988; the first to declare Estonian the official state language, in June 1988; the first to declare republic sovereignty, in November 1988; and the first to adopt legislation setting rules governing the use of Estonian as the state language, in January 1989. From then on, Estonian was to be brought into use in all official business and by all officials and individuals in positions of authority, who, the law said, were to be given four years to learn the language in order to comply with the regulation.

The Estonian language is similar to Finnish, and as part of the Finno-Ugric family of languages, is further from Russian than the English language is. Its structure offers a clue to the Estonian national character.

"Estonian has no future tense," a member of the Estonian Popular Front informed us, "that is, no future tense in the abstract. We have to think in terms of 'What is possible must be done today,' " she explained, trying to be helpful. "Maybe that is why Estonians consider things very carefully before acting. The whole of our culture is based on this approach."

Perhaps that is why the Estonians have found it so difficult to be convinced that the system of Communism, with its promise of a radiant future full of enticing benefits, would ever be attained. The Estonian language is just one sign of the cultural gulf between the Estonians and the Slavic giant on their doorstep. Most Estonians speak Russian with a distinct accent, even the younger ones who have never known a time when Estonia was not "occupied," as they refer to the period under Soviet rule.

Tallinn is a fairy tale town. The streets are cobbled and the buildings that surround the old town square have the uneven look that comes with centuries of wear. The old town hall on one side of the square dates from the fourteenth century. At the top of the hill, where Pikk Hermann and the other remains of the city's old fortress are located, sits the Upper Town, which offers a view of the Baltic Sea shimmering in the distance. The Upper Town itself was the ancient fortification; today it is still home to several government buildings, and an ocher-colored Russian Orthodox church.

February 23, the day before Estonian independence day, is celebrated all over the Soviet Union as the Day of the Soviet Army and Navy. When we visited Tallinn on that day in 1989, each storefront was equipped with a flagpole from which hung the Soviet Estonian flag—a sheet of red, pulled through with a thin wavy blue line. The appearance of this flag all over Tallinn was particularly irksome to the Estonians; one of their demands is the withdrawal of the 150,000 Soviet troops stationed in the tiny republic—one soldier for every ten people, Estonian nationalists like to point out. The following day, the Soviet flags were replaced by the clear white, blue, and black of the national flag, colors that more accurately reflect the Estonian soul.

Public commemorations of important events are a recent phenomenon for the Estonian national movement. The first public demonstration against the Hitler-Stalin pact took place on August 23, 1987. Although the authorities had officially sanctioned the meeting, they nonetheless caused difficulties by changing the venue at the last moment. One of the people at that demonstration retold the story for us:

"Who would have thought it possible? As we stood there we were afraid of what the future might hold. . . . We were being photographed and watched by the security police, we thought it would only be a matter of time before they set the dogs on us. But today you can see, we are no longer afraid . . . and how far we have come. . . .

"We were so surprised by the turnout. We had to move into the park as there were far too many people to continue the meeting where we were. . . . Nobody even thought to bring a megaphone, we didn't realize we would need it. People brought their own banners, and stood and listened to the impromptu speeches. We never expected the people to support us in this way."

Tunne Kellam, our source for this information, is chairman of the Congress of Estonia. He is also a founder member of the Estonian National Independence Party, which was formed four months after that demonstration, even though some of the group's leaders had already fallen victim to Soviet reprisals. Tiit Madisson, a charismatic young organizer of the August 1987 demonstration, was expelled from the country almost immediately, and within the next month five of his colleagues joined him in forced exile. For many years, those who considered themselves Estonian patriots worked clandestinely and concealed their identities, to avoid the gulag. There were only a few people courageous enough to sign the declaration of intent to establish the Estonian National Independence Party in January 1988. Even now its membership is only a few hundred. The party is still regarded a minority party, honest people prepared to suffer for their views. But its members enjoy a moral authority and tacit support unrivaled by the other new groups, Kellam believes. Many people who might have wanted to join were still afraid of losing their privileges were they to take the step into overt opposition that the party represented. Their apartments, jobs at the university, and at prestigious journals could have been taken away.

Demands for independence and sovereignty in Estonia were once the domain of the courageous dissidents and, later, the brave group around the Estonian National Independence Party, but now they are the everyday slogans of the Estonian Popular Front, and have been taken up even by the Estonian Communist Party. Such has been the rapid growth of confidence and patriotic feeling in this republic. One event in Estonian history is now the starting point for most discussions of Estonia's current situation: Estonia's independence was guaranteed under the terms of the Treaty of Tartu, negotiated by Lenin and the Estonian government, in 1921, and thus the occupation by Soviet troops in 1940 was a violation of the treaty. The Estonian National Independence Party continues to insist on the withdrawal of Soviet troops from Estonia and regards them as an army of occupation.

The Estonian Popular Front is less radical than the Estonian National Independence Party and claims many more members. It was formed during the summer of 1988. On April 13, 1988, Edgar Savisaar appeared on Estonian television on the program *Let's Think Once More* and proposed the creation of a "Popular Front in Support of Perestroika." During the summer, hundreds of thousands of Estonians became accustomed to attending mass meetings of one kind or another: 170,000 gathered to see off the delegates to the Nineteenth Conference of the Communist Party of the Soviet Union in Moscow. Weeks later, many more, almost one in every three Estonians, participated in the Estonian Song Festival, held once every five years. This was the summer of Estonia's "Singing Revolution," when the Estonian people united in thoughts toward their homeland. By the end of the summer, there were 250,000 who supported the Estonian Popular Front, which was formally constituted at its first congress on October 2, 1988.

Rein Veidemann, editor of the progressive literary journal *Vikerkaare*, is one of the seven members of the Estonian Popular Front's executive committee. He lives in an apartment block specially reserved for literary critics and writers at the center of Tallinn's old town. As he is a mere editor and literary critic, the apartment he shares with his wife and child is by no means the largest—the best are set aside for the novelists and poets.

"The Estonian Popular Front was formed to support perestroika," Veidemann explains, offering us the ubiquitous sandwiches of Baltic sardines. "The front was formed to mobilize the people to put up an opposition to the bureaucracy. But more practically," he adds, "the Baltic peoples were beginning to lose hope; the Popular Front has renewed our hopes that our aspirations will be achieved. The political school behind this move was the school of democracy."

Veidemann explains that there are two aims: to create an independent Estonia and to transform the Soviet Union into a democratic state. He outlines the issues, starting with the most important: the economy, language, citizenship, the electoral system, the Estonian constitution, the recognition of the Treaty of Tartu. "We want to be part of the Soviet Union in a 'special way,' just as we were first occupied 'in a special way.' These are every Estonian's ideals, even among Party people."

In the middle of 1989, the Estonian Popular Front was the leading force in the Estonian republic, enjoying the support of 35.2 percent of the entire population and 50.3 percent support among Estonians. The Communist Party of Estonia mustered only a 16.2 percent popularity rating in the same poll, with only 7.2 percent among Estonians. Veidemann's moderate views probably represent a consensus of opinion among Party and non-Party members of the Popular Front. Most Estonians believe that there should be a variety of forms of ownership of land and property, including the "independence to own private property," as one member of the Popular Front put it. Discussions on land reform and farming occupy a special place in the minds of most Estonians and so take on a special intensity. Here they rely on elements of Estonian mythology and the essence of Estonian national consciousness that is so hard for the outsider to grasp. An Estonian ethnographer offers this insight: "We Estonians have occupied this piece of the earth for over five thousand years. It is not an easy place to live; it is not naturally fertile and it has rejected many of the peoples who tried to conquer it by force—the Swedes, Germans, the Russians—only we Estonians, with our hard work, patience and persistence, have managed to eke a living from this land. And from this hardship developed the bond that now holds us to the land. That is why we defend its interests so fiercely."

Estonia has been hailed as the laboratory where the new Soviet reforms can be tested. It is true that there are many cooperative ventures now operating in the republic, but they have not been greeted with much enthusiasm by the majority. Many Estonians feel that the cooperatives are just one more way in which the Russians can take advantage of them.

Behind the Estonian Popular Front's economic program is the underlying fact weighing on every Estonian's mind: 90 percent of Estonia's industries are directed from Moscow. Even before the Popular Front was formed, Estonian economists had put together a plan, in September 1987, to restructure Estonia's economy and make it self-financing and thus more independent of Moscow's control. The acronym for the Estonian economic plan is IME, which means "miracle" in Estonian. Estonian economists have also taken part in joint discussions with Lithuanian and Latvian economists. But the problem still remains. When Moscow speaks of *khozraschet*, or republican self-financing, it refers only to the 10 percent of the economy not controlled directly by the all-Union ministries.

Many Estonians are not interested in the intricacies of self-financing and relationships with Moscow. One Tallinn housewife we spoke to pointed out, "We were much better off when we were independent. All we want now is to have a market economy and to be able to get back to

Europe where we belong. Imagine how I feel every day when I switch on the TV and watch the commercials on Finnish television, for washing powder, yogurt, shampoo—all the things that are normal in a normal society, but here I have to stand in line, or know someone who can save me something. In 1940, Estonia had the same standard of living as Finland, and now, Finland's is seven times higher!"

The tantalizing proximity to Finland is a particularly irksome reminder of Estonia's predicament. Three channels on Finnish television are easy to receive in Estonia and there is no difficulty in understanding as the languages are very closely related.

Estonians have always been people of the land; they never developed any significant urban presence as the towns always belonged to the Germans, Russians, Swedes, or whoever ruled over the territory at the time. The Estonians' special relationship to this tiny strip of territory pushed into the extreme northeast corner of the landmass that is dominated by today's Soviet Union is a strong element in their sense of national consciousness. Collectivization left searing memories for many Estonians. Estonian farmers were not easily to be herded into the Sovietized system of farming. Many have consistently defied orders from the center, only to be vindicated by higher yields and better-quality products. Nonetheless, when the question of land leasing is discussed, Estonians shake their heads and explain that Gorbachev's proposals allowing up to fifty years for a lease are not likely to convince Estonian farmers. Most of them remember how easily the land was taken away from their parents and grandparents. Until there are guarantees that ensure control over the land for at least three generations, the farmers will be unlikely to agree to terms set out by bureaucrats in Moscow.

The Estonian attachment to the earth may be an explanation for the popularity of the Estonian Green Movement. It ranks high in popularity among Estonians, and started out as by far the most popular group, before the Estonian Popular Front gained strength and recognition. Vello Pohla is one of the Greens' leading figures, a deputy to the Congress of People's Deputies, and also a member of the Estonian Popular Front. He looks like any number of people now in their early to mid-forties, who were influenced by the wave of radical movements throughout Europe in the 1960s. But the difference in Eastern Europe was that 1960s radicalism was felt but not allowed to take root. Many of the present-day Estonian Greens have nurtured their ideals through periods of repression and inactivity, ready for this, their day in the sun. The Estonian Greens now form the heart of Estonian national consciousness, and it is no surprise to hear that their group has been accepted as the first Soviet affiliate of Friends of the Earth.

The issue that stirred the ire of all patriotic Estonians, bringing the Greens together—and arguably also giving the impetus for the formation

of the Estonian Popular Front—was the government's decision in 1987 to
conduct phosphite mining in eastern Estonia. The Estonian government
had consented to a plan of the USSR Ministry of Fertilizer Industry without
the knowledge of the Estonian people. Largely owing to the efforts of the
journalist Juhan Aare, the plan was publicized and the Estonian public rose
in outrage. Not only were these lands among the most fertile in Estonia,
but they also constitute the source for Estonia's major rivers. The pollution
of Estonia's major water supply and the prospect of the phosphite mining
laying bare the country's best arable land galvanized the public into a protest campaign.

During that campaign, ideas began to form and groups of intellectuals
and others got together to broach the wider problems facing their nation,
putting Estonia's specific problems against the general background of
economic and ideological crisis in the USSR. The Greens worked out
their own specific agenda, but defined it broadly to accommodate many
diverse trends. The first commitment was to protect the environment; the
second, to help protect a distinct life-style for Estonia and the Estonians.
These points were based on the premise that the only way to protect
nature is to protect the rights of individual nations.

Among all the Estonian informal groups, there is one that has a visible
presence in the center of Tallinn. The kiosk of the Estonian Heritage
Society by the side of the old town hall is open most days. The kiosk
displays a range of Estonian flags in the form of pins and small ornaments
together with the Estonian and Tallinn coats of arms. The proceeds from
sales go to the society's activities. The president of the society is the
energetic Trivimi Velliste.

A man with long-standing service in the Estonian patriotic movement,
Velliste believes that political symbols are very important to Estonian
national identity; his organization was largely responsible for restoring the
flag, the Estonian tricolor. The Heritage Society was the organizer of the
Heritage Festival where the still-banned flag was publicly displayed in
large numbers for the first time in Tartu in April 1988. It was impossible
for the Estonian authorities to do anything about it once it had occurred.
From then on, they grudgingly accepted the public display of the flag and
eventually made it legal. The event also led to a summons from a high-
ranking Moscow official for a discussion with Velliste: After an hour of
discussion, the official recommended that the Estonian flag should be
kept in a museum. But it was already too late for that solution.

The Heritage Society has been around for only a couple of years, but
already has over ten thousand registered members in over two hundred
local clubs. In addition to the society's usual activities of restoring monuments, preserving graveyards, and collecting historical memoirs, the
summer of 1989 brought a minor coup. The Heritage Society sponsored

the restoration of the statue of Konstantin Pats, the last president of Estonia just before the Second World War. Velliste reported on its progress; it had been the subject of some interest from a Canadian film crew: "They went to look at it being made. There were many dusty Lenins lying around too, but work on the Pats statue took priority." The statue was unveiled on June 25, 1989, in the presence of thirty thousand spectators exactly fifty years to the day after the original unveiling, and forty-nine years after its destruction by the Soviet regime.

Together with the Estonian National Independence Party and others that favored full independence for Estonia, the Heritage Society determined a way to resolve the problem of Estonian sovereignty. On February 24, 1989, these groups launched a campaign to register all citizens of pre-1940 Estonia and their descendants, through a network of citizens' committees, to establish a Congress of Estonia that would be the only authentic representative body empowered to decide the fate of Estonia. A year later, 850,000 people had registered—around 93 percent of the total of those who were eligible to be citizens of the Estonian Republic under those criteria. Registration was also accepted from thousands of non-Estonian residents wishing to become citizens.

When voters went to the polls in the last week of February 1990, they elected a congress of 499 delegates: 109 unaffiliated; 107 supporters of the Popular Front; 104 supporters of the Estonian Heritage Society; 70 supporters of the Estonian National Independence Party; 39 from the Estonian Communist Party; and others. The Congress of Estonia is the body that now holds both a moral and a certain kind of legal authority in Estonia. Thus, the Estonians have rendered unto the Kremlin what was supported by the Kremlin—the Supreme Soviet continues to function for the moment—while looking to the Congress of Estonia for leadership.

Latvia

Despite the upbeat tone of most of our meetings and encounters in Estonia, we found in many Estonians a creeping fear that they were becoming the minority in their homeland: They number only 61 percent of Estonia's population and their low birth rate does not give cause for optimism for the future. Latvians have the same worry: According to the last census, Latvians make up barely half of the population of Latvia, which now numbers 2.6 million.

A short drive through the center of Riga, Latvia's capital, suggests that the Latvians have a far more serious problem on their hands. Riga is the largest city in the Baltic States and has a population of almost a million, only 27 percent of which is Latvian. The city's broad roads and massive

Soviet architecture indicate the heavy hand of Gosplan, the Soviet State Planning Bureau. Vilnius and Tallinn have preserved much of their attractive style and architecture that set them apart from other Soviet cities, but, in Riga, only the Old Town shows evidence of the city's former role as a thriving port and a commercial center of the Hanseatic League.

Riga was founded at the beginning of the thirteenth century as a Catholic Church mission and home of the Livonian Brothers of the Sword. An influx of Westphalian nobles and immigrant peasants brought to the area a strong German presence, which it has never entirely relinquished. The architecture of the old city reveals the connection with the Germans. The two huge churches that stand next to each other in the Old Town look solid yet airy inside and are sparsely decorated according to the later Lutheran tradition. One of them, the Cathedral Church built at the beginning of the thirteenth century, houses the largest pipe organ in the world, which is used for concert performances. The church itself is now a concert hall but there is some talk of returning it to the jurisdiction of the small but influential Latvian Lutheran Church. The cobbled, traffic-free streets of the Old Town are lined with houses, shop fronts, and cafés that show signs of Riga once having been a much livelier and more colorful place.

Outside of the Old Town, Gothic and Teutonic architecture gives way to Soviet-styled monuments and buildings. Teams of Young Pioneers regularly change guard at the monument to the Latvian Riflemen, goose-stepping and swinging their arms in the exaggerated gestures this particular Soviet ceremony requires of the young people. The monument they guard is dedicated to the battalion of Latvian marksmen that helped Lenin to secure the revolution at a crucial point in 1917, and then went on to fight in the civil war on the side of the Bolsheviks. The Latvian response to the Riflemen is ambivalent: They occupy a revered place in Soviet history books, yet Latvians generally look for their heroes elsewhere.

Our guide in Riga is eminently suited to take us through the recent history of his country. Eduard Berklavs was a Communist youth leader before the Second World War in independent Latvia. After the Soviet takeover, he quickly rose through the ranks of the Party to become first secretary of the Riga City Party Committee and a deputy chairman of the Latvian Council of Ministers. He fell afoul of the Party leadership at the end of the 1950s for his pro-Latvian policies and received a reprimand from Khrushchev himself. He was sent into exile in Siberia for his mistakes. When he returned, he became an ordinary worker. He turned to writing protest letters to the Communist Party and government and was expelled from the Party for his trouble in 1972. Today, this stocky, white-haired man with thick, heavy-rimmed glasses is once more in the vanguard of change, but this time as a leader of the Latvian National Independence Movement, which counted over ten thousand members by mid-1989.

Before the Soviet takeover of Latvia, there were never more than 250 members of the Communist Youth League in the underground in Latvia, and no more than 500 to 600 Communist Party members. According to Berklavs, "It's patently clear that these kinds of forces could not even contemplate overthrowing the Latvian government, which had, after all, its own army. . . . When the tanks rolled into Riga on June 17, 1940, we Communists were as surprised as anyone else." The Latvian Communists were invited to a meeting in an apartment in the Old Town, but were soon informed by a liaison from the Soviet embassy that a government had already been formed.

Berklavs explains that Latvia was singled out for industrial development in the 1950s and that meant importing not only technology and hardware, but also large numbers of Russian workers. Once he saw that the large-scale immigration was changing the very fabric of the country, Berklavs used his position of power to try to impose limits. "There were people coming in at the rate of two to three thousand a month," he recalls. "The situation was getting out of hand. In Lithuania, they resisted immigration, and they are much better off today. But here in Latvia . . . we managed to stem the flow for a while. Then they branded me a 'bourgeois nationalist'—me! a son of poor workers who had never owned anything in his life—and you know what happened to me after that."

In the center of Riga is a monument held in great esteem by Latvians all around the world: the Freedom Monument that stands in the middle of Lenin Boulevard on the approach to the Old Town. The monument is a column topped by a female figure, "The Lady of Liberty," holding three stars, arms outstretched to the sky. It was constructed in 1933, during the period of Latvia's independence. During the Soviet period, it has been reviled by the official media as a symbol of the bourgeois regime, but secretly venerated by a population struggling for its national rights. For much of this time, it was as if the monument were invisible; people were afraid openly to acknowledge its existence, although its powerful presence was felt throughout the city. Sporadic demonstrations took place here, and from time to time the area was cordoned off or closed to traffic. Yet, the monument grew to symbolize the freedom Latvians craved, and existed as a permanent reminder of the people's aspirations. Today, the monument has become a focal point for the newest wave of nationalist activity in Latvia and a place for regular gatherings. Flowers laid out in apparently permanent display adorn the base of the monument in Latvia's national colors, deep red and white.

Lithuania

Lithuania is the southernmost of the three Baltic States and the far-thest inland. It is also the largest and the most ethnically homogeneous of the Baltic States: 80 percent of its 3.6 million people are Lithuanian. Of the non-Russian republics, only Armenia has a higher percentage of tit-ular nationality in its native population. Lithuania's geography also re-veals a different historical evolution than that of its two Baltic neighbors. Unlike Riga and Tallinn, both port cities, Vilnius, Lithuania's capital, is located some distance inland, reflecting its past role within a larger land-based kingdom.

At the beginning of the fourteenth century, when Latvia was a thriving realm of the Livonian Knights and Estonia was ruled by Denmark, Lithua-nia constituted one of the largest areas of land in Europe. While the areas to the north of Lithuania were participating in the world of the Hanseatic League, Lithuania, blocked by the Livonian Kingdom to the north, had expanded its territories southeastward toward the Dnieper River. Gedymin (1316–41), the real founder of Lithuania, made Vilnius the capital of the new state. The state remained heathen—one of the last refuges in Europe—until Jagiello, Gedymin's grandson, married Jadwiga of Poland, thus linking the two states by a personal union and introducing Roman Catholicism as the state religion of Lithuania in 1387.

Pre-Christian influences have remained intertwined with Roman Ca-tholicism in the distinctive Lithuanian culture. The Lithuanian language is believed to be derived from Sanskrit; it bears only a slim resemblance to any of the languages of the surrounding peoples, and is one of the most ancient languages in the Soviet Union today. It is written in the Latin alphabet and has the appearance of a medieval Latin gone wrong with its *ius* endings. You know you are in a country where time went its own way when you come across men named Ringaudas, Vaidotas, Sigitas, Zigmas, and Arunas, and women called Ginte, Angonita, Jurate, and Mirga.

Vilnius must have been a beautiful city, a Florence of the North with its stunning Baroque architecture and pastel-shaded buildings. Many buildings in the old city are now shabby and falling apart, plaster peeling and scaffolding around walls marked with rust and years of neglect. Some have been earmarked for restoration and stand surrounded by scaffolding bearing the plaque of PKS, the Warsaw-based firm that specializes in restoration, whose services are increasingly in demand in the Baltics' historic cities. Vilnius University is one of the oldest seats of learning in Europe. Its buildings still form the heart of the old city, and it is a dynamo for Lithuanian culture and intellectual life whose influence is still strongly felt, particularly during the past few years of Gorbachev's rule. Many leaders of the Lithuanian reform movement are connected with the university in some way and many of the most active members are students, or people in their twenties or thirties.

Sajudis, the Lithuanian Popular Front, was formed at the same time as the popular fronts of Latvia and Estonia; it was conceived in the summer of 1988 and held its first congress in October. Of the three fronts, Sajudis has the most solid support from its population. There has been no Lithuanian independence group formed to rival Sajudis, which has managed to bring together under its umbrella most of the new informal groups. Only a few of the most radical groups remain outside Sajudis's organization. But the differences are differences only of tactics and timing: The radical groups want full and unconditional independence for Lithuania immediately, while Sajudis has worked through constitutional channels to ensure a stable transition that will at the same time ensure a democratic system. Differences among Sajudis members also seem to be nominal, although many are also members of the Communist Party. The same refrain can be heard here as elsewhere in Eastern Europe: People became members of the Communist Party for many different reasons. One Sajudis Council member admitted in a candid moment that many jobs, especially more influential ones in the universities or in the Academy of Sciences, were virtually unattainable to non-Party people. In the past, there was no alternative employment, and there was no reform movement to join to attempt to improve the situation. Many members also make the point that the Lithuanian Popular Front's main goal, in accordance with its name, is to support and put into practice Gorbachev's policy of perestroika—the restructuring of society and the economy—to better meet the needs of the Lithuanian people.

The selection of Vytautas Landsbergis for the president of Sajudis reflects a commitment by its members to deep-rooted, exclusively Lithuanian values. He is a musicologist by profession: a quiet man with a full dark beard and thick heavy glasses. In 1988, he was voted the most popular figure in Lithuania. An opinion poll gave him 78 percent of the vote and named him Man of the Year. The Party first secretary, Algirdas Brazauskas, lagged behind with a poor 22 percent at that time. Landsbergis's manner is unassuming and matter-of-fact and he guides the organization in purposeful activity. Yet when he stands at the podium to address two hundred thousand people, his tone is clear, his message strong, and the spirits of his ancestors line up behind him in triumph. The Landsbergis family's fate has been interwoven with the fate of Lithuania for generations. Landsbergis's ancestors have long been involved in the struggle for Lithuanian independence: His father fought for independence in the First World War and one of his maternal ancestors, of the Jablonskis family, was responsible for the development of the literary Lithuanian language.

Outside the building where the Sajudis headquarters is located on the corner of Gediminas Square, lines of people gather regularly to buy Sajudis publications. After the former Party ideological watchdog, Aleksandr Yakovlev, paid a visit to Lithuania in August 1988, Sajudis was given limited access to the official media. It has published the newspaper *Atgimimas (Rebirth)* in the Lithuanian language since then, and puts out a parallel Russian-language version. The first few issues were published without censorship, which was introduced only after the twelfth issue early in 1989.

"The idea behind that move was fairly simple," explains a young editor of a mass-circulation unofficial bulletin. "The authorities thought they would wean the readership away from the unofficial publications— numbering around twelve at that time—and then once they had closed them down they would crack down on the one official paper. But it didn't work out that way. Our unofficial press is thriving."

There are now around two hundred independent publications in Lithuania; some official and some unofficial. Each of the forty-four administrative regions has its own Sajudis-run newspaper and many informal groups have their own publications.

"There is a newspaper published in Kraje," a young Sajudis member told us. "In fact it is the revival of a newspaper published in independent Lithuania. Kraje has only one thousand inhabitants, but the newspaper comes out in a print run of three thousand. It is an official publication of the Sajudis 'Kraje Group.' " This is yet another of the anomalies that have become the norm in this period of national reawakening.

On our visit to Vilnius in February 1989, the city buzzed with excitement. The Sajudis headquarters there, three floors up in a corner building overlooking Gediminas Square, was packed with people, some manning the information desk, some visiting, some just sitting around. The walls were decorated with the yellow, green, and red of the Lithuanian flag and with the representations of the medieval knight Vytautas on his steed emblazoned in red across one wall. Here and there hung wall decorations made out of bank notes that were the currency in independent Lithuania. In the corner was an antique-looking East German Robotron computer, and a couple of telephones, each attached to a single line. Apart from these, and a television in the main office, there were no other items of technical equipment to suggest that this was the nerve center of an organization of hundreds of thousands, supported by a couple of million more people. The office was given to Sajudis after the organization's founding congress in November 1988. With only a few full-time staff, the office is nonetheless fully staffed every day and evening; many Sajudis officials stop in when they can to catch up on business. For many of the young people, it is also a place that they feel is their own, a place where something is happening. Part carnival, part permanent campaign headquarters, the office is reminiscent of the main office of the independent trade union Solidarity in Warsaw in the heady days of its legal existence in 1980.

The scope of activities of the Sajudis organization is truly awesome; it has penetrated all sectors of Lithuanian society. In October 1988, it took the organization three days to collect a million signatures to protest against amendments to the Lithuanian constitution proposed by Moscow. The entire country mobilized: Bus drivers were entrusted with carrying petitions out to the villages and bringing them back signed. The outpouring of dissatisfaction was there to be harnessed, and, more than the other popular fronts in Latvia or Estonia, Sajudis skillfully united the entire spectrum of people in its movement from the merely discontent to the politically astute.

The balcony from the Sajudis office's inner sanctum, where the leaders sit and receive foreign visitors, is the perfect vantage point onto Gediminas Square and Vilnius Cathedral. On independence day at around noon, people began to converge on the square, emerging silently from the surrounding side streets as if beckoned by an invisible Pied Piper. Young people, old people, people in groups, a lone Lithuanian striding along with a full-sized national flag unfurled across his shoulder. The day's proceedings were about to begin with a solemn mass in commemoration of the day, seventy-one years ago, when Lithuania's political leaders declared independence in Vilnius.

Lithuanians, like the Poles, have always looked to the Catholic Church for refuge against the tyranny of Soviet rule, so it is natural that the revival of national spirit should be ushered in by a religious ceremony. Yet, the Catholic Church could not play as great a role in the resistance against totalitarianism in Lithuania as it did in Poland: It was itself the victim of severe repressions. In the years of Soviet rule, Vilnius's Baroque cathedral served as a storehouse and then as an art gallery. It was returned to the Catholic Church in February 1989, just two weeks before the independence day celebrations. Lithuania's Catholic clergy suffered exile and repressions: Bishop Julijonas Steponavicius of Vilnius was exiled for twenty-seven years in a remote village in Lithuania before his joyous return to the city in 1989; Cardinal Sladkevicius, now the highest-ranking Lithuanian prelate, was also exiled for twenty-one years before his release in 1982.

Official religious life in Lithuania is reviving in fits and starts. There are over three dozen Old Believers churches in Lithuania today; thirty Orthodox churches; twenty or so, Lutheran; a few Calvinist and Baptist; one Pentecostal; two mosques; two synagogues without rabbis; and one Krishna temple. But the overwhelming majority of people in Lithuania today are Catholics, around 80 percent of the population. There are over six hundred Catholic churches and the number is increasing. For many years, the Lithuanian Catholic Church was especially reviled by the authorities and systematically suppressed, because of its close links to Lithuanian nationalism. The *Chronicle of the Lithuanian Catholic Church* was one of the longest-running samizdat journals in the Soviet Union. Begun in 1972, it helped to foster a sense of unity among Lithuanians and established the Lithuanian Catholic Church as an alternative to the Party's monopoly over ideological thought and activity.

Father Vaclovas Aliulis of the Lithuanian Catholic Church is a member of the Sajudis Council; he is the only man of the cloth among the leaders of the reform movement. He lives and works at the *kurija*, the church center, by the side of one of Vilnius's old churches set in the midst of the twisting roads and cobble-stoned alleyways of the old town. The furnishings in his reception room are sparse: There is no item that would give away the current year or even the decade apart from the portrait of Pope John Paul II. Father Aliulis has lived through all the vicissitudes meted out to the Lithuanian Catholic Church. He recalls the situation twenty years ago when the seminary for training young priests was allowed to accept only 25 students per year; now the number has risen to 141, although the authorities still reserve the final decision on admission to study for the priesthood.

"There were four seminaries for training priests in Lithuania before the war," he intones. "Now there is only the one in Kaunas. It all comes down to the same question. Who is the master here? *Kto khozyain?*" he repeats in Russian, shrugs his shoulders, and smiles an enigmatic smile. There is certainly no rancor or bitterness in his response, but more a sense of resignation that there is a transcendental battle to be fought. The Lithuanian Catholic Church has 7 bishops and 680 priests, but this still leaves 150 churches without a resident priest, he explains.

Father Aliulis has worked at translating and editing liturgical texts since 1965. Today, he is the editor of the first Catholic journal to be published legally in the Soviet Union. He modestly admits to his position and points to the top cupboards of his cabinet. "There is the editorial office," he says, smiling. For years, Father Aliulis and many like him persevered despite the persecution of their Church. The damage wrought by militant atheism still requires some work to undo. Children are no longer reprimanded by their teachers for attending church, and the Museum of Atheism has been closed down, but there are now two generations of Lithuanians who grew up without formal Christian or Catholic instruction. But the future looks bright for Lithuania's Catholics.

Lithuania's remaining Jews have not fared so well. It is hard to picture it now, but before the war, Lithuania was home to over a quarter million of Europe's Jews, who had lived here for centuries; today, there is still no working synagogue with a rabbi. Lithuania's Jews had developed a distinctive culture and spoke a variant of Yiddish that set them apart from their fellow Jews in the rest of Europe. The war swept it all away; there are currently only some eight thousand Jews in Lithuania and the rich and distinct culture has all but disappeared. Today, some of the Jews in Vilnius have hitched their fortunes to Sajudis.

Emanuel Zingeris is the leading force behind the newly established Jewish Cultural Association, and is also a member of the Sajudis Council. He is a mercurial figure, a mass of energy and a difficult person to find; he is in constant motion between the Sajudis office, the newly established Jewish Cultural Center, and any number of projects he has on the go at one time. During the early 1980s, he tried to stage exhibitions of Jewish art and culture, but was stopped by the authorities. Now the Jewish community has plans to establish teachers and doctors associations and to build a hospital. But for the moment, they must take things one step at a time. Zingeris firmly believes that the fate of the Lithuanian Jews lies with Sajudis and its program for more autonomy and independence. He is aware of the long road ahead. Many of the younger generation of Lithuanians are only dimly aware of the history of Jewish settlement in the Baltic lands; so well have the Soviet history books rewritten the past. He views with skepticism those who have sought to emigrate; the struggle is here, he maintains, in coordination with Sajudis, for a better future for both Jews and Lithuanians.

The striking feature of the Lithuanian movement is the number of young people who are actively involved. Back at the Sajudis office, the staff over the weekend are in their teens and early twenties. The older members, in their thirties, are home with their families, a rare respite since the movement began to grow. The exuberance and determination of these young people are sometimes hard to understand—where did it come from? They do not remember anything other than the day-to-day reality of life under the Soviet system; nor are they old enough to have experienced the Khrushchev years, which were the formative years for many Russian and Ukrainian dissidents who are now in their early fifties. Not many of them would remember even the Soviet invasion of Czechoslovakia of 1968. What is it that drives them onward?

"We are all Lithuanian, and we want to be free" is the simple answer given by one young man, who struggles to speak English even though his Russian is much more fluent. "We feel in our hearts that independence is the only way." He looks around and receives the affirmative nods from everyone else in the room.

One young woman makes an attempt to explain: "It's not as if we were ever taught to strive for independence. It depends, from family to family, how much real history a person managed to learn. I don't remember my parents ever telling me directly that the Russians were bad, or that we should struggle against Communism for an independent state once more. I'm not sure why we all feel so involved in this struggle: It's something that's always been with us, it's hard to explain."

Arvydas Juozaitis, in his mid-thirties, is one of the group of young radicals who are the dynamo of Sajudis. A bronze medal winner on the Soviet swimming team at the Montreal Olympics of 1976, he is now a philosopher at the Lithuanian Academy of Sciences. We first met him in early 1989 in his offices at the academy, located just next door to the Sajudis headquarters. At that time, the trappings of a makeshift campaign headquarters lay all around the office—he was the Sajudis candidate pitted against Party first secretary Algirdas Brazauskas in the elections for the Congress of People's Deputies. Helped by a campaign manager well versed in Western techniques, he looked set to give the Party veteran stiff competition. But a couple of weeks later, he withdrew his candidacy after he had deliberated with the Sajudis Council. The Party first secretary continued his campaign and won the seat. Juozaitis had been set not only to challenge the Party first secretary, but to deliver a crushing defeat. The council conceded that humiliating and antagonizing a moderate Party leader, who was generally sympathetic to Sajudis, was not a risk they were willing to take, perhaps for fear of creating the circumstances for his replacement by a hard-liner.

Juozaitis has pondered the prospects for Lithuania's future and has a ready answer for the first question on everyone's mind: Will Moscow use military force in the Baltics? He thinks not. "We have won every step thus far, and each time we win another, the possibility of such action becomes more and more remote. . . . The possibility may exist, but the chance of its actually happening is remote, because it would clearly mean the end of perestroika."

He shares the belief of many Lithuanians that Gorbachev will try to hang on to the Baltic States, in order to preserve the empire. But if somewhere along the line the Soviet president is confronted with the decision of whether to save the empire or to save Russia, then, clearly, the Baltics will diminish in their importance. What about the possibility that the Baltics' striving for independence can destabilize the Soviet Union and be harmful to Gorbachev's attempts at perestroika? He has been asked that question many times before. "I think that as far as destabilizing the Soviet Union," he replies, "the Baltics no longer bear the primary responsibility. The Soviet Union is being destabilized from all directions, and most importantly, from the economic direction." He paints a grim picture of the shaky Soviet economy and the danger to political structures throughout the USSR. Economic instability is a danger for both Moscow and Lithuania. Moscow will continue to be very important to Lithuania in the economic sphere under any political arrangement, as the largest potential trading partner. But the leaders of

Sajudis project that the relationship will be even more beneficial to Moscow once Lithuania has gained full independence and has regained control over the 80 percent of the economy currently directed from Moscow. On September 9, 1989, economists from the three Baltic popular fronts met in Panevezys, Lithuania, and drew up a series of economic guidelines, which proposed, among other things, that by 1993 there should be a common Baltic market.

A whole new set of relationships will be established between Lithuania and Western Europe, even if, as Juozaitis assumes, an independent Lithuania will tread the neutral path of Sweden. He shows no sign of pessimism. His clearly articulated statements reflect not only his own views but are also the result of months of careful and prolonged discussion in the Sajudis Council.

Not all pro-Lithuanian forces belong to Sajudis. The radical Lithuanian Freedom League is a small proindependence group that wishes to see less compromise with the Communist authorities and a swifter transition to independence. The league's leader is the former political prisoner Atanas Terleckas. His weather-worn features show the years he spent in labor camps. When we met him in February 1989, he complained that the people in Sajudis were faint-hearted; too attached to their possessions and jobs to strike out for the independence everybody craved. The league's relations with Sajudis were cool, Terleckas stated; but the group's final aim appeared to be the same, at least to the outside world.

Independent activity in the Baltic exudes a particular urgency and determination rarely found elsewhere in the USSR. The three Baltic nations are precariously close to the point of marginalization: Even though they have withstood the considerable pressures of Russification and the calculated resettlement of Russians into their region, there is the threat posed by their catastrophically low birth rate. Latvian women, for example, have the lowest reproduction rate in the USSR; Estonian and Lithuanian women are not far behind.

As the 1990s began, the proindependence forces in all three Baltic republics were in the paradoxical position of having to modulate and restrain the demands of the people. One Sajudis official informed us that the organization's role was to explain to the people the necessity for moving in gradual and systematic fashion. By the end of 1989 there was no longer any question that independence was a platform supported by almost all Lithuanians. The Sajudis meetings became less interesting, and all the action shifted over to the Communist Party headquarters where the contagious fever for independence caught on in a big way.

The Lithuanian Party's First Secretary Algirdas Brazauskas was somewhat in sympathy with the reform movement from the beginning of his tenure, although his low popularity rating in 1988 showed he did not enjoy much support among Lithuanians. But in the course of the following year—always walking a delicate tightrope between the warnings from the Kremlin and the increasing pressure for independence from the Lithuanian population—he began to chart a new course for the Communist Party in Lithuania, taking the initiative in the next stage in the struggle for independence. After several months of deliberation, the delegates to a special congress of Lithuania's Communist Party voted by an overwhelming 855 to 160, with 12 abstentions, to reconstitute themselves as an independent Party, separate from Moscow, with its own programs and statutes. In its "Declaration of Independence of the Communist Party of Lithuania," the goals of the new Party were described as Lithuania's "independence, a democratic society and the implementation of the ideals of humanistic socialism."

The reason for this astonishing move was clear to all. On December 7, 1989, Lithuania followed in the fresh footsteps of Poland, Hungary, East Germany, and Czechoslovakia, and became the first Soviet republic to formally drop the guaranteed "leading role of the Party" from its constitution, thus opening up the political field for a multiparty system. Facing an open competition with Sajudis candidates and other parties, in order to survive the Communist Party could not risk being trounced at the ballot box once more, as it had been in the elections to the Congress of People's Deputies in March 1989. The only way to remain alive was to declare "independence" from the Communist Party of the Soviet Union and to stand with, if not at the head of, the independence movement. Brazauskas's popularity ratings shot up, and suddenly the Communist Party became a real contender for political power. Patriotic Party people in the Baltic felt that they could use their Party posts to further their national activities. Nowhere was there a sense of the reverse, that the newly revived national feelings were seeking to resurrect Marxist-Leninist ideology.

In the face of the growing assertiveness of the Baltic Communists, Gorbachev himself decided to pay a visit to the wayward republic in January 1990. A top-level delegation was convened, led by Vadim Medvedev, the Kremlin's current top ideology watchdog, to prepare the visit of the president and his wife. By any account, the purpose of the visit was not clear, especially as the Lithuanian Party had already made its break with Moscow—the horse was out of the stable. Nonetheless, Gorbachev spent three days in and around Vilnius, debating, cajoling, and coming up short with Communists, workers, and even people on the street. The visit was highly publicized on Soviet TV, but the overwhelming impression was one of a peaceful, mass movement, totally in disagreement with the president and leader of the Communist Party of the Soviet Union. The most interesting of Gorbachev's statements during his visit indicated that the Kremlin might be prepared to accept Lithuanian demands. Instead of ruling out secession from the Union of Soviet Socialist

Republics, Gorbachev prevaricated and stated that the process should be regulated and that new laws were under discussion to provide the framework for such a move.

Roads to Independence

Within the next two months, events took a dramatic turn: The newly elected Lithuanian parliament voted Vytautas Landsbergis as president of Lithuania and on March 11, 1990, voted to take Lithuania out of the USSR. At the same time, the name Lithuanian SSR was changed to the Republic of Lithuania. The move to reestablish independence took place just days before Gorbachev was voted wide-ranging powers and promoted to the position of president of the USSR by a vote in the Supreme Soviet. Faced with the reality of the declaration of independence, Gorbachev made his intentions clearer. Within hours of the Lithuanian decision, tanks were rolling through the streets of Vilnius and Soviet soldiers had seized buildings belonging to the Communist Party and had forced their way into the offices of the republic's procuracy and leading newspapers. At the same time, young Lithuanian army conscripts who had deserted their posts in the Soviet Army seeking refuge in Lithuania were brutally rounded up in a surprise raid in the hospital where they were sheltering.

Lithuania's declaration of independence should not have come as a surprise to Gorbachev and his leadership in Moscow. The new Lithuanian government stressed that the majority of members of the Supreme Soviet, or Supreme Council as they now preferred to be called, were elected on a proindependence platform. But in the few tense weeks that followed, Gorbachev had few arguments with which to support his strong-arm tactics in the republic. The war of words escalated as the world media focused full attention on developments in the renegade Baltic republic. Officials in Moscow claimed the Lithuanian government had perpetrated an illegal act. The Lithuanian government countered that the Soviet occupation of Lithuania in 1940 was the illegal act; they were merely reinstating the legal existence of a republic that had been on hold for fifty years.

Several ultimatums were issued from Moscow instructing the Lithuanian Supreme Council to rescind the declaration of independence; foreigners, including young people of Lithuanian parentage who had come to help Sajudis from North America, were ordered to leave. Lithuanian requests for negotiations were swept aside as Gorbachev took decisive action and imposed an economic embargo of the republic. The embargo was reinforced by a blockade, which effectively prevented goods being delivered from Poland or via the sea route on Lithuania's east coast. At the same time, the new law on secession was rushed through the Supreme Soviet in Moscow, creating a procedure so lengthy and cumbersome that many national democrats began to refer to it as the "antisecession law."

The Lithuanians pledged to stand firm on their declaration of independence, but expressed willingness to compromise through negotiation on other issues. Gorbachev remained adamant on the economic embargo and refused to enter negotiations with one of the constituent republics of the USSR as if it were a foreign country. There was little sympathy for Lithuania in Moscow even among liberal Russians, including members of the Interregional Group of Deputies. For several weeks the situation looked desperate. On April 26, Stanislavas Zamaitis, a Lithuanian national, set fire to himself and burned to death in Moscow in protest against the Soviet government's refusal to recognize Lithuania's declaration of independence. In his suicide note he wrote: "Lithuanians will not live in a Lithuania that is not independent."

Lithuanian deputies were dispatched around the Soviet Union to seek assistance from democratic groups and deputies in other republics; and in the international arena, Lithuania urged recognition of its new status, particularly from the United States and other countries that had for years professed a policy of nonrecognition of the incorporation of the Baltic States into the Soviet Union. The delegations received a positive response from the newly elected Moscow City Soviet and the Democratic Bloc in the Ukraine among others, but Lithuania's request for assistance, or even unqualified moral support, from the governments of the Western democracies met with a cold shoulder.

While Moscow continued its coercive tactics against Lithuania, and the tense standoff dominated headlines in the West, the two other Baltic States were quietly planning their own moves toward independence. On March 11, the Congress of Estonia was convened by Estonians who had been citizens prior to the Soviet occupation and their descendants. Following through to the logical conclusion, there was no need to announce independence when, the Congress decided, independence had never formally been given up by the citizens of Estonia. The newly elected Supreme Soviet of Estonia was a potential rival center of authority, but when it convened later that month, it voted to recognize and cooperate with the Congress of Estonia. On March 30, the Supreme Soviet went even further and declared the continuing de jure existence of the Republic of Estonia and announced a transitional period that would lead to full independence for the republic.

On May 4, 1990, the newly elected Latvian Supreme Soviet followed Estonia's lead and declared Latvia's incorporation into the USSR to have been illegal. It adopted a resolution calling for a period of transition leading to full independece for the republic. Gorbachev's response to these events was unequivocal. The declarations were judged to be in contravention of the Soviet constitution. And as long as Lithuania continued to uphold its declaration of independence there would be no negotiations and the economic blockade would continue. Feeling the pressure, but buoyed now by a sense of solidarity, the three republics signed an agreement reestablishing the Baltic Council of the interwar period to coordinate their moves toward independence.

During the blockade, Lithuania's prime minister, Kazimiera Prunskiene, visited all the major capitals of the West in an attempt to gain support. Although she reported a warm welcome in most places, very little concrete assistance came out of her tour. Interestingly, the leaders of the fledgling democracies of East and Central Europe were not so reticent in their support for Lithuania's independence. President of Czechoslovakia Vaclav Havel invited Vytautas Landsbergis for a two-day visit to Prague. The Polish Sejm adopted a resolution of support for Lithuanian independence and sent a high-ranking delegation of Solidarity parliamentarians headed by Bronislaw Geremek to Vilnius for talks. Asked in an interview what he would say to Mikhail Gorbachev about Lithuania, Solidarity leader Lech Walesa stated: "I would say what I said a long time ago: The only solution is to dissolve the Soviet Union. And then you can establish ties founded on completely different principles—free will, freedom. You cannot try to prevent an unavoidable trend by force because this dissolution must come."

Closer to home, Lithuanian independence was greeted with enthusiasm in the republics: The Ukrainian popular movement Rukh organized pro-Lithuanian demonstrations in Kiev and Lvov, and several thousand people attended a rally in the Georgian capital of Tbilisi. All this time, the people of the Baltic States were subjected to provocations and pressure from anti-independence forces. Military helicopters dropped leaflets over Vilnius urging the population to oppose Lithuanian independence. In Latvia and Estonia, members of the pro-Moscow Interfront organizations stormed buildings and created ugly scenes. In all three republics, the supporters of independence remained calm and maintained the strategy of peaceful progress.

A major breakthrough came at the Bush-Gorbachev summit at the beginning of June 1990. Without bestowing any greater measure of diplomatic recognition on the Lithuanian state, U.S. President George Bush warned the Soviet president that as long as there was an economic blockade against Lithuania, further progress on negotiating favorable trade agreements between the United States and the Soviet Union would not be possible.

By mid-June 1989, Gorbachev was facing a radically new situation at home: Boris Yeltsin, his erstwhile supporter turned principal challenger, now president of the Russian Republic, had declared for republican sovereignty, and every day, demands for more democracy and autonomy in the other republics were increasing. All of this was taking place against a backdrop of continuing inertia and crisis in the Soviet economy. When Gorbachev called in the three Baltic presidents—Vytautas Landsbergis from Lithuania, Anatoly Gorbunovs from Latvia, and Arnold Ruutel from Estonia—for talks to break the deadlock he had perhaps finally realized that the tide could not be turned.

Far from discouraging national democratic movements in other republics, the Baltics' dash for freedom created a precedent on many levels for organizing citizens' efforts, establishing parliamentary procedures, and referring to national and international law. In the process, the courageous stand of the Lithuanians won the sympathy of a large segment of public opinion in the West and showed the other nations of the USSR that patience and fortitude can be rewarded. The peaceful revolution demonstrated that the first stage of the dissolution of the empire need not automatically unleash forces of destruction nor signal a descent into interethnic violence, particularly when freedom is the goal and democracy the means.

Ivan Gel (*left*), a leader of the Ukrainian Catholic movement. A political prisoner for over a decade, Gel is now a deputy in the Ukrainian Parliament—the Supreme Soviet.

A rally in support of the Ukrainian Popular Movement, the Rukh. Lvov demonstrators endorse a call to build a statue in honor of the nineteenth-century Ukrainian poet Taras Shevchenko.

Iryna Kalynets, former political prisoner, addresses a rally in Lvov in the summer of 1988.
Just a year and a half later, Ms. Kalynets was
elected overwhelmingly to the Ukrainian Parliament.

Lvov, Ukraine, July 1988. Tens of thousands of protesters gather in a large unofficial demonstration on behalf of national rights and democratic elections.

Thousands of Ukrainian Catholics gather for an open-air mass in January 1989 as part of a campaign to win back the legalization of their banned church.

Kiev, Ukraine, September 1989. International Solidarity: (*left to right*) Polish Solidarity leaders Zbigniew Janas and Adam Micknik meet with Ukrainian ecological activist Yuri Shcherbak at the founding congress of the Ukrainian Popular Front, the Rukh.

As part of the upsurge in patriotism among young Ukrainians, student volunteers help repair formerly despoiled cemeteries of the Ukrainian Sharpshooters of the post–World War I independent Ukrainian state.

A statue of Saint Volodymyr (Vladimir), Christianizer of the Kievan Rus state. The statue, located in Zbarazh, in Western Ukraine, was desecrated during antireligious campaigns of the 1950s.

The Crimea in 1988. A Crimean Tatar village, razed during the Stalin era, awaits the return of the indigenous population, which was exiled to Central Asia.

Tallinn, Estonia, June 1988. The Singing Revolution: part of a crowd of Estonians, who gathered for a patriotic song festival that turned into a manifestation of mass support for independence.

Tallinn, Estonia, summer 1988. Several hundred thousand Estonians gather under the banner of their formerly independent state to press for independence.

Tallinn, Estonia. A candlelight vigil organized by nationalist demonstrators commemorates the victims of Soviet repression.

The airport near Yerevan, Armenia. Thousands gather to block the arrival of Soviet aircraft bearing troops. The protest, in the summer of 1988, was brutally suppressed by Soviet authorities and resulted in the deaths of several protesters.

Opera Square, Yerevan. A crowd of some half a million gathers to press for national self-determination and to demand that the region of Nagorno-Karabakh be handed over to Armenia by Azerbaijan.

The airport near Yerevan. An ambulance carries off protesters wounded in assaults by Soviet authorities. The violence, which resulted in several deaths in the summer of 1988, only served to strengthen the determination of pro-independence forces.

Child labor in Uzbekistan. The exploitation of children in the cotton fields of that republic is one among many complaints against colonial exploitation leveled at Moscow by Uzbek popular front activists. This photo, taken in November 1988, is from the Khotirchi region in the Samarkand district.

BIRLIK

Taking tea. In a cotton field poisoned by the misuse of chemical fertilizers, Uzbek cotton gatherers take a break for tea.

ANDREW TKACH

Tashkent, Uzbekistan. A clash of cultures. Women in traditional dress stroll past a looming banner of Karl Marx.

ANDREW TKACH

Samarkand district, Uzbekistan. Uzbek women gather around a traditionally prepared dinner table.

Samarkand district, Uzbekistan. Uzbek elders play chess in a typical open-air *chaykhana*—a teahouse.

Town of Girchak in the Tashkent district of Uzbekistan. The Soviet militia moves in to arrest Crimean Tatars at a May 8, 1988, gathering to commemorate the forty-fourth anniversary of the forced expulsion by Stalin of all Tatars from the Crimea.

Leader of the "Black-shirts." Dmitry Vasiliyev, leader of the Russian ultranationalist, neofascist Pamyat organization, at his home on the Moscow Ring Road.

The Caucasus:
Three Nations in
Ferment

When will the blood cease to flow in the mountains?
When the sugarcane grows in the snows.

—Caucasian Proverb

For visitors and the residents of Moscow, firsthand acquaintance with the peoples of the Caucasus begins in the Soviet capital's open-air marketplaces. Even before perestroika, the privately sold produce brought in for Moscow's more prosperous housewives often came from distant Georgia, Armenia, and Azerbaijan. Since Mikhail Gorbachev's encouragement of private enterprise, Caucasian merchants are even more keen to capitalize on the economic potential of their lands. Speaking in heavily accented Russian, the vendors tell of driving two thousand miles to market with a truck full of vegetables from Azerbaijan, or of transporting plump radishes and ripe tomatoes from Yerevan by airplane.

The mountainous Caucasus region is lodged squarely between the Black Sea and the Caspian Sea. It is the gateway from the Russian north to the Middle East. The thousands of daily travelers from Moscow leave behind dreary Domodedovo Airport and the oppressive constraints, shortages, and rudeness of everyday life in the empire's capital. For the people in the Caucasus, the period under Soviet rule is a mere blip in the region's history, which stretches back through the mists of time to the era of mythology, when Jason and his Argonauts landed in Colchis, in present-day Georgia.

This land contains diverse and rich terrain. One of the peaks of the

Caucasus Mountain range, Mount Elbrus, rises to over 5,500 meters (about 18,000 feet) above sea level. The oil fields in Azerbaijan produce around 10 percent of the Soviet Union's total output of oil; Georgia's vineyards produce some of the best wine and champagne in the country. The lush and comfortable resorts of Sochi and Sukhumi on the Black Sea coast are among the most popular in the Soviet Union, while just a few miles inland, the Armenian towns of Spitak and Leninakan were at the epicenter of perhaps the century's most devastating earthquake. All this is located within less than 72,000 square miles that contain the three Caucasian republics of Armenia, Azerbaijan, and Georgia.

True to the region's turbulent past, each of the republics has been the scene of dramatic events in the past two years. In 1988, the trend of mass street gatherings that has astonished the world began in Armenia. It was the first time that crowds numbering in the hundreds of thousands were seen taking part in peaceful demonstrations on the streets of Yerevan. These scenes, more than any of the previous declarations from Gorbachev or assurances from the Soviet press, showed that there had been dramatic change in the structure of the Soviet Union. In April 1989, tragedy struck in Georgia. People praying in front of the government building were brutally cut down with sharpened shovels and poisoned with chemical gas. In Azerbaijan, the movement was slow to take off, but by September 1989, the crowds were with the Azerbaijani Popular Front: Hundreds of thousands demonstrated in the main square in front of the statue of Lenin. And in January 1990, the entire country went on a month-long general strike.

The massive demonstrations by hundreds of thousands of Armenians, Azerbaijanis, and Georgians, and their general strikes, have changed the West's perceptions of nationalism in the Soviet Union. The explosion of nationalist feeling in the Caucasus forever laid to rest the notion of the USSR as a happy family of nations living in harmony under one rule.

The people of the Caucasus look different; they behave differently. Their view of the world does not revolve around Moscow, but is firmly rooted in the lands where they have lived for centuries.

Relations between these three distinct and ancient peoples, now numbering around 15.6 million, have not always been easy. The Russian czar Alexander I annexed part of Georgia in 1801 and by 1810 had consolidated his rule over the country. The annexation of the rest of the Caucasian region was complete by 1829, after a war against Persia, when the Armenian territories together with the city of Yerevan were signed over to Russia. The Azerbaijani principalities in the region were conquered by Russia at the same time.

The nineteenth century was a period of uneasy coexistence among the Georgians, Armenians, and Azerbaijanis. While each nationality existed under czarist domination, borders were fluid or nonexistent. Azerbaijani

Turks, as they were known, lived in Armenia, and Armenians lived in Azerbaijan and Georgia. Of the three peoples, the Georgians were the most geographically compact, occupying a well-defined area in the western Caucasus. Nonetheless, Tbilisi, or Tiflis as it was then called, was more an Armenian city because of the predominance of Armenians in the urban merchant class at that time. Up until the recent strife between Armenians and Azerbaijanis, there was a strong Armenian presence in Baku.

When the Russian empire disintegrated in 1917, major political groups consolidated primarily along ethnic lines in the Caucasus. For a time after the Bolshevik coup of October 1917, the three Caucasian nations maintained a federation. But by the spring of 1918, internal dissension made that arrangement untenable and each state in turn declared its independence: the Georgians on May 26, the Azerbaijanis on May 28, and the Armenians on May 30. Independence did not last long as, one by one, the national states that had broken free of the czarist empire were reabsorbed into the new Soviet state.

Under Soviet rule, the three Caucasian nations became part of the many nations and peoples that make up the USSR. The designation of Soviet citizens has not been a comfortable one. Although none of the three nations was an enemy of Russia, their subjection to Soviet nationalities policy through the years has only fueled the desire for independence from the Russian-dominated state in the north.

Georgia

Today, the Georgia of popular imagination is a land of dancing ensembles whose dark-eyed women glide like clockwork dolls and whose mustachioed men perform an array of acrobatic feats on tiptoe. But it is also the birthplace of Stalin, about whom many Georgians remain ambivalent—at once proud and critical. For years, the Georgian Republic has enjoyed a special status, and its Communist Party has earned the reputation of being insular and corrupt. The central authorities let Eduard Shevardnadze (now Soviet foreign minister) run the Georgian SSR without direct interference from Moscow, so long as he maintained Party discipline and kept nationalism in check.

Tbilisi, the capital city of Georgia, is located in a picturesque basin surrounded on three sides by mountains; the fifteen-hundred-year-old city has a population of more than one million. Its name comes from the Georgian word *tbili*, which means "warm": The city is home to a district of sulfurous springs. A city of citadels, cathedrals, castles, and cable cars, Tbilisi has a long history as a center for trade and commerce and intellectual life. Its various districts reflect three distinct periods in Georgia's history: pre-Russian times, the nineteenth century under czarist rule, and the last seventy years under Soviet rule.

On Rustaveli Boulevard, the central artery that runs through Tbilisi, everyday life appears to be proceeding as normal in this bustling Caucasian metropolis. There is little trace of a Russian presence in this Soviet city. But for the lack of advertising, shabbiness of the minor roads, and the occasional youth dressed in a military uniform strolling the streets when off duty, it could well be taken for one of the poorer towns of southern Italy. It is surrounded by mountains that treat its inhabitants to many spectacular sunsets.

But there is a seething resentment that lies just below the surface, shared by every Georgian here. On April 9, 1989, nineteen people, mainly women, were killed and many more injured when troops from the Ministry of Internal Affairs attacked a peaceful demonstration outside the government building. The unprovoked attack on law-abiding citizens was carried out by soldiers using sharpened shovels, backed up by the use of a lethal gas. Many of the victims died of chemical poisoning, and countless others were hospitalized suffering severe effects.

Bloody Sunday, as it is now referred to, stunned and shocked the Georgian people, and provided a compelling reason for resistance to Soviet rule for those who had hitherto stood on the sidelines of demonstrations. There were some who claimed a knowledge of ulterior motives by the authorities on that night. There was a secret plan, informed sources claimed, to force the crowds to enter the government building as if in a spontaneous, storming surge. Troops had flanked the crowd on three sides, leaving open the side toward the government building, and had been ready to force in the crowd. A telegram addressed to Moscow from the then first secretary of the Georgian Communist Party, Djumber Patiashvili, explaining how troops were obliged to put down the rioting masses when they broke into the government building, had already been drafted. But the plan backfired. The crowds refused to be incited and remained calm, most of them on their knees praying in front of the building.

Months after the horrible tragedy, passersby could still detect a faint whiff of chemicals in the air, even though the stone slabs and turf in front of the government building had been pulled up and a fence erected to block off the site from public view.

The events of April 9, 1989, will be remembered here and throughout the Soviet Union as a national tragedy. For the Georgian movement, the date marks a watershed. Since the killings, the population has been galvanized behind the various groups that make up the movement for Georgian rights. Shaken by the wanton violence against their own people, the authorities have ceased to obstruct and prosecute the activities of the Georgian patriotic organizations. Hardly a Georgian can be found now who does not condemn the April 9 events and who does not advocate independence for the Georgian nation.

The Georgian case has been bolstered by official investigations of the killings. In October 1989, the Georgian Supreme Soviet issued its report, including that the military operation in Tbilisi "had the appearance of a deliberately planned slaughter carried out with extraordinary cruelty." A committee of the Supreme Soviet came to a similar conclusion on the facts; its findings implied that high-level officials in Moscow—among them Defense Minister Dmitri Yazov and Politboro members Yegor Ligachev and Viktor Chebrikov—had made key decisions concerning the operation.

Across the street from the site of the massacre, the Kashveti Church has become a memorial sanctuary, with candles set up to honor the dead in the age-old Georgian religious tradition. The constant stream of faithful people of all ages keeps the church open now at all times.

The Union of Cinematographers building, about half a mile up the road from the scene of Bloody Sunday, has turned into the intellectuals' and reformers' meeting place. Georgia's filmmakers have always been somewhat independent—Tengiz Abuladze's film *Repentance*, shot in a Georgian setting, was one of the first to reach a mass audience with its explicit criticism of Stalinism.

In the summer of 1989, Eldar Shengelaya, people's deputy and supporter of Georgian rights, gave over the use of his office in the union's building to proindependence groups for their meetings. Almost all groups were represented: the newly formed Georgian Popular Front, the Ilya Chavchavadze Society, the National Democratic Party, the radical Society of St. Ilya the Righteous, and several others. Discussions proceeded in an amicable yet determined atmosphere. Although there was no disagreement on the fundamental issue of independence, the moderates, such as the Georgian Popular Front, were in favor of achieving this aim through participation in the Soviet electoral process, while the radicals within the Society of St. Ilya the Righteous and the National Democratic Party were for a boycott. Anxious crowds gathered outside the building day and night throughout the summer. Still suffering from the trauma of the April massacre, they gathered to hear the latest news, to give each other moral support, and to feel a sense of solidarity with their countrymen at a time of crisis. Across the road, the statue of Shota Rustaveli, the medieval Georgian bard, joined them in silent vigil.

There are almost no Soviet-style slogans left in the center of Tbilisi. Only a few remain in the workers' districts, the last bastion of Party influence. But one panel shows Georgia's evolution over the past few years. At the end of the main drag of Rustaveli Boulevard, just outside one of Tbilisi's major theaters, stands a billboard that has always been used for political purposes. In Brezhnev's day, it displayed a large picture of the venerated general secretary, dressed in a dark suit in the winter and a light suit in the summer. When Gorbachev took over, the portraits disappeared, to be replaced by sayings from the new leader and exhortations for more effort toward perestroika. In the last few months, all semblance of lip service to the regime has been abandoned and the billboard now shows the sayings of the Georgian poet Rustaveli displayed with a Georgian-style folk pattern around the border.

The paraphernalia of Georgian independence is for sale on the streets of Tbilisi for those who have not yet fashioned their own version of the national symbols. The newsletters and literature of proindependence groups and pins depicting the national flag can be bought for a modest price. Young people walk down Rustaveli Boulevard carrying the national flag. That act would have provoked immediate arrest not long ago, but now it passes almost unnoticed. The Georgians' growing national assertiveness is literally changing the city's appearance. For many years, a statue depicting Sergo Ordjonikidze, Stalin's right-hand man in the conquest of Georgia for the Bolsheviks, stood in a small square to the north of the boulevard. He was an officially venerated figure in Georgia—until recently. The town named after him in Georgia has reverted to its old name. The statue in Tbilisi suffered a less dignified fate: After months of being pelted with rotten eggs and vegetables, and futile efforts by the authorities to keep it clean, the local government finally gave in and ordered its dismantling.

The Georgians' upsurge of national feelings and grief after the April 1989 massacre has served as the catalyst for demands for Georgian independence and has politicized the population. But the foundation was already present: The Georgians have always maintained a strong sense of their unique and separate national identity. Seventy years of Soviet rule have merely sharpened their sensibilities.

Ghia is a philosopher who works at the Georgian Academy of Sciences. He completed his candidate's dissertation (equivalent to a Ph.D.) in 1981, but because of bureaucratic procrastination it was not published until 1986. As a subtle act of protest, he refused to delete the quotes and references to Brezhnev that had been mandatory when it was first written. "I had fulfilled my duty," he says. "I left them to sort it out."

Ghia lives in one of the new apartment blocks not too far from the center of Tbilisi. The surrounding blocks are shabby and already crumbling even though they were built just three years ago. Sections of wall still have gaping holes in them, but work will never be completed because the materials have long ago disappeared from the building site. Ghia has a large apartment by Soviet standards, four large rooms and a spacious hallway shared with only one adjoining neighbor. But when we arrive for dinner at his home, we find the bathtub filled with water, to provide reserves for the evening when there is no water: Ghia's family still suffers the same indignities as the rest of the population.

One of the other dinner guests is a second Ghia who signs himself "George" and sports a thick mustache and stubbled chin, *de rigueur* for all Georgian men. George is a member of the Caucasian Club, an informal organization that takes up ecological issues in the Caucasus. It is hard to tell how serious is his concern for the environment; one gets the distinct impression that George's club has a more Georgian focus to it than he acknowledges. As the evening wears on, we discover that George hails from a blue-blooded family of the Georgian nobility. We are reminded that the Georgian monarchy was deposed by the Russians when Georgia was annexed to the empire at the beginning of the nineteenth century. Another of George's forebears was involved in the settlement of the Abkhazians in the north of Georgia, and another took part in the 1924 uprising, the last stand of anti-Bolshevik forces that ended in the defeat of the rebels in Western Georgia. The Georgians are fierce defenders of their history; they are also renowned for their pride and passion. A traditional anecdote explains why there are no lines of people waiting to purchase goods in Soviet Georgia: The reason is not that there is plenty to go around, but that Georgians are too proud to stand in line.

The Georgians have much to be proud of. Mtskheta, the ancient capital of Georgia, was at the junction of important trade routes—from east to west down the Mtkavari River, and from north to south down the Argvi River, then onward to Armenia and Persia. The old Jvari Church, built in the fourth century, sits on top of a precipitous peak just outside the town. In the center of the town below is the huge Svetitskhoveli Cathedral: Built in the eleventh century, it is the spiritual center of the Georgian Orthodox Church. It is a breathtaking edifice, stunning in its simplicity, yet aesthetically complex with its asymmetrical construction. Priests dressed in long, black raiments and conical, black hats walk by, as if the tourists were not there. The cathedral draws many native Georgian visitors, as it is the burial place of many of the Georgian monarchs.

The Georgians today display an aristocratic bearing. The women are renowned for their looks, not pretty but striking. And the men usually wear a beard, mustache, or a five-o'clock shadow that is definitely the mark of manliness here. They are the principal actors in the political game, the organizers and the contemporary defenders of the national honor. Women play hardly any role in the business of politics.

Zviad Gamsakhurdia has the dark eyes and brooding good looks of a true son of Georgia. Even though his hair has turned gray since his first independent political activities, he is a popular hero whose time has come. Georgian nationalism runs in his family. His father, the renowned Georgian writer Konstantine Gamsakhurdia, was expelled from the Georgian Writers Union in the early 1930s as Stalinism moved into high gear. In the 1950s, he was once more singled out for attack for "idealization of the past" in his works—in other words, for attempting to present history as it was, rather than as the Party had dictated it should be written. The young Zviad must have suffered these indignities together with the rest of his family.

Until a few years ago, Zviad was virtually an unknown figure despite many years of activity. As a teenager, he was arrested for distributing proindependence leaflets and served a short sentence. In 1972, now a teacher of American literature and English language, he made a protest against the poor state of Georgia's architectural monuments. When it was discovered that precious Georgian religious artifacts were missing, Gamsakhurdia pressed the authorities into an investigation that eventually led to the wife of the Georgian Communist chief, Vasily Mzhavanadze. In 1974, Gamsakhurdia and his colleagues regrouped to defend human rights, and in 1977, to monitor violations of the Helsinki Accords that the USSR had just signed. He was arrested with his longtime friend and colleague Merab Kostava, and sentenced to five years' incarceration. The authorities did their best to make sure that news of the arrests and imprisonment was kept away from the public in Georgia. Gamsakhurdia's plight was known mainly in the West, publicized through links he had established with Russian dissidents in Moscow.

Today, when he appears in public, people flock around him to air their grievances or merely to shake his hand, and at meetings the crowds wait in anticipation, cheering when he arrives. He has a brisk, businesslike demeanor and his sentences are clipped and precise. True to the Georgian character, there is no room for equivocation in what he says:

"The Georgian government is Moscow's puppet. . . . There are no Marxists in Georgia, even in the Party, they are all businessmen, hiding behind Marxist and Communist ideas. It's a party of businessmen." He pauses, to make sure we get the message.

He sees independence as the only way out for Georgia and alludes to hundreds of thousands already engaged in the movement—"practically the whole of Georgia," he stresses. But the path toward this goal will be different from the one taken by the Baltic nations:

"The Baltics have their own way, a parliamentary way. . .this is possible for them as they have nationally conscious people in the Communist Party and in the government. Ours are corrupt and antinational."

He stops to search for an analogy, then continues: "Our movement is more like the movement in Poland. We are forming workers committees throughout the country; we are working to establish a free trade union. We will be better organized in the future."

Gamsakhurdia's assessment of the national question in the Soviet Union is common among the thoughtful dissidents who have grappled with the issue for many years, both in the gulag and outside. He believes that many interethnic conflicts are orchestrated from Moscow, and are a way of exercising "Moscow's imperial policy." Close to home, he believes that the Georgian conflicts with the Abkhazians and Azerbaijanis fall into this pattern. On the issue of Georgia's independence, Gamsakhurdia's voice has been consistent for many years. When he was unknown to the Georgian population, his views were the cry of a dissident figure isolated from his people, but now he voices the feelings of the majority of the Georgian population. Other leaders of informal groups emphasize different points, but he is, for the moment, the unofficial leader.

Until his untimely death in a motor accident in October 1989, the fifty-year-old Merab Kostava had been one of Georgia's preeminent political leaders. His funeral was a huge event attended by thousands. In the summer of 1989, this silver-haired firebrand stood together with other leaders of proindependence groups, but towered above them as a moral force. Speaking in heavily accented Russian, Kostava stressed the need to introduce Christian values and teachings into Georgia: "The empire *will* fall apart, and Georgian independence will be achieved in these circumstances." For him as for increasing numbers of Georgians, there were no compromises. He believed Georgians should strive for their ideal of Christian brotherhood and independence without succumbing to a system imposed by an illegal power: They should boycott the Soviet elections.

Not all Georgia's leaders are so radical. Nodar Notadze, the head of the Georgian Popular Front, is a philosopher at the Academy of Sciences and a relative latecomer to the ranks of the organized opposition. He explains that the Popular Front also is for an independent Georgia, but favors a gradual approach. The front will not boycott elections, but works to achieve its aims through constitutionally established channels. The idea of a gradual approach is new and much more difficult for Georgians to grasp than the goal of unconditional independence, clearly articulated and publicized by radical dissidents for so many years. The Popular Front has a difficult task ahead if it is to mediate between moderates and radicals.

Support for Gamsakhurdia and the radical wing of the independence movement becomes evident at a meeting of workers at the Stalin Rail Carriage Repair Factory. A bas-relief of Stalin's face, flanked by Maxim Gorky on one side and Mikhail Kalinin on the other, stands outside the entrance to the building. Not allowed to hold the meeting indoors, Gamsakhurdia addresses the workers outside in a small amphitheater that is decorated with panels depicting scenes from working life. Over two hundred people in tattered and shabby overalls stand and sit on the steps awaiting his arrival even though he is already more than half an hour late. The assembled workers cheer and applaud as he strides up to the platform to join his colleagues from other radical groups. He is the center of attention, the main speaker, and his message to his growing constituency of supporters is clear, he wants their support for a one-day token strike. He promises the formation of a free trade union and urges the workers to send in their grievances. He lashes out at the official trade unions and Communist Party for their failure to defend the interests of Georgia's workers. The crowd breaks into tumultuous applause as he finishes: "Long live a democratic, independent, Christian Georgia!"

Spurred on by the success of Poland's Solidarity trade union, the Georgian radicals have wasted no time in taking their discussions out of the circle of intellectuals and into the factories, where there is fertile ground for the organization of a mass movement. Like the Poles, Georgians are polarized into "us and them": government and opposition, with little firm ground in between for a moderate tendency to gain strength. It is unlikely that a "Hungarian solution" would work here; there is no constituency for the formation of a range of moderate groups and parties to fill in the political spectrum between the government and the former dissidents.

Swept up in the maelstrom of nationalist activity is Georgia's youth. Many young people are alienated from the Communist Party and the current political system in Georgia, but are instinctively drawn to the independence movement. There is one youth organization group, the Christian Democratic Group, that explicitly excludes young Communists from the Komsomol, the Communist Party's youth organization. The Christian Democratic leaders intend to supplant the Komsomol with their own organization with its once forbidden ideology that endorses the idea of private property, and calls for a multiparty system. It impatiently demands a constitution formulated on the basis of the Helsinki Accords and the Universal Declaration of Human Rights. These young Georgians epitomize all the energy and radicalism that are characteristic of their nation as a whole. As young Soviets, they are going through the strains and stresses of life under a system where they can expect to wait twenty-five years for an apartment of their own. As young Georgians, they are filled with the confidence that the way forward lies through Christian values and the reassertion of Georgian national and political rights. Occasionally, in informal conversation, the radicalism and hotheadedness that is under the surface inadvertently emerge. One of the young Christian Democrats asserts that "Georgia should be only for the Georgians"; all Soviet troops and eventually all other nationals should leave the republic. What he and many other young Georgians lack is the accumulated knowledge of world affairs that only exposure to uncensored information can provide. For generations, the Georgians have been isolated from events in the rest of the world, without even a significant diaspora, like that of their neighbors, the Armenians, to give them a window on a different way of life and a vision of a different way of organizing their political affairs.

Young people from Georgia have only just begun to travel abroad. They show little enthusiasm for exploring other parts of the Soviet Union. Poland and Hungary are strong attractions. Israel is considered a desirable place to visit, but they fail to see that a future independent Georgia, like Israel, might find itself surrounded by potentially hostile states. Their limited political experience has given them no basis for recognizing a situation that might one day be their own.

Sitting around in their offices, in a building of faded splendor off Rustaveli Boulevard, the young Christian Democrats have gained support at a rapid rate since the congress that founded their group in May 1989. The group's emblem, a stylized sign of a cross, is emblazoned on a wall poster next to a poster of the Georgian national flag. The young Christian Democrats interrupt each other to voice their opinions, which span a broad range of topics. Their youthful enthusiasm brings forth a string of expressions couched in the language of democracy, but behind the rhetoric, we get the uneasy feeling that Western values are little more than a reservoir for anti-Soviet slogans.

There is as yet little of the meticulous, careful planning of strategies and moves in Georgia that has characterized the national movements in the Baltic States. Nonetheless, passions here run deep, and most Georgians will tell you that they want nothing short of full independence.

The infectious enthusiasm for independence and the shortage of democratic ideas, especially among the youth, may be seen partly as the result of Georgia's location and historical development. Situated on the periphery of the Western world, Georgia never had a Magna Carta, nor the same traditions of justice and law that developed in Western Europe. The Georgians lived under constant threat of being conquered by Persia or Turkey. Nonetheless, a rudimentary understanding of democracy and social and political rights evolved through the years between the Georgian nobility and the peasantry. After Georgia's annexation by the Russian empire, the Georgian nobility was gradually absorbed into the imperial social structure or else became so impoverished as to be virtually indistinguishable from the rest of the Georgian population. The social contract broke down and responsibility for creating the foundation for a modern democratic tradition passed to the Georgian intelligentsia in the nineteenth century. One of them was Ilya Chavchavadze, who proposed the preservation of Georgia as a homogeneous agricultural society based on respect for Georgia's language and historical traditions, and a political system that extended voting rights to peasants. One of present-day Georgia's most prominent informal groups has named itself the Ilya Chavchavadze Society. But the development of the Georgian national democratic tradition was squashed, as were many other national democratic movements in the nineteenth-century Russian empire, by restrictions imposed by an increasingly conservative czarist government. In the twentieth century, democratic traditions were hardly given a chance to develop before the independent Georgian state constituted under the Social Democrats was brought under Bolshevik rule.

After seventy years of Soviet rule in Georgia, as in Armenia, interethnic problems are arising that could further complicate current efforts for reform and democratization. The dispute between Georgians and Abkhazians has been festering for some time. The Abkhazians, who live in an autonomous republic within the borders of Georgia, have proposed leaving the Georgian SSR to join the Russian Republic to the north. The Georgians object, because they consider the territories of Abkhazia and, in fact, the Abkhazians themselves to be part of the traditional Georgian heritage. The Abkhazia issue has mobilized the people around the Georgian leaders in a way that talk of peaceful democratic change has not. This dispute, which could turn into another Nagorno-Karabakh, is just another example of how ethnic differences can be exploited for antidemocratic ends.

Merab Mamardashvili, a philosopher who lives in Tbilisi, is troubled by recent events in Georgia and by the widespread radicalization of the national movement after the April 9 killings. Sitting in his study in a comfortable Tbilisi apartment, he sucks on his pipe and pronounces, "Georgians are so taken with the idea of freedom that they have lost the ability to think rationally."

Mamardashvili has walked the fine line between official approval and banishment for his pursuit of philosophical truth. He taught himself English and other languages in order to have access to the philosophical traditions that were outlawed by Soviet philosophy. He deals deftly with terms such as "liberty," "democracy," "perestroika," and "bureaucracy." He believes there is no bureaucracy in the Soviet Union in the strict sense of the word: "A bureaucratic system is predictable and runs according to set rules. This, we do not have. Gorbachev has brought into use all the words in the European political lexicon, but their meaning"—he shakes his head with regret—"bears no relation to reality." This wisest of men in Georgia fears for the future of his country, but is powerless to divert the mounting swell of nationalist feeling onto a path that will ensure peaceful evolution toward democracy.

Armenia

In Armenia, the turbulent republic to the south of Georgia, interethnic tensions run high. For the Armenians, the current troubles are a mere continuation of hundreds of years of struggle. Even the association with the Russians to the north is a short episode on the path of their history. Armenians trace their origins from the dawn of civilization. Their capital,

Yerevan, is reckoned to be one of the world's oldest cities—over twenty-eight hundred years old. Armenia was on the map of the Middle East as early as the sixth century B.C. Then it was one of the most powerful states in the region, stretching across lands that are now part of Turkey, Syria, Iraq, and Iran. Although not always an independent state, Armenia maintained a precarious existence between Persia and Rome up until the ninth century, when it fell to the Turks. During the wars over her territories that followed—fought by Mongols, Turks, and Persians until the nineteenth century—Armenia nonetheless remained a culturally unified entity. Christianity and the Armenian Church were the most important elements that sustained the strong sense of identity among Armenians, wherever they eventually ended up. The Armenian Church is separate from both Byzantium and Rome, and the catholikos of the Holy Etchmiadzin monastery is the head of the Church and moral leader of the nation.

The Armenians in Moscow feel at home in the USSR's capital city. The community here numbers between 30,000 and 40,000 and has its own church and cemetery. In Moscow, we visited the Old Lazarian School, a center for Armenian studies, to find out more about the Armenians. In the uncomfortable heat of mid-July 1989, we turned into Armenian Street, not far from the center of Moscow. It was midday and the narrow street was packed with people waiting in line. "Refugees," we were told, as we pressed past them to a side door of the institute. The flow of refugees to Moscow is just another problem caused by the current dispute with the Azerbaijanis over Nagorno-Karabakh, the predominantly Armenian-populated territory within Azerbaijan.

The Old Lazarian School, or the Armenian Institute as it is sometimes referred to, is an oasis of elegance in the otherwise grotesque architectural landscape of Moscow. It was built by the Lazarevs, a wealthy Armenian family, as part of the reconstruction of Moscow in the aftermath of Napoleon's invasion of 1812. For many years, it was the Institute of Oriental Languages, then a House of Culture under Soviet rule. Recently, it has been returned to the Armenians for use by official representatives of the Armenian Republic in Moscow. It now functions as a cultural center providing language classes for Armenians who no longer speak the language and for anyone else who wishes to learn, monthly exhibitions, a service for helping Armenians emigrate, and a highly successful dating service for lonely Armenians in the big city.

Inside the building, there is not a trace of the decorative paraphernalia that usually adorns public buildings in the Soviet Union. There is no portrait of Lenin, or of Gorbachev for that matter, just long, well-proportioned hallways and high-ceilinged rooms, painted in subtle shades. At the heart of the institute is the Lazarev family museum, which holds the original charter for the Institute of Oriental Languages and displays many old Armenian books, all from before the 1917 Revolution.

They are the pieces of Armenia's noble and ancient heritage, and Armenians come from all over the world to study the collection. An Armenian diaspora has existed since the Middle Ages, when the population scattered before foreign invaders. Today, it stretches from Los Angeles to Moscow to Syria, and other parts of the globe. Yet, wherever they are, the Armenians' sense of identity has always remained strong.

Armenians all over the world share a heritage that reflects their history of survival. Their collective memory combines stories from biblical times with the sufferings of the twentieth century. Every Armenian knows, for example, that Noah's Ark came to ground on Mount Ararat after the Flood. Mount Ararat used to be located at the center of the Armenian state in classical times. But today, the most famous Armenian landmark is clearly visible from Soviet Armenia, but barely accessible at its new coordinates in the northeast corner of Turkey. For Armenians, whose national consciousness has been impregnated with anti-Turkish feelings as a result of a history of animosity between the two peoples, this is more salt to the wound.

The horror of the 1915 massacre of Armenians at the hand of the Turks is another haunting memory shared by all Armenians. The massacre, considered by some historians to be the first instance of genocide of modern times, decimated the Armenian population in the Anatolian region of Turkey, killing up to one and a half million people of all ages. The motivation behind the atrocity, according to some historians, lay in the pan-Turkic ideal of uniting the Turkic peoples from Constantinople eastward through Central Asia—the two and a half million Christian Armenians in Eastern Turkey were in the way of such a scheme. The Anatolian Armenians were also considered a security risk by Turkey, which was at war with Russia. The proximity to their Armenian Christian compatriots just across the border in the Russian empire was felt to endanger the success of the Turkish war effort.

After World War I, when the Ottoman Empire was broken up to form Turkey, Syria, and other countries in the Near East, the new Bolshevik regime in Moscow protested vigorously against the proposition to form an Armenian state between Lake Van and Mount Ararat in the traditionally Armenian territories of Eastern Turkey—a proposition that was supported by Woodrow Wilson. Any hope for the return of their ancestral lands was thwarted. Thus, the only territory left to the Armenians was the tiny tract of land within the Soviet Union where Armenians had formerly lived under the protection of the Russian czars. Once a state that bordered three seas, the Armenian Republic has been shaved down to a landlocked state. Throughout most of the twentieth century, the Armenians have been struggling to retrieve their lands and their dignity.

Armenia is the smallest Soviet republic; its territory amounts to just

11,306 square miles, slightly larger than the state of Maryland. (Neighboring Georgia takes up 26,911 square miles, slightly larger than West Virginia, and Azerbaijan is 33,400 square miles, about the size of Maine.) It is the most ethnically homogeneous republic in the USSR with a native Armenian population of over 90 percent. Yet, this figure accounts for only 66 percent of all Armenians in the Soviet Union, a total population of 4.6 million. The Armenians' list of national grievances is enhanced by their tragic, historic sense of loss over the massacres of their people and confiscations of their lands. For seventy years under Soviet rule the territorial predicament has remained unresolved. Indeed, the Soviet Armenian emblem, which shows the twin peaks of Mount Ararat now located in Turkey, is a constant reminder of the Armenian predicament. The Armenians' sensitivity to the decimation of their lands and their people is one of the deep-rooted elements that has fueled the dispute over Nagorno-Karabakh.

On December 7, 1988, tragedy struck the Armenian nation once more in the form of an earthquake measuring 8.0 on the Richter Scale. Housing built in the last twenty years collapsed like a pack of cards, and an estimated twenty-five thousand people were killed. Thousands of people were left wandering around piles of rubble searching for loved ones in the freezing cold of the approaching winter. Sensing a crisis of confidence, Mikhail Gorbachev dramatically cut short a USA-USSR summit in Washington to rush to the scene of the disaster. When he got there, he succeeded only in making a tense situation worse. He expressed his exasperation at finding an unresponsive and angry Armenian population that was still insistent on raising the Nagorno-Karabakh issue at this moment of tragedy. The disordered and slow-moving relief effort organized by Soviet officials did little to raise Gorbachev's already flagging prestige.

The arrest of five members and some supporters of the Karabakh Committee, and their detention for thirty days, at this time exacerbated already high tensions. The Karabakh Committee had become the moral authority and the principal political force in Armenia throughout that year. Arising out of the February 1988 demonstrations as an informal group, its leaders became the spokesmen for the aspirations of the Armenian people. The committee began to organize within Armenian society and quickly became an alternative source of authority to the long discredited Communist Party in Armenia. Its credibility was further enhanced by the arrest of its leaders. Their incarceration without trial in 1988 continued to galvanize the Armenians into opposition.

The loss of faith in Moscow's leadership and the new intensity of national feelings became evident in the aftermath of the earthquake. Rumor spread that Armenian orphans were to be taken to the Russian SFSR to be cared for. There was an immediate outcry and the Karabakh Committee organized a relay of women to guard and take care of the orphans, just as it had already mobilized a relief effort for victims, far sooner than any planned by the Soviet authorities.

Against this backdrop of natural disasters, the Armenians feel they have suffered a man-made catastrophe—the dispute over Nagorno-Karabakh—which has mobilized the nation. The Armenians were the first of the Soviet nations to take to the streets in mass demonstrations of hundreds of thousands in February 1988. At the first rumors of such demonstrations in Yerevan, a disbelieving world waited for concrete news of what was happening. Western reporters based in Moscow were banned from traveling to the area; telephone communication was cut off and trips suddenly canceled. Then came the confirmation: The resourceful ex-political prisoner Sergei Grigoryants, himself part Armenian, procured a video film of the demonstrations in Yerevan and passed it on to the Western news media for rebroadcast. The scenes were unbelievable: A sea of dark-haired heads stretching into the distance filled the screen. Hundreds of thousands of Armenians sitting peacefully or swaying in unison to one chant.

Almost two years before the pictures of thousands in the streets of East Germany and Czechoslovakia stunned the world, the Armenian nation underwent its own baptism of fire in Yerevan. Almost a third of the population of the Republic of Armenia demonstrated in peaceful protest over a territory, officially known as the Nagorno-Karabakh Autonomous Oblast, a place little known even by the average Soviet citizen at that time, but one that now ranks with Ulster and Lebanon as the scene of conflict between warring factions whose varied interests will not be resolved easily—if ever.

Situated within the Azerbaijan Republic, Nagorno-Karabakh is the size of Long Island. Its population of 180,000 is three quarters Armenian—and that's where the problem lies. It has been a source of dispute between the Azerbaijanis and Armenians since the territory was first given over to Azerbaijani jurisdiction in 1923. The Armenians who live there feel themselves to be cut off from their people and discriminated against by the Azerbaijanis. The Armenians regard Nagorno-Karabakh as historically a part of ancient Armenia. They refer to the territory by its old Armenian name, Artsakh. In czarist times, the region was at the center of important cultural developments for the Armenian nation, but in 1923 territorial boundaries were drawn in order to prevent any contiguous border with the Armenian Republic.

The painful issue of Nagorno-Karabakh was raised time and again, after 1923, as just one item among others, which affected Armenia's sovereignty. The Soviet authorities had it within their power to undo at least this injustice, even if they could not or would not press for the return of territories within the borders of Turkey. Moscow's continuing lack of response gradually bred anti-Soviet sentiments in a population that had traditionally welcomed Russian protection. Underground groups formed; people were arrested and imprisoned. Through the years, the population swung between silence and sporadic outbursts of anger and mass demonstrations.

Throughout 1987, small groups of Armenian activists had gone about, enjoying more relaxed conditions under glasnost, to collect signatures on a petition demanding the return of Nagorno-Karabakh to Armenian control. A similar movement was stirring in Nagorno-Karabakh itself. Paruir Hairikiyan, now living in forced exile in the West, was a leader during the events of February 1988.

"In Yerevan," he recounts, "before the mass demonstrations about Karabakh, there had been two demonstrations about the ecological situation—one in the center of Yerevan and one in the suburbs. Thus, already the atmosphere and the groundwork for the events had been created. February twentieth was a day on which we had planned a large demonstration about the ecological situation. But we learned that precisely on that day a delegation was due to arrive in Yerevan from Moscow, because of the emergence of the Karabakh problem. It was believed this delegation would offer some answers to a series of public declarations that had been issued by Armenian groups.

"At that time, we were aware that the situation in Karabakh was becoming more and more tense. There, the Armenian nation was pressing its deputies to reflect its views on the self-determination of Karabakh and its unification with Armenia.

"We were fully aware of these expectations and so we decided to end our ecological demonstration before the delegation arrived. But the people would have none of it. And so the Moscow delegation was surprised to find such a large group of people gathered in Yerevan.

"That was Saturday. The crowd kept getting larger and larger, and the demonstration was no longer on the ecology. That evening we learned that the Karabakh regional Soviet had called for independence from Azerbaijan. Thus arose the expectation that all that remained to be done was for Moscow to confirm this decision, inasmuch as we considered it now to be a period of democracy."

Hairikiyan was arrested soon after the events he describes here. Sitting in an office in downtown Washington in September of 1988, he still feels a part of the unfolding story in his native land. Speaking slowly and distinctly, he describes the events and feelings of the crowds during the uplifting few days when Armenians had taken over their capital city.

"None of us had supposed that ten thousand Armenians could have gathered without incident, peacefully and without conflicts. But here you had a gathering of one million and this, without the utterance of a single vulgarity. This was because for a moment, at that time, the Armenians became an independent nation. They subordinated themselves to their own collective consciousness."

He stops for a moment to ponder the implications of his words and continues his account: "Various orators gave speeches. But in time, these speakers would pass through a filter—the filter of public opinion. If someone spoke nonsense he was hooted and jeered. These people would not come back to speak. If a speaker spoke truthfully and intelligently, he was applauded. It was a case of natural selection. The nation elected who should speak . . . out of this process a leadership emerged, a leadership selected by the hundreds of thousands who gathered to protest. This was a remarkable phenomenon. It cannot adequately be described in words. In the end, the nation was opting, more and more, for self-determination, for the right to determine one's own fate."

It is hard to believe that this dark-haired, bearded man with deep brown eyes has spent seventeen of his thirty-nine years in prisons and labor camps. He has been an Armenian rights activist since he was a teenager. After so many years behind bars, his resolve is as strong as ever. His imprisonment without a formal charge and without a trial at the height of the Armenian demonstrations became a cause célèbre, and demands for his release were included in chants taken up by the crowds in Yerevan. Human rights activists in Moscow soon joined the chorus. The authorities were at a loss what to do; and in July 1988 they unceremoniously stripped Hairikiyan of his citizenship, expelled him against his will, and sent him to Ethiopia. He shakes his head in disbelief and still cannot come to terms with his exile, vowing to return to Armenia as soon as he can.

The dispute over Nagorno-Karabakh has now become a major problem for the Moscow leadership. Each side in the dispute claims to have history and legality on its side. The legislature in Nagorno-Karabakh voted to unify with Armenia, and the legislature in the Armenian Republic voted the same. But under Soviet law, any change of borders must be agreed upon by all entities concerned. In this case, the Azerbaijani legislature voted to retain control over the area. All three territories have been convulsed with general strikes, protest rallies, and armed conflict. The dispute has provoked a great deal of violence, which has further fueled nationalist feelings. Just after the Yerevan demonstrations in February 1988, Azerbaijanis went on a rampage in the industrial city of Sumgait, near Baku, killing thirty-two people—twenty-six of them Armenians. Intellectuals in Baku were reluctant to believe that Azerbaijanis, unprovoked, could have perpetrated what became known as an "anti-Armenian pogrom." Yet in January 1989, Armenians in Baku were hunted down in the same fashion. These ugly scenes of murder and violence have set the stage for the unfolding events that had left a total of ninety-one dead by the end of 1988, and many more by the end of 1989.

For several months in 1989, Moscow removed Nagorno-Karabakh from Azerbaijani jurisdiction and exercised direct rule from Moscow through a special commission, experimenting with a new constitutional amendment giving the Presidium of the Supreme Soviet new authority to introduce "special forms of administration" to protect the safety of Soviet citizens. But the territory was then returned to the jurisdiction of Azerbaijan without any noticeable progress in resolving the conflict.

By the end of 1989, relations between Armenians and Azerbaijanis reached a low point and the conflict looked poised to break out into full-scale war between the two nations. Both Armenians and Azerbaijanis were arming, and skirmishes had taken place along the border and around the Nagorno-Karabakh region. The two sides seemed irreconcilable and Soviet troops sent into the region on Moscow's orders were ineffective in countering guerrilla tactics. The first glimmer of a possible breakthrough came from an unexpected source. In January 1990, representatives of the Armenian National Movement and the Azerbaijani Popular Front accepted an invitation from the leaders of the Baltic popular fronts to come to Riga to open talks. One of the first issues on which Armenians and Azerbaijanis were agreed was the lack of effective action from Moscow.

It will take a long time for the Armenians to recover from the natural and man-made disasters of the 1980s. Even if an agreement is reached with the Azerbaijanis, there are still hundreds of thousands of Armenian refugees to accommodate. The devastation wrought by the earthquake has left thousands still without a home. These misfortunes have encouraged an almost mystical belief among Armenians that their nation is doomed to extinction as victim in a predetermined cosmic drama. There is a pervasive sense of isolation and having been abandoned, especially as Armenia is still located between two Turkic neighbors. Traditionally, the Armenians had always looked to the Russians for protection against the threat from the surrounding Muslim population, but today's Russians have thus far disappointed them. Seventy years of Soviet rule have done little to dispel their fears. If anything, Soviet policies have increased the possibility for feuding and conflict.

Azerbaijan

Azerbaijan is the odd man out in the trio of major nations in the Caucasus. Pushed in between the Black and Caspian seas together with its Christian neighbors, Georgia and Armenia, it differs from its neighboring republics in that it is a predominantly Muslim country. Although many Azerbaijanis assert their Caucasianness—and occasionally they claim to be the original inhabitants of the entire region—their culture attaches them to their Muslim cousins in Soviet Central Asia.

Baku is the most important city in the Caucasus region because of its proximity to the oil fields that were exploited first by the Russian czars, then by the Soviet regime in Moscow. The oil rigs, some distance out in the Caspian Sea, are not easily discernible from the city, but everywhere there is evidence of the culture that has evolved through the centuries because of the presence of oil. The name Azerbaijan itself is believed to have evolved from the word *Adurbadagan*, which means "land of flames." Baku's coat of arms bears three torches on a field of sea waves.

In ancient times, according to mythology, the people in these regions were fire worshipers. They were prone to experience spontaneous manifestations of their god in unexpected places. The science behind the belief is hardly mysterious. Near the village of Mahomedly there is a rock that has been "burning," it is thought, almost since the time of Alexander the Great. The escaping methane that keeps the flames alight must truly have seemed a miracle to the fire worshipers. Azerbaijan is also the birthplace of Zarathustra and historical bastion of Zoroastrianism. Zoroastrianism vied with Christianity here before Islam supplanted them both to become the dominant religion under the Arab Caliphate in the middle of the seventh century.

The oil wells of the Baku region were jealously guarded, even in medieval times. As well as being used for lighting, heating, and medicinal purposes, the oil was used in warfare by special detachments of flamethrowers right up until the spread of firearms in the sixteenth century. By the mid-nineteenth century, the first deep borehole had been drilled and an oil-processing plant had been established near Baku. Today, downtown Baku bears the signs of a nineteenth-century boomtown. European-style houses and streets fan out from the walls of the old city, and the wide promenade constructed along the seashore in the 1860s lends the atmosphere of a British seaside town. On summer evenings, Bakintsy (the people of Baku) stroll up and down and up and down the promenade; young men play snooker on specially constructed tables and their elders play chess—or else they sit in one of the teahouses, or *chaykhanas*, drinking tea Turkish style, in small glasses with sugar cubes, discussing the events of the day. Throughout 1989, however, this happy routine was interrupted. By the designated curfew hour, everyone scattered homeward and anyone left on the streets listened nervously for the sound of tanks. From January to September 1989, Baku was under the rule of martial law, with only a brief respite before the military crackdown of January 1990.

On a hill in the southwest corner of the town sits a famous house built by former Party boss Geidar Aliyev for a one-day visit by the then general secretary Leonid Brezhnev. Many people speak of the "legacy of Geidar Aliyev" in the same derisive tones they apply to Brezhnev's period of stagnation. Aliyev was the only Azerbaijani to have broken into the predominantly Russian Party leadership in Moscow. The existence of the house was a badly kept secret for many years—neither the high walls nor barbed wire surrounding it could prevent the stories of its lavish interiors and fabulous decorations purchased for hard currency that went to adorn the one-day wonder. A fifteen-foot-high mirror specially made in Austria cost 118,000 rubles, and the intricate light fixtures were equally expensive. No one knows whether Brezhnev was impressed.

Today, the house serves as the Palace for Weddings, and is open to the public. Every half hour or so, a wedding party pulls up outside the entrance and the band that sits on the doorstep strikes up a nuptial march as the couple enters. The house is set on the hillside that leads up to the enclave of apartment blocks where Baku's Party elite live, a short distance from the Central Committee and the republic's Party offices, set apart from the rest of the city. By Western standards, the apartments are hardly alluring; the brickwork is already crumbling from the balconies despite the shabby attempt at style, but to the average Soviet, they are an unattainable luxury.

It has been one of the misfortunes of Soviet town planning that the largest open space in the center of the average Soviet city is usually the square in front of the statue of Lenin. Originally constructed for local May Day and October Revolution parades suitably near the Party building—so that portly Communist Party dignitaries would not have to walk too far to mount the dais—those open spaces are now being put to different use.

In Baku, Lenin Square is a widened roadway that comfortably accommodates half a million people. The guidebook describes it as being as large as Moscow's Red Square and Leningrad's Palace Square put together. For eighteen days in November 1988, the square became the site of a continuous demonstration of thousands of pro-Azerbaijani protesters. At its height, the crowd swelled to five hundred thousand. Many who were there described it as a turning point. The normally conciliatory Azerbaijanis had stood by and watched throughout the year as the situation in Nagorno-Karabakh grew steadily worse and the Azerbaijani Party leadership seemed powerless to assert authority over the enclave that legally lay within its jurisdiction. Frustration with the leadership spilled over into other national and political issues to fuel the protests.

The November demonstration was joined by Azerbaijani refugees from Armenia who had nowhere else to go. The protest finally came to a head at 4:00 A.M. on December 4, 1988, when a reduced contingent of demonstrators (women and children, except for the refugees, had been sent home) was left facing four lines of armed soldiers. The *spetznaz* troops were armed with clubs. Lashing out at the protesters, they cleared the square, leaving an official total of three dead and thirty wounded from the civilian population. The demonstration had mobilized the population, including the workers, who had put forth their own leader, the twenty-six-year-old Nemet Panakhov.

Emboldened by the people's response, the fledgling Azerbaijani Popular Front, the Azerbaijan Halq Jabbasi, began to strengthen its organization and press for registration. Within a few short months, the membership had grown to over seventeen thousand. In April 1989, the leaders of the front went to meet Abdul-Rakhman Vezirov, the first secretary of the Communist Party in Azerbaijan.

"He was not happy to see us, and questioned us on why we wanted to set up the front," says Leyla Yunusova, press liaison for the front. So enraged was the Party first secretary, he told them that if they had been in Stalin's time he would have had them all shot. He was especially incensed by her comments. "As a woman—in fact I was the only woman in the delegation," she points out, "according to Azerbaijani tradition, once he had insulted me the men were obliged to defend my honor."

Harassed when they tried to meet, and refused an office and access to the media, the Azerbaijani Popular Front leadership nonetheless continued to gain support.

The Azerbaijanis were late in organizing a popular front. There is an impression among Soviet oppositionists and also in the West that somehow the Muslim regions cannot spawn a Western-oriented and pro-democratic movement; that Islamic fundamentalism will be the way forward for the mass of people in Soviet Central Asia, beginning with the Azerbaijanis. The reality appears somewhat different. The urban intelligentsia is looking toward the West—even though this often means toward the Baltic States—for their ideological inspiration. In fact, the draft program of the Azerbaijani Popular Front is very similar to the programs of the popular fronts in the Baltic States.

The Azerbaijani Popular Front's demands reflect the desires of most of the Soviet population to have a local leadership that is responsive to the people. The Popular Front objected to the way the deputies to the Congress of People's Deputies were selected in March 1989. Their complaint is that the candidates who might have represented the true interests of the people were blocked from standing at the nomination stage. They consider the Azerbaijani Party leaders and the members of the Azerbaijani Supreme Soviet to be corrupt and unrepresentative of the people.

In August 1989, the Azerbaijani Popular Front organized a number of successful mass demonstrations. Up to six hundred thousand people gathered on several occasions that month to put pressure on Party leadership to support the Popular Front's demands, which included recognition of it as an official organization, release of members of the Pan-Turkic Birlik Society who had been arrested, a revision of the March elections, greater local autonomy, and continued control over Nagorno-Karabakh. On September 4, the Azerbaijani Popular Front called a successful general strike, which brought the republic's transportation and industry, including the precious oil industry, to a standstill for over a week. The republic's Party leaders finally gave in and agreed to recognize and register the Popular Front and consider its demands.

Apart from their grievances over the lack of representation at the local level, there is a strong perception among Azerbaijanis that their interests are not adequately represented in Moscow, and not just in political circles. Frequently, Azerbaijanis will reel off the names of Armenians who have influence in Moscow, then bemoan the media's domination by the Armenian interpretation of the news, especially on the Karabakh issue. The visit of Andrei Sakharov to the Caucasus in December 1988 brought no joy for the Azerbaijanis; it appeared to many people there that he had taken the Armenian side before he had heard them out.

Throughout most of 1989, Baku's inhabitants experienced the Karabakh dispute and the tensions with the Armenians only at second hand. Many were dimly aware of the refugees that had flooded into the city since the troubles began. But perhaps it is the Azerbaijani character that discouraged them from sharing the grim facts with strangers. Azerbaijanis, so the traditional wisdom goes, do not shout their misfortunes from the rooftops. If there is anything wrong, it is kept "in the family."

Most Bakintsy know about Khutor, but very few will volunteer the information to strangers. Khutor is a shantytown, one of several on the edge of the city, which has now become so overcrowded with Azerbaijani refugees from Armenia that the authorities have built a wall around it to shield it from view. Over two hundred thousand people live in these conditions, and more arrive every month. Whole families now share small cramped rooms in the jerry-built dwellings, or *samostroiki*, as they are called in Russian. Many were forced to leave their homes in Armenia on short notice, often having been called into the local Party offices and informed that the authorities could no longer ensure their safety if they stayed; whether they were Party members or not made no difference. Most Azerbaijanis left behind a lifetime's accumulation of possessions; some had to abandon newly built homes; others, in their hurry, left behind vital documents, such as the *trudovaya kniga* (Soviet "work book"), without which it is difficult to secure work. Without residence permits and other documents required by the Soviet system, many new arrivals found it extremely difficult to find work and to gain access to services such as hospitals and polyclinics. Many still suffered the trauma of being under attack by armed Armenians, being airlifted out by Soviet troops in helicopters, and barely escaping with their lives. To cap it all, the people vacating the houses where they now live demanded huge sums of money for the shabby dwellings. With only a one-time fifty-ruble handout from the authorities, many of the displaced Azerbaijanis are angry.

But they are resigned to the attempt to rebuild their lives somehow in these desperate circumstances.

Since the start of the conflict between Azerbaijan and Armenia over Nagorno-Karabakh, almost half a million people from both sides have been made refugees, through coercion or choice, in some cases fleeing for their lives from their homes and lands. Many Azerbaijani intellectuals feel that the Armenians are to blame for stirring up the enmity. They point out that *Karabakh* is a Turkish word meaning "dark vineyard" or "garden." The area holds great significance for Azerbaijanis as the home of many cultural figures, writers, and musicians—such as Uzeir Hajibeyli, composer of the first operas with Muslim themes as well as the composer of the national anthems of both the Republic of Azerbaijan and the Azerbaijan SSR.

Religious differences between the Muslim Azerbaijanis and the Christian Armenians have been held up as the root of the conflict, but most Azerbaijanis would disagree. The Muslim religion still plays an important role in Azerbaijan today, but its influence falls far short of the mobilizing power of the fundamentalism of other Islamic states outside the Soviet Union. Nonetheless, the Caucasus region is still considered a stronghold of Sufism. There are many holy places very close to Baku and on Azerbaijan's northern border, where Sufism and mysticism were traditionally the strongest. Throughout much of Azerbaijan, unofficial mullahs can be hired to perform circumcisions, weddings, and burials—to keep the traditions. But they are usually old men and have little to tell the younger generation. Young intellectuals in Baku still consider their cultural traditions to be Muslim: They are at the forefront of the revival of language and traditions. But they draw a distinction between themselves and the older generation: "Our parents still think of themselves as Muslims, but we the younger generation, we consider ourselves to be Turks."

When Iran's Hashemi Rafsanjani visited Baku at the beginning of July 1989, he was greeted by a disappointing turnout of around three thousand at Baku's main mosque. Although Azerbaijan's Muslims are predominantly Shiite, they have little sympathy for their Iranian neighbor. The Azerbaijani population in Iran has suffered waves of persecution under the shah's regime and more recently at the hands of Ayatollah Khomeini's pro-Farsi functionaries.

Baku has two working mosques, the main one is the Tazapir Mosque. It is the home of Sheik Ulislam, one of the four official spiritual leaders of the Muslim faithful in the Soviet Union. There are signs of the gradually reviving status of the religious community: A new *medresseh*, an Islamic school, is under construction nearby. Traditionally, Shiites and Sunnis would have worshiped separately, but both are accommodated at this mosque. Both Sunni and Shiite symbols are found in the building's decorations, and Sunnis mingle with the traditionally Shiite Azerbaijanis without much attention to their differences. The mufti has not been a crusading advocate of fundamentalism or, indeed, of spreading his faith among the lapsed intelligentsia, although he has expressed his tacit support for the Azerbaijani Popular Front. There has been a modest revival in the building of medressehs, and mosques are reopening throughout Azerbaijan, but as yet, the movement is far from attaining the fervor and momentum of Islamic fundamentalist movements.

The Azerbaijan Halq Jabbasi, or Popular Front, is the largest informal group in Azerbaijan, but there are many others. The Gala, or Castle, is an association with a few hundred members that focuses on history and culture. Its student members seek out holy and historical places and organize work groups to restore them. Yurt, or Fatherland, is an ecological group concerned with the increasing pollution of Azerbaijan's environment; its members have discovered several inches of oily slime at the bottom of the Caspian Sea. The informal group IRS, an umbrella organization for numerous cultural activities, is housed in a caravansary at the edge of Baku's old town. Not all informal groups are cultural and ecological. Dirchalish, or Rebirth, is a clandestine group dedicated to the idea of establishing a constitutional assembly in Azerbaijan. The group has already published its own newspaper, although its statutes have circulated hand to hand. The group proposes to work within the limits of the existing constitution of Azerbaijan to defend the sovereign rights of the Azerbaijani nation on the territory of Azerbaijan; to secure the establishment of a democratic Azerbaijani government bound by law; to change all political and economic agreements that are against the interests of the Azerbaijani people; and to aim for the transition of Azerbaijan into an emerging economically viable state. Nobody knows yet how many members belong to the Dirchalish or how influential it will be in the future, but enough people had heard of it in 1989 for it to have had some impact.

There are still other groups, including Azerbaijan's Pan-Turkic Birlik (not to be confused with Uzbekistan's Birlik organization). The Azerbaijani authorities quickly recognized the threat from this group and imprisoned several of its members in the turbulent summer of 1989. A major force behind the Birlik group is the divided nation issue: There are millions—figures range between eight million and seventeen million—of Azerbaijanis in Iran. The members of Birlik pay more attention to religious issues than do other informal groups in Azerbaijan. The young workers' leader, Nemet Panakhov, was reportedly being advised by leaders of the Birlik throughout the mass demonstrations of November 1988. Since mid-1989, however, the secular wing of the Azerbaijani movement has become the dominant one and all leaders appear to have thrown their support behind the Azerbaijani Popular Front. In January 1990, Azerbaijanis in the Nakhichevan Autonomous Soviet Socialist Republic (located between Armenia and Iran) took matters into their own hands and set about making contact with their ethnic brothers and sisters across the border in Iran. Spurred on, no doubt, by the image of the crumbling Berlin Wall and the joyous reunion of Germans who had been forcibly kept apart for so many years, the Azerbaijanis attempted their own re-union across the border. In some places, the people tore down fences and barriers to reach the other side.

January 1990 also marked a sudden escalation in the violence between Armenians and Azerbaijanis. Armed clashes occurred along the border between the two republics and armed men of both sides took to the hills in and around Nagorno-Karabakh, prepared for prolonged guerrilla war-fare, having procured sophisticated arms and in some cases even armored cars and helicopters. At the same time, violence struck in the heart of Baku, a place where many Azerbaijanis up until then had been bewil-dered by the animosity between their people and the Armenians. Baku, traditionally an ethnically mixed city, has been home to Armenians, Jews, Russians, and many other nationalities. The planned attacks of January 1990 singled out Armenian families and caused most to flee from the city, abandoning their homes and friends. The city, once home to over two hundred thousand Armenians, now contains hardly any. Rumors soon spread, just as they did after the killing of Armenians in Sumgait in February 1988, that the pogrom had been provoked by the authorities.

Garri Kasparov, world-famous Armenian chess player and resident of Baku was a witness to the events of January 1990. In his assessment, there was some prior knowledge of the pogrom by the authorities, and a pur-pose behind its instigation: "Provoking these events led to the creation of a situation in Baku that would permit tanks to crush the movement for independence in the republic. That is, to strike not against those respon-sible for the pogroms but against those who were demonstrating for changes in the republic, for an end to Azerbaijan's dependence on Mos-cow, for a chance to sell their oil and cotton."

Whatever the truth, the pogrom provided the pretext for a military crackdown in Baku and the declaration of a state of emergency in Nagorno-Karabakh and the border areas. KGB troops were sent in together with regular army and navy forces to assist the Interior Ministry troops already in the republic.

The military intervention ordered by the Kremlin temporarily diverted the anti-Armenian violence, but ultimately served only to further alienate the Azerbaijanis from both the central regime in Moscow and their own republic's Communist leaders. Leaders from the Azerbaijani Popular Front claimed that attacks against Armenians had already been under control as a result of the front's efforts before the tanks rolled into Baku. Many Azerbaijanis suspected that ethnic unrest had been used as the pretext to suppress the increasingly assertive national movement. State-ments by the minister of defense, Dmitri Yazov, later provided the confirmation: The military crackdown was necessary, he claimed, to prevent a takeover of the government by Azerbaijani nationalist forces.

Thousands turned out for the funerals of those killed in the action, and a massive show of civil disobedience in the form of strikes shut down transportation and industry for days in Baku. Once again, as in Georgia, the use of troops had served only to activate broad masses of the population against the Soviet system, and encouraged the idea among those masses that secession from the USSR provides the only solution.

In the rising swell of grief and protest in Azerbaijan, there is a risk that the moderate nationalists who originally formed the Azerbaijan Popular Front will be swept aside. Their emphasis on the struggle for democracy, representative government, and a free press has become submerged in the mass emotions engendered by the conflict with the Armenians over Nagorno-Karabakh. While the rest of the world stood by and accepted the view propounded from the Kremlin that Soviet intervention was the only way to mediate between Armenians and Azerbaijanis, representatives of the Armenian National Movement and the Azerbaijani Popular Front held a historic meeting in Riga, under the supervision of the Baltic popular fronts with Moscow deliberately excluded. That meeting between representatives from Armenia and Azerbaijan was a real breakthrough, and achieved a temporary truce and preliminary agreement on some issues. But it raised the question why such a meeting could not have been arranged by the Kremlin, which continued to perpetuate the notion of an insurmountable "interethnic conflict."

For centuries, the English and French regarded themselves as sworn enemies, but times change; political systems evolve, as do perceptions of nationhood. Throughout the nations of Western Europe, the implacable foes of yesteryear now rely on their freely elected representatives to maintain the peaceful status quo and conduct the day-to-day business of economic and political exchange. There are two successful methods of resolving conflicts in the world today; total suppression of both sides, or negotiated settlement between the trusted representatives of each group. Now that the Soviet Union has moved away from the first, it can only be hoped that all obstacles to the second arrangement will soon be removed.

Soviet Central Asia:
The Muslim Factor and
the Turkic Continuum

> We cannot do without the petroleum of Azerbaijan or
> the cotton of Turkestan. We take these products which
> are necessary for us, not as the former exploiters, but as
> older brothers bearing the torch of civilization.
>
> —Grigori Zinoviev, 1920

IN THE Soviet Union, there are sixty million people of the Muslim faith, most of whom live in Soviet Central Asia. Only Indonesia, Pakistan, India, and Bangladesh have larger Muslim populations. Yet the Muslim factor is the least familiar piece in the jigsaw puzzle of nations and peoples that make up the Soviet Union. The rich and ancient cultures of Central Asia have not adapted well to Sovietization. And after seventy years of central planning, the region has been reduced primarily to a producer of raw materials. Without a strong presence in Moscow and without a significant émigré community in the West to publicize their existence, the Soviet Muslims have been regarded as mysterious, exotic peoples with impenetrable traditions and esoteric agendas. Yet, the authorities in Moscow are acutely aware that the Muslim population could pose a severe challenge in the very near future. Their high birth rate and low level of assimilation into the USSR's Russian-dominated culture make them a growing risk to the stability of the Soviet state.

Soviet Central Asia—the heartland of the Muslim faith in the USSR— is made up of five republics: Uzbekistan, Kazakhstan, Turkmenistan, Kirgizia, and Tajikistan. The Muslim region reaches Turkey through Azerbaijan in the West and borders Iran, Afghanistan, and China to the south and east. The Soviet border separates the Muslims of the USSR from Muslims within the vast region of Asia. To the north, the Tatars and Bashkirs form a Muslim bloc at the center of the Russian Republic. All of these major Muslim groups are considered Turkic peoples, except the Tajiks, whose ethnic origins can be traced to Iranian roots.

The Russians were not always the dominant power in this region. The territory in Central Asia now claimed by the Soviet Union was once part of the Mongol empire where Genghis Khan held dominion. His empire stretched as far as the medieval principality of Moscow. The Russians were one of the few Christian peoples of Europe to experience the "Tatar Yoke" from the thirteenth to the fifteenth century, a period of domination by Mongols who converted to Islam. This period left a deep imprint on the Russian psyche and on Russian-Muslim relations. Although the newly centralized Muscovite state began to drive back the Muslim conquerors in the sixteenth century, the two states coexisted for a time in an uneasy balance of power. During the sixteenth and seventeenth centuries, important Muslim territories were conquered and incorporated into the Russian empire, including Kazan, Astrakhan, and Western Siberia. It was not until the mid to late nineteenth century that Central Asia, or Turkestan as it was known, was finally conquered. Tashkent fell in 1865, followed by Bukhara and Khiva in 1873. And in 1875 the Russian Army invaded the khanate of Kokand. Last to be taken over were the Turkmen territories.

The Russian Revolution and Bolshevik victory brought about a distinct turn in fortune for the Muslims. Although the czars had not encouraged Islam, the religion was left more or less unhindered under their rule. Lenin's new atheistic state, on the other hand, sought to eliminate Islam as part of a policy of the wholesale destruction of religion. Much of the history of those first years under Soviet rule has been lost to the population of Soviet Central Asia. During the 1920s, when Bolshevik rule was being consolidated in the former territories of the Russian empire, fervent young Bolsheviks went into Soviet Central Asia to promote the Bolshevik creed. Their mission was to spread enlightenment and dispel years of illiteracy and backwardness. Official records of the era abound in pictures of Kazakh herdsmen marveling at the phenomenon of an electric light bulb; and of Uzbek women, seeing the light of day for the first time after emerging from behind the Muslim veil.

The 1920s also saw the rise and fall of Mirsaid Sultan Galiev, and thus the rise and fall of national Communism in Soviet Central Asia, a story that is only just being revealed to three generations of Soviet Central Asians. The policy of suppressing the history of the national republics in the 1920s began with Stalin as a way of eliminating from public consciousness any memory of an alternative to the state he had created. The first significant departures from this policy came only after Gorbachev became Soviet leader.

A Tatar, Sultan Galiev was one of the highest-ranking Muslims in the Communist Party hierarchy. He joined the Bolsheviks in 1917, and, like many other Muslim intellectuals, was taken up by the optimism of the revolutionary spirit of the time. Those men believed that the new Communist system would liberate them from the tyrannies of czarism, and would provide for the welfare and economic prosperity of the Turkic and Tatar peoples. Sultan Galiev refined the Communist doctrine into a specific blueprint for revolution not only for the Turkic peoples of Russia but also for their Turkic brothers still oppressed by imperialist powers beyond its borders. He had a bold vision of all Muslim peoples living together in a kind of Turkic commonwealth within the new socialist order.

But Stalin had a different vision and he called for Sultan Galiev's arrest and expulsion from the Party in 1923 on charges of "nationalist deviation." Then Stalin made it very clear that national Communism would have no independent role to play in the newly established union of socialist republics.

By the late 1920s, the Muslim leadership gave up hope that Communism would improve the lot of their people. Under the Bolsheviks, the new system gradually reverted to the old, familiar practices of Russian domination and great-power chauvinism. But the Bolsheviks' system was even more limiting: Instead of leaving the people to worship and educate their children in the age-old traditions, as czarism had allowed, they began to systematically wipe out the old faith and to indoctrinate the people into a new way of life. The aim was to clear Soviet Central Asia of its indigenous religion, history, literature, and ancient culture.

The people's disillusionment soon turned to active opposition. Some groups of Muslims had taken to the hills in Fergana as early as 1918 to form an armed resistance in response to the crushing of their autonomy. The Basmachi, as they were known, became an effective fighting force that proved a formidable challenge to the Red Army until 1923. Guerrilla fighting and anti-Soviet opposition continued until at least the end of the 1920s. (Needless to say, the history of the Basmachi movement has never been taught in Soviet schools.)

By the end of the 1920s, the Muslim national Communists' plan to preserve the unity of the Muslim region had been severely undermined by the policies of the new Soviet leadership. Their plans to codify a language for all Turkic territories came to an abrupt halt. Instead, the Soviet Muslims were divided into some thirty-six separate nations, and literary languages were established—and sometimes invented—for each. At the same time, the Latin alphabet was introduced to replace the Arabic script that had been used throughout the region for centuries. In 1939, another alphabet change, this time to Cyrillic, was forced on the people, further distancing the Central Asians' ties to their rich culture, traditions, and history.

Today, the five republics that make up Soviet Central Asia are sometimes referred to as the "soft underbelly" of the Soviet empire. Kazakhstan is the second largest republic in the Soviet Union in terms of territory. It takes up almost 1.1 million square miles, but has a population of only 16.5 million; Uzbekistan has the largest population, 19.9 million; Kirgizia, on the border with China, has a population of 4.3 million; Turkmenistan, which borders Iran and Afghanistan, has a population of 3.5 million; and Tajikistan, the republic that borders on Afghanistan and China, has a population of 5.1 million.

Today, there is a growing sense of confidence among the Soviet Central Asians. With a consistently high birth rate set against a stable if not declining birth rate in the European parts of the Soviet Union, the Central Asians know that their potential power is growing. Already one out of every five conscripts undertaking obligatory military service in the Soviet Army is from Central Asia.

The role of Islam, too, appears to be changing. Its importance for the Soviet Central Asians' identity cannot be overestimated; it has been the force that has held them together and has provided cultural and spiritual nourishment when they were under pressure to Sovietize. But travel throughout the region suggests that its appeal is weakening among the intelligentsia. In its place a new, unifying force is emerging—Pan-Turkism. Young Central Asians are beginning to rediscover what their ancestors always knew, that from the Kazakhs and Uighurs in the northeast to the Tatars, Turkmen, and Azerbaijanis farther west, they are part of a Turkic continuum that, when aroused, could provide a powerful counterweight to the Slavs.

Increasingly, the Turkic peoples of the USSR are becoming aware of their common heritage and are seeking to bridge what they regard as an artificial gulf imposed upon them by the policies of Stalin and his successors. The combined population of Turkic peoples in the Soviet Union, now over fifty million and rapidly rising, must drive forward this sense of reviving strength and cultural unity.

One Uzbek writer explained the revival this way:

"The Uzbek intelligentsia has always regarded its culture as part of a broader Turkish culture. Our history is tied to the history of the Kirgiz and the Kazakhs. . . . In the 1920s and 1930s, we understood each other and could read the same texts. The languages are very close. You could even say that Kirgiz, Kazakh, and Uzbek were dialects of one great language."

The Uzbeks

The Uzbeks are the third most numerous ethnic group in the Soviet Union after the Russians and the Ukrainians. They are poised in a central position among the Soviet Central Asians and hold the key to the region's future development.

Tashkent, capital of Uzbekistan, is touted as the "showcase" of Soviet Central Asia, or the gem of the Soviet south. In truth, that is far from the reality. Tashkent has many wide boulevards lined by large antiseptic government buildings and identical apartment blocks. The monotony of the sprawling city's architecture is relieved by plenty of parks and trees that provide shelter against the fierce, scorching summers. The earthquake of 1966 destroyed much of the old Tashkent. The buildings constructed since show all the signs of the creeping stagnation of the Brezhnev era. Shoddily built from the outset, there are some buildings under construction that are already crumbling. Rows of apartment blocks have risen up among the rubble left by the earthquake, but there are still expanses of wasteland in the middle of the city, which give it a stark, Orwellian appearance. It is here and not in the arbored, better-maintained residential areas that many newly arrived Uzbeks are now sheltering, six or eight to a room.

Parts of Tashkent are sensibly planted with trees and greenery and the older parks are crisscrossed by *aryks*, small canals constructed for irrigation. Tashkent's statue of Karl Marx sits in the middle of just such a park. His sculpted facial features bear more resemblance to Genghis Khan than to a German of Jewish extraction.

The combination of earthquake damage and socialist city planning has left Tashkent a city without a heart. Its shopping districts offer little in the way of goods. Very few people carry shopping bags or containers of any kind as they move about town. Uzbek men wear the *tubateyka*, a square skullcap that sits on the back of the head. For everyday wear, the tubateykas are usually of one color and embroidered with a simple design. More lavishly adorned tubateykas made of velvet and embroidered with sequins and gold and silver thread are reserved for special occasions. The striking thing about Tashkent's female population is the limited selection of dresses available to them. On any day in the city, the same dress and fabric can be spotted on hundreds of women.

Tashkent still has a district called the Old Town, located in the vicinity of the old Chigotai Gate, once a part of the Old Silk Road, the most famous medieval trading route, which ran from the Black Sea in the west to China in the east. But there are no old or exotic buildings, no Eastern architecture, harking back to antiquity. The road is a dust track and the buildings are barely above the wattle-and-daub stage; at a junction, a pile of rubbish lies smoldering.

There are fly-infested restaurants every few courtyards along, where Uzbeks go to eat *shashliks* cooked over an open fire. There, tables under canopies are open to the street. In one restaurant, a large bathtub in the center serves as a sink for washing the plates. Traditional Uzbek green tea is served and Uzbeks go through an elaborate procedure of swilling out the teacups before drinking in order to "disinfect" them, as Uzbekistan is in the middle of a major hepatitis epidemic.

The roads are lined with buildings that have only an entrance onto the street. The typical layout of an Uzbek house includes a courtyard inside, with a small patch of land on which herbs and small vegetables are usually growing, and perhaps a goat tethered to a post. The building surrounds the courtyard; it has a porch and rooms for the members of the extended family and their children. Prior to the earthquake, much of Tashkent looked like this. The new apartment buildings are, on the whole, inhabited by Russians or other people who have moved more recently into the region.

Tashkent's Uzbek population, for the most part, has been only recently urbanized. Uzbeks were never city dwellers, and they are only just beginning to establish a significant urban presence. Thus, the Uzbeks have no historical attachment to any major city, unlike the Tajiks, who point to the stunning architecture of Bukhara and Samarkand as a product of their long history of urban settlement. But the Uzbeks do have a growing sense of their numerical importance in the region, which can only fuel their demands for national parity.

Uzbekistan's most serious problems today stem from the republic's economy. According to the Soviet plan designed in Moscow, Uzbekistan has been turned into a huge cotton-producing farm, to the virtual exclusion of any other crop. Throughout history, the Uzbeks have produced not only cotton, but a wide variety of foods: all kinds of grain; rice; vegetables such as carrots, peppers, radishes; and fruits, grapes, apricots, melons, walnuts, and many other things. As recently as twenty years ago, people used to travel to Uzbekistan to buy fruit and vegetables, but now they cost more there than in the bleaker, less fertile regions of the country. The concentration on the cultivation of cotton—the monoculture, as it is called by Uzbeks—has led to innumerable social and ecological problems.

According to statistics for 1983, the USSR was the world's second largest cotton producer after China. Uzbekistan plays a major role in this industry: Two thirds of all cotton produced in the USSR comes from Uzbekistan, which alone produced almost as much cotton as the United States in 1983. And the crop accounts for over half of the agricultural output in the rest of Soviet Central Asia. Despite its key role in the production of such an important commodity, Uzbekistan has not reaped the benefits. The cotton is grown and harvested in Uzbekistan, primarily using methods abandoned in the cotton-growing regions of the United States at the turn of the century. The raw cotton fetches fifteen kopeks (under three cents) a kilo and is exported out of Uzbekistan to be processed and made up into goods in other republics, which sell them for a far higher profit.

Mohammed Salih, a secretary of the Uzbek Writers Union, has emerged as a leading spokesman for the Uzbek people. He is concerned about Uzbekistan's economic problems, and has spoken out on the subject on many occasions, despite the Uzbek authorities' disapproval:

"There is a direct link between the deteriorating ecological situation in Uzbekistan and the cotton monoculture," he tells us. "We have lost not only our lands and waters, we have forfeited the health of our people. The land is ailing and also the people who work on it. Around eighty percent of Uzbeks live in *kishlaks*, traditional rural Uzbek settlements, where they work the cotton fields. This part of the population is basically in a state of ill health."

Salih runs down the list of Uzbekistan's grievances in a matter-of-fact way. He is not pleading for special consideration for the Uzbeks, merely stating facts and statistics that are well known among the increasingly active Uzbek intelligentsia. Threatened with reprisals by the authorities for his outspokenness, he was vigorously defended by student demonstrators and all charges against him were dropped. He was on the record as speaking out against corruption in the ranks of Uzbekistan's Communist leaders, Rashidov and Usmankhodjayev, long before glasnost made it fashionable to do so. Asked about Uzbekistan's new first secretary, Islam Karimov, Salih adopts a tone of determined resignation: "He is said to have very democratic views, so we have hope for him. We'll see. We can only hope. Apart from hope, we have very little else."

Salih is also a member of the presidium of Birlik, the Uzbek Popular Front, which has based its program on relieving the social and economic injustices resulting from the imposition of the cotton monoculture.

The Uzbeks remain tied to the land as agricultural laborers without any chance of improving their skills in industrial production, as cotton-processing plants and textile factories are generally located in other republics, according to the plan determined in Moscow. Finished goods would translate into a stronger economy and more power for Uzbekistan's people.

Ironically, Uzbekistan is not an ideal place to grow cotton. Although the climatic conditions provide enough heat and sunlight, the lack of adequate rainfall means that huge reserves of water are diverted to the region from the rivers that used to run into the Aral Sea. The final stages of irrigation to feed each thirsty cotton plant and to prevent the soil from drying up in the arid heat are generally still performed by hand. The land itself is exhausted from the harmful chemicals, artificial fertilizers, and pesticides used to cultivate cotton. The traditional system of crop rotation, which prevailed until the 1940s, has now vanished and the cotton plant has been in continuous production on some lands now for over fifty years. Harmful pesticides, long-banned in Western Europe and North America, are routinely used in Uzbekistan in quantities that exceed even the permissible Soviet norms.

The systematic poisoning of the land is accompanied by an abysmal state of health care. Cancers, anemia, and hepatitis are ravaging the Uzbek population. The average incidence of child mortality in Uzbekistan is around 47 per 1,000, but is closer to 100 per 1,000 in the area around the Aral Sea.

The situation of women is particularly harsh. Mainly women and children work the cotton fields, while the men try to find scarce higher-paying jobs elsewhere. The average pay for work on the cotton fields is around 35 to 40 rubles a month. Self-immolation, a method of suicide among Soviet Central Asian women that is on the increase, is now frequently discussed in the Soviet press. Many Uzbek intellectuals take the view that there is no cultural or religious tradition behind the practice. The women do it out of sheer despair at the hopeless conditions in which they live. The birth rate is very high, and there are few opportunities for prosperity in many regions.

Child labor on the cotton fields at harvesttime, a widespread practice rarely mentioned in the press until recently, is now supposed to be discontinued. But owing to official inertia, children of ten, eleven, and twelve years were brought out to work during the 1988 harvest for two to three months. The children are deposited in the cotton fields for the entire day, without shelter in the scorching sun, and often with little refreshment. In some areas, they are taken away and housed in barracks close to the work while the harvest is in progress.

Uzbekistan's fate is decided primarily in the corridors of Gosplan, the Central Planning Bureau in Moscow. It is unlikely that the republic will go over to a system of self-accounting, or *khozraschet*, that will include the part of Uzbekistan's economy devoted to cotton production. The fabled principle of perestroika, touted as a fundamental necessity for encouraging greater productivity, will not be put into effect in Uzbekistan as long as Moscow perceives Uzbekistan's cotton production as crucial to the economy.

Ecological disaster simmers at the edge of people's consciousness. The Aral Sea, one of the world's largest inland expanses of water, has almost dried up, causing a huge imbalance in the region's ecosystem. The two great rivers, the Amu Darya and Syr Darya, that used to flow in to replenish the sea no longer reach its shores. Their waters were diverted years ago to provide irrigation for the land to enable it to support rice and cotton. The resulting catastrophic drop in water levels in the sea has exposed miles of seabed, now made up of a mixture of salt, sand, pesticides, and defoliants. The lethal pollutants have caused a sharp increase in cancer of the throat in the area. Child mortality in this area is among the highest in the world. The environment is so polluted that mothers often contribute to the poisoning of their infants through their own breast milk. An ambitious plan to divert rivers from Siberia to flow into Soviet Central Asia was discussed for many years as a possible solution to the region's water shortage. It was abandoned in 1987 partly as a result of opposition from Russian writers and intellectuals.

These and other problems are now on the agenda for the newly formed Unity Movement for the Preservation of Uzbekistan's Natural, Material, and Spiritual Riches, the Uzbek Popular Front, usually known by the Uzbek word for "unity"—*Birlik*. Indeed, the growing sense of unity among the Central Asians has encouraged close relations between the popular fronts of Uzbekistan and Azerbaijan. The Azerbaijani Popular Front sent a representative to Birlik's founding congress.

Birlik occupies a temporary office on the ground floor of the Uzbek Writers Union building. People drift in and out in a continuous stream. The variety of people in the office at any one time reflects the Birlik's diverse and growing membership. One woman volunteer in her mid-thirties is the mother of four children. She has worked in a research institute for ten years, but now feels she must do something that will contribute to a better future for her children. Most of Birlik's members are in their thirties to early forties or younger, which is also the average age of the group's leadership and the average age of the Uzbek intelligentsia. In Uzbekistan, there is no old intelligentsia. During Stalin's rule, anyone who could remember how to read the Arabic script was sent to prison, and usually never heard of again.

Some visitors to the office have come to purchase the Birlik bulletin, some to inquire about joining the organization, and some simply to bring in a complaint that has met with no response in the appropriate government offices. Common grievances include: the poor state of health of the Uzbek population; the lack of ability to influence the choice of Uzbek deputies to the Congress of People's Deputies; the oppressive bureaucracy that stifles any initiative; and—one of the most sorely felt—the Russification of Uzbek culture. Despite the fact that only 19 percent of the population in Uzbekistan is Slavic, most television programs are in Russian. In the Russian SFSR, there are an average 12.5 books per person; in Uzbekistan there are only 2.5 books per person in the native language. Even in the realm of popular culture, Uzbek sensitivities are rarely taken into account. Many Uzbeks were gravely insulted when a film about Uzbekistan was prepared in Russian. To make things worse, the Russian actress invited to play the part of an Uzbek woman made no attempt to portray the traditional, modest behavior instilled in all Uzbek women from an early age.

Some Uzbeks still remember the 1960s when they were told Uzbekistan would become a model—an example of the success of the Soviet system. But the reality of the 1990s is very different: Statistics paint a bleak picture. Uzbekistan falls well below the USSR average in most areas of consumption and stands high on the list for infant mortality and other illnesses as indicators of the population's ill health.

The growing social and economic divide between Russians and Uzbeks in the republic is another major issue for Birlik. Class differences have essentially been shaped by differences in nationality; a person's access to work and living quarters in a city often depends on fluency in the Russian language. The production of cotton ties people to the land and, especially in the case of children, robs them of a significant part of their education. As a consequence, they fail to master the Russian language well enough to take the specialist courses in technical schools that are taught only in Russian. Breaking out of the cycle of poverty and manual work is very difficult for the majority of Uzbeks.

To make matters worse, when Russians come in from the Russian SFSR to fill jobs where no qualified Uzbeks can be found, they are offered the desirable apartments in the city, thus perpetuating the Russian-Uzbek divide. Out of a few thousand workers at the aviation factory in Tashkent, only 12 percent are Uzbeks. The Uzbek working class is very small, and the factory environment is essentially Russian-speaking and often hostile to Uzbeks who come in from the countryside and have only a poor command of the language. "It's like being an immigrant in your own country," one Birlik supporter commented.

The poverty in Uzbekistan is striking. The statistics are dismal: Around 45 percent of the population earns less than 78 rubles per month, the officially designated Soviet poverty line. There are over a million unemployed in Uzbekistan and still the government has no concrete plans to change the structure of the work force and the society.

Birlik is hoping to correct the social and economic inequities in the republic. The group was founded in the summer of 1988, as a response to protests against the proposed construction of a factory in the Bostonlykskiy district, which had been formally designated as an area of recreation. The authorities, as usual, had not consulted the residents of the area. The Uzbek Writers Union joined in the protest, whose purpose was to make clear to the Party apparat that arbitrary violation of the area's recreational status would not be tolerated. Gradually, people began to coalesce around issues that concerned them. Students came out to demonstrate, and in March 1989, thousands of people attended a demonstration sponsored by Birlik in favor of making Uzbek the state language in the republic. By mid-1989, there were three hundred thousand members in the organization. Their primary concern is to improve the social and economic conditions in Uzbekistan, and for that reason they have already gained a large following, even without any access to the mass media.

Abdurrakhim Pulatov, one of the founding members and leaders of Birlik, is not a writer but an engineer. For him, the social and economic issues are the most important items on the agenda for the Uzbek national movement. He is acutely aware of the poverty and hardships of everyday life for Uzbeks. "When people hear there is an organization for Uzbeks," he says, "they know immediately what its program must be; even without access to the media thousands of Uzbeks have given their support." He regrets only that the Russian-speaking population has no access to information about Birlik and its program. "They are fed all kinds of inaccurate information about us. We would like to straighten out the record." Drawing on a comparison with the Baltic popular fronts, he points out that Birlik focuses more on the pressing problems in Uzbekistan. The humanitarian and national cultural concerns of the Baltic popular fronts are not yet priorities for the Uzbek people.

In October 1989, Birlik organized demonstrations in support of greater official standing for the Uzbek language and against the official law that sought to limit the language's use. An estimated fifty thousand people demonstrated, and Pulatov together with around one hundred other demonstrators were arrested at one of the events. The following month, Birlik held its second congress, attended by delegates from Uzbekistan and representatives of informal groups from other parts of the USSR. A difference of opinion among the leadership arose at this meeting; part of the newly elected central committee voted to open up discussion with the republic's authorities, while part decided to continue the antigovernment strategy of the previous leadership. Another major decision taken at this congress, in keeping with the organization's name, endorsed the acceptance of members from other Soviet Central Asian republics.

The name *Birlik* ("unity") suggests an identity that attaches Uzbekistan to the broad continuum of Turkic peoples stretching through Asia. There is certainly a growing interest in other Turkic peoples and especially in Turkic areas outside the Soviet Union. Well-thumbed copies of Turkish-language journals from the West circulate among those lucky enough to gain access to such rare literature. Turkey is a country that has remained a mystery, however, for most Soviet citizens. The vicissitudes of Turkey's political scene and economy have rarely been discussed in the pages of the Soviet press. Only recently has there been some information published in *Izvestia* on the country that was taboo for so long. Surprisingly, the new line on Turkey expresses admiration for the country's economy and the variety of goods it provides for its people. The comparison with their own situation cannot be lost on readers in the Turkic regions of the USSR.

In the summer of 1989, the idea of brotherhood between the Turkic peoples seemed strained, however, with news of violent attacks by Uzbeks against Meskhetian Turks in the Fergana region of Uzbekistan. Within one week, rampaging Uzbeks had killed almost a hundred people. Figures differed, official statistics claimed that of the total seventy-nine were Meskhetian Turks and the rest Uzbeks, but unofficial investigators have evened out the figures of fatalities between the Meskhetian Turks and Uzbeks.

In Tashkent, there were growing suspicions that the whole episode had been contrived as a provocation. Most people acquainted with the area confirmed that the situation in the region was ripe for a confrontation. The Meskhetian Turks in general enjoyed a higher standard of living than the native Uzbeks. Moreover, just before the tragic events there was growing apprehension among them, encouraged by then Georgian Party first secretary Djumber Patiashvili, that forty years after their deportation they would finally be allowed to return to their ancestral lands in southern Georgia. There were rumors that they began to behave as if these were their final weeks in the country to which they were forcibly moved.

In Margilan, where the violence started, there are ten thousand unemployed and in Fergana, twenty thousand. This is just a portion of the one million unemployed in Uzbekistan, most of them Uzbeks. Many of the Uzbek intelligentsia fear that the violence was a well-planned provocation aimed at sabotaging efforts for perestroika in the republic. Among the many rumors and assumptions about the attacks that immediately began to circulate were some that directed full blame to Islamic groups, informal associations, and especially implicating Birlik.

Uzbekistan's chief of security blamed "Pan-Islamic" agitators for inciting the violence. But members of Birlik deny the possibility of such a force. They themselves were spurred to register their dismay over the events: A joint statement was drawn up together with representatives of the Crimean Tatars and Meskhetian Turks as an appeal to end the violence. There is an anecdote that brings a touch of humor to the otherwise tragic situation: In Uzbekistan, the optimists are learning Uzbek, the pessimists are learning English, and the realists are learning how to use a Kalashnikov (rifle). Everyone hopes this is not an accurate prediction for the future.

Tales of corruption in Uzbekistan are legion. Not long ago, revelations worthy of the Arabian Nights came to light in Uzbekistan. A local strongman had built himself a luxurious fortified estate in Uzbekistan, complete with slaves and a private prison. Uzbekistan's reputation has been tarnished lately through the revelations of investigators Telman Gdylan and

Nikolai Ivanov, the supercops of the Soviet crime-fighting force. This team has uncovered corruption throughout the Soviet establishment, reaching formerly untouchable people such as Leonid Brezhnev's son-in-law. Archconservative Yegor Ligachev himself has also been implicated, though never directly accused by the prosecuting team. And as a result of these investigations, hundreds of Uzbek officials have been dismissed from their posts and punished for wrongdoing, usually taking many other officials with them. The scandal has created an atmosphere of unease throughout the Uzbek apparat, which has slowed many officials into a passive, unresponsive mode, hardly exemplary of the new enthusiasm required by perestroika.

A publisher we met lives in a chic neighborhood of Tashkent—not all Uzbeks suffer from poverty and corruption. He acknowledges his good fortune, referring vaguely to a time when he was not so well accepted by the powers-that-be in Uzbekistan, after he had made statements against the Soviet invasion of Afghanistan, where over a million Uzbeks live. Nonetheless, he feels alienated among the other predominantly Russian residents of the neighborhood, and there is no Uzbek-language kindergarten to which he can send his young son. He regrets that his three other children had to attend Russian-language schools. Despite his own success, he feels deeply the desperate situation of his people. "They say perestroika will help us," he laments, "but how can you construct something new and viable in a cemetery?" He and his wife are a modern couple, yet she does not take part in our discussions, but drifts in and out of the room serving sumptuous dishes of *plov* and other Uzbek specialties, according to the traditional practice. The young girls of the family are, of course, nowhere to be seen. He and his family represent a growing trend among the Uzbek intelligentsia. For many years, they were weaned away from their national traditions and discouraged from identifying with the national minority population by the lure of a position within a new "internationalist" class, in exchange for loyalty to the dominant culture centered in Moscow. The benefits of this arrangement have proved illusory for the younger members of the intelligentsia, who are now turning back to their roots, and to their people.

The return to tradition has been accompanied by a revival of religion in Uzbekistan, although, as in other Soviet Central Asian republics, Islam was never suppressed among the broad masses of the population. There have been numerous reports in the Soviet newspapers of respected Party officials, who had maintained a public face as atheists throughout long and successful careers, suddenly becoming unofficial mullahs on retirement.

There are only four or five mosques now in Tashkent and a total of seventy in Uzbekistan. Before the 1917 Revolution, there were over twenty thousand in Uzbekistan alone. The staying power of Islam in this region was reinforced by the incorporation of its rituals into the national traditions of the people. The Islamic way of conducting circumcisions, marriages, and, particularly, funerals became partly secularized after 1917 in the transition to national tradition. The only existing translation of the Koran from Arabic into Uzbek was prepared before the 1917 Revolution. Specialists are presently preparing another to be published very soon. The Muslim sharia law (Islamic law) has been maintained purely through its survival as an oral tradition, which has been subsumed into the developing Uzbek national tradition. The religious revival has provided many people with an alternative to Russified Communism for their cultural and spiritual needs. Islam in Soviet Central Asia has not taken a fundamentalist turn as many feared it might. The spiritual and political "awakening" in this region's cities looks decidedly secular. Fundamentalism does not provide ready solutions for an urban intelligentsia raised during the cult of envy for the West and its material progress.

Sherali, the most popular singer in Uzbekistan today, professes to be a devout Muslim. His enormous success among both young and old may be attributed to the reviving interest in the Uzbeks' cultural heritage. To the accompaniment of the traditional eleven-stringed *tor*, he weaves lyrics by Alisher Navoyi, Omar Khayyám, and more recent Uzbek poets into renditions of his own poems. He is the Uzbeks' bard, the keeper of the ancient verses. The richness of the Uzbek cultural heritage that spans the centuries is revealed in these songs, which speak of the eternal themes of faith, love, and passion. Yet, the descendants of that culture, the present-day Uzbeks, are a people now struggling for their very existence.

With a population of 16.6 million, Uzbeks are reproducing at a rate surpassed only by the Tajiks in the Soviet Union. The dismal circumstances of the majority of this population and their lack of power to achieve change will become increasingly untenable in the coming months and years. The Uzbeks have not matched the other, more established nations in the USSR in their demands, but the Uzbek nation itself is a newcomer to national consciousness. The process of nation building and development among the Uzbeks has taken place primarily during the Soviet period. Their evolving sense of a need for self-determination and the perception of having been exploited can only spur this development— to what end, and whether it will be in concert with the other Turkic nations or alone, only time will tell.

The Kazakhs

Alma-Ata, the capital city of Kazakhstan, is a secret closely guarded by the people who live there. Close to the Chinese border, the city appears to have avoided much of the dismal construction and pollution that are the hallmark of most major Soviet cities. The stunning Tien Shan Mountains,

higher than any others in the Soviet Union, form the border with China
and are an omnipresent backdrop to the cityscape. The air is clear and
sharp and much of the town still preserves the atmosphere of an outpost
of the empire, as it was in the nineteenth century.

Vernyi (the Faithful), as the town was originally called, was founded in
the mid-1850s with the arrival of 470 soldiers and officers to establish a
fortified garrison outpost for the Russian empire. Russian and Kazakh
families soon followed and by the end of the decade the town had 5,000
inhabitants, and soon gained a reputation as one of the most lively market
towns in Central Asia. People came from miles around to the five market
squares in the town where there was trade in fruit, agricultural produce,
wood, horses, and livestock, and anything that needed to be bought or
sold. The largely Russian population and the function of the town as a
frontier outpost of the Russian empire resulted in the town having very
few characteristics of a region populated mainly by the nomadic Kazakhs.

Alma-Ata is filled with delightful parks and the occasional Russian
Orthodox church, with its onion-shaped domes made up of bright, multi-
colored tiles of pink, ocher, blue, green, and white. The city has not been
subjected to the typical ravages of war and destruction, followed by reconstruction, as have the Soviet cities farther west. The legacy of the
Russian imperial presence in the late nineteenth century is all around and
permeates even today's relations among the nations.

Until they began moving into Alma-Ata, the nomadic Kazakhs had
invested little energy in constructing buildings and cities, traveling instead from place to place and living in their distinctively shaped yurts.
During the period of Sovietization, many were forced into a sedentary
life-style against their will.

Today, less than half of the population of Kazakhstan is composed of
native Kazakhs. The way Kazakhstan's borders were drawn in the 1920s
ensured the republic a mixed population. The southern and western
regions are inhabited by the core Kazakh population, while in the territory to the north—the vast virgin lands of Communist myth—Kazakhs are
the minority. Nonetheless, the latest statistics show that the Kazakh share
of the population is increasing. The 1989 census shows that for the first
time in the postwar period, the Kazakhs are the largest national group.
The percentage of Russians in the republic has now dropped to 37.6
percent, and the Kazakh share has increased to 38 percent. The increase
is due partly to the higher birth rate among Kazakhs, but also to the minor
exodus of Slavs migrating back to their ethnic homelands. In the last
decade, over 780,000 people—more than in any other republic—mainly
Russians, have migrated out of Kazakhstan to take up newly created jobs
in European Russia where there is a labor shortage.

Despite Soviet claims that the republic is a haven of internationalism,
Kazakh national consciousness is developing at a rapid pace. It was the

Kazakhs in Alma-Ata who staged the first major ethnic disturbance of Gorbachev's tenure in December 1986. News of the demonstration that turned into a riot swept through the Western press corps in Moscow, but direct information was difficult to come by as reporters were not allowed to travel to the scene. According to the official Soviet accounts, thousands of Kazakhs had taken to the streets and had rampaged through the city in violent clashes with the militia. The official account reported two dead and many injured. The culprits were arrested and subsequently many young people were dismissed from their colleges and universities. Several people received very harsh sentences. One young man was sentenced to death, the sentence later commuted to life in prison.

The immediate pretext for the demonstration was the replacement of longtime Party first secretary Dinmukhammed Akhmedovich Kunayev, a native Kazakh, by Gennady Kolbin, an ethnic Russian and supporter of Gorbachev. Kunayev had been in power since 1959—except for a two-year period, 1962–64, when he fell afoul of Khrushchev—and was closely identified with the Brezhnev clique. It was assumed that Gorbachev would soon move to replace him, as he had with several of the Brezhnev holdovers in the Politburo. For the first time, it became clear that Gorbachev was either unaware of national sensibilities or had grossly underestimated the power of ethnic allegiances. It was the first step in a series of blunders and miscalculations by Gorbachev over the next three years that showed he had no plan for perestroika in nationalities policy. What became increasingly clear, moreover, was that he showed no sign of understanding the need for restructuring national relations and the situation of the nationalities in his Soviet Union. The Alma-Ata riots were a rude awakening.

From Gorbachev's point of view, Kolbin was the ideal choice for cleaning up a republic that still bore signs of functioning "stagnation." He was young and energetic and had proved his loyalty to Gorbachev and his policies in his previous appointments as second secretary in Georgia and Party leader in the Ulyanovsk Oblast. But, as one Kazakh writer put it: "He was completely unaware of our customs, our way of life, our language. How could he understand our problems?"

The true story of the December 1986 events was not widely known until many months after, but Alma-Ata residents are now ready to fill in the details. The Soviet press at the time had reported that an armed gang of Kazakh youths—"hooligans, drunks, and other rowdies"—had damaged public buildings and had attacked the militia. A young man present at the demonstration relates a different version of the events:

"It was a peaceful demonstration, without excesses. Mainly young people gathered for three days on the square. There must have been a permanent contingent of around five thousand. But can you imagine, in December it is very cold in Alma-Ata."

The demonstration included both workers and students, who were already organized before the event. Faced with a potentially unruly crowd, the authorities tried to regain control by urging Party leaders to speak to the crowds; but that only made matters worse, because few of them could speak in the Kazakh language. Then some Russian and Kazakh workers began to fight and the Interior Ministry troops moved in. According to eyewitness accounts, they were armed with heavy truncheons.

Three years later, the Kazakhs have only just begun to press for an official commission to investigate the events. During the first historic session of the Congress of People's Deputies, the well-known Kazakh writer Olzhas Suleimenov raised the issue and compared the 1986 demonstration with the April 9, 1989, massacre in Tbilisi, Georgia. Brushing aside all the official information released on the demonstration, he confirmed that it had been peaceful, similar in its origins to the Georgian gathering. He urged a thorough and public review of the incident.

Dinmukhammed Kunayev was not an enthusiastic supporter of Kazakh nationalism. He was nothing like his fellow first secretary Petro Shelest, the Ukrainian Communist Party boss who lost his position in 1972 for allegedly supporting Ukrainian nationalism. Kunayev did not speak out in defense of Kazakh national rights; neither did he pen any historical works of nationalist subtext; nor did he seek to preserve monuments with particular significance for Kazakhs. Nonetheless, Kunayev's Kazakhstan appears to have been a much more livable place than other republics over the past twenty years or so. This feat was accomplished by skillfully balancing the demands imposed from Moscow against the needs of the republic while maintaining a regime of strict control at the same time. Alma-Ata, for example, boasts new housing complexes that are not the standard Soviet-built fare. In the districts at the edge of the city, new apartment blocks have been built on a fairly regular schedule. They are decorated with Asiatic motifs and look quite attractive from a distance against the backdrop of mountains. Certainly, public architecture here is more in tune with the surroundings, a rare treat compared with Moscow's monumental cinderblock projects. There was no warning before Kunayev's retirement. No criticism had been published in the press and the people still believed in the image of him as the great man that careful propaganda had created. The suddenness of the change of pilot for the republic must have come as a shock to the population that had borne with him for twenty-seven years.

Although Kazakhs benefited under Kunayev's rule in some ways, in other ways they suffered discrimination. Alma-Ata's population is about one-quarter Kazakh, and rising, but there are no kindergartens for Kazakh children, and Kazakh-language instruction in schools is often unavailable. Some Kazakhs wish to see their language legally introduced as the official language of the republic, but they are ready to admit that even

Kazakhs are now used to working in Russian. Some refer wistfully back to the time in the 1920s when officials received 15 percent more in salary if they knew the Kazakh language.

Many Kazakhs have a strong sense of their history. Sherhan Murtaza-yev is a well-known Kazakh writer and also the editor of Kazakhstan's only literary weekly newspaper. Together with a few of his colleagues in the Union of Writers of Kazakhstan, he has a passion for history. He is currently working on his fourth book about Turar Ryskulov, a leading figure in the Kazakh national Communist movement in the 1920s. With other Turkic Communist leaders such as Mirsaid Sultan Galiev, Ryskulov forged a new sense of identity for the Kazakh and Turkic peoples under Bolshevik rule. For a time, it looked as if the peoples of Soviet Central Asia really could free themselves of the shackles of colonialism and move into the modern era under the guiding hand of the Bolsheviks. But when the leading figures in this movement began to be denounced one by one by the Bolsheviks in Moscow, it was all over for national Communism.

Sherhan Murtazayev recounts details about Ryskulov's life that have not been part of the permitted span of official Soviet history: his upbringing as an illegitimate child before the Revolution, his imprisonment for taking part in an uprising in 1916; his key role in the formation of policy toward Turkestan as one of the first Central Asian Muslims to join the Bolshevik party; the decline of his career after the Twelfth Party Congress in 1923; and his posting to faraway Mongolia by an irate Stalin, where he wrote a constitution for the new republic. These are now acceptable subjects for study, but they were not always so.

Even today, there are still taboos. There is still no objective study of the Alash Orda, a liberal nationalist Kazakh political party that formed an independent Kazakh government from 1917 to 1920. There is a subtlety in discussing historical subjects here, as in most non-Russian republics. Turar Ryskulov's history as a Bolshevik with nationalist inclinations was on the fringes of what could be officially discussed for many years, when any subject that had Kazakh substance was nurtured and explored as far as possible by those who sought to preserve the national heritage even in those constricting circumstances.

Feelings of national pride are very close to the surface and there is an undercurrent of resentment among the Kazakh population that their people have suffered severe deprivations throughout their history. In 1930, the Kazakhs outnumbered the Uzbeks, but today, there are twice as many Uzbeks as Kazakhs in the USSR. In 1932–33, the Kazakh population was cut down by a famine at the same time as the Ukrainian famine. A Kazakh demographer has calculated that between 2.5 million and 3 million Kazakhs perished at that time. The famine was followed by Stalinist repressions in 1938–39 and soon thereafter by the war. If the Kazakh population had not suffered such severe setbacks, it would, according to one Kazakh authority, number around 30 million today. Slowly, their population is increasing, but the Kazakhs feel they have a lot of catching up to do.

Conflicts between Kazakhs and other ethnic groups flare up from time to time. In the summer of 1989, they clashed with immigrant workers in Novy Uzen, in Western Kazakhstan. Novy Uzen is a new town with a modern oil industry to which immigrant workers from outside Kazakhstan come to earn high wages, while many of the native Kazakhs remain unemployed. One writer clarifies the situation: "It is easy to see what has happened. Next to Novy Uzen [New Uzen] there is Stary Uzen [Old Uzen], the old settlement. Its population is exclusively Kazakh, around sixteen thousand, and not even one telephone between them! In that area there is nothing but sheep and camels. Is it any wonder that the native population vents its frustrations every now and again?"

Many Russians consider Kazakhstan to be their homeland. The sheer beauty of Alma-Ata has created a deep-rooted sense of attachment. Sergei is one such example; he studied in Moscow, but couldn't wait to finish in order to return to his native Alma-Ata. Now he works with a group eager to create joint ventures and encourage tourism in Alma-Ata. His colleague Marat is a Kazakh. They work together in the new enterprise, putting perestroika into practice, but there are certain subjects Marat does not discuss in Sergei's presence. He points out that urbanization has been severely limited to exclude migration by Kazakhs from the surrounding countryside into the city. Kazakhs who do manage to find work in Alma-Ata often have to give up and return to their *aul*, their settlement in the countryside, after failing to find an apartment.

Marat is one of the lucky ones. He, his wife, and two children share a three-room apartment with his brother, his wife, and their child. The kitchen accommodates only two adults standing and the bathroom is not much bigger. Marat's room is almost filled by a bed and the children's cots. The living room sofa doubles as his brother's bed at night. A beautiful handmade rug covers one wall. "It's a traditional Kazakh design," Marat explains, "a present from my family for our wedding." The two young families try not to be at home all at the same time and Marat hopes to make some money in business so that he can move out soon and leave the apartment to his brother, a doctor.

Alma-Ata is a beautiful city that has drawn many people to it over the years. The classical film directors Vsevolod Pudovkin and Sergei Eisenstein lived out the Second World War here. The Luna Park, with its landscaped flower-beds, paths, and ornamental ponds, was laid out just two years after the first contingent of the czar's Russian soldiers arrived at the garrison in the 1850s. Its mature trees and elegant walkways exude an atmosphere of more bourgeois times. The only signs of Sovietization are a small statue of Maxim Gorky, for whom the park is officially named, and a portrait of Lenin, tastefully tucked away to the side of a walkway. As in most Soviet cities, districts in Alma-Ata bear names connected with the 1917 Revolution or with its leaders. But increasingly, people are reverting to use of the old names. For example, "Tatarka," just north of the park, named after the Tatar settlement there, was one of the three original districts of the garrison town.

These days, young Kazakhs increasingly profess a deep commitment to the Kazakh cause. Many Kazakh children are passed from one grandparent to another, to learn their native language. College-educated Kazakhs often study Arabic to try to regain something of their heritage. Together with the growing respect for their Kazakh heritage comes the conviction heard elsewhere in Soviet Central Asia. "The Kazakhs," one youth leader pronounces, "are part of the great Turkic race which stretches from the Uighurs of Northwest China to the Magyars of Hungary." The addition of Hungary to the continuum of Turkish peoples is somewhat unexpected, but the youth assures us that the Magyars migrated westward from the region around Alma-Ata. "Almaty was the name of the old settlement here before the garrison town of Vernyi; *alma* is the Hungarian word for 'apple.' This was known as the City of Apples."

Kazakhs are not the only Turkic nation in Kazakhstan. There are just over 200,000 Uighurs in the Soviet Union and most of them live in Kazakhstan. The Soviet-Chinese border cuts off the Soviet Uighurs from the main body of their people—estimates range between 5 million and 10 million—who live in the Xinjiang Province of China. Travel and immigration were relatively easy until the early 1960s when the border closed after the breakdown in relations between the USSR and China. Many families that had settled on the Soviet side of the border were cut off from their relatives for many years. Since 1988, family visits have been possible across the border, and a revived railway service between Alma-Ata and Urumchi will soon restore the link to the Uighurs on the Chinese side of the border.

While Alma-Ata is the capital city of a republic whose titular nationality is Muslim, it does not appear as Muslim as the cities in Uzbekistan or Tajikistan. The Kazakhs adopted Islam much later than many other Central Asians did, and the religion never became as great a cultural force in their society as it did in the others. Because of their nomadic life-style and isolation from centers of Muslim culture, the Kazakhs developed a form of Islam that retained elements of their earlier beliefs. Today, the Muslims of Kazakhstan fall under the jurisdiction of the Spiritual Directorate of Central Asia and Kazakhstan, one of the four official bodies for Muslims in the Soviet Union, but the seat is located in distant Tashkent. Alma-Ata has one functioning mosque, which is hardly discernible from the road apart from a small minaret rising just above the fence. The structure is old but has no lavish adornments. Each day, elderly Kazakhs sit on a bench by the entrance, some leaning on their walking sticks, dressed in Astra-khan hats, trousers tucked into boots.

The administrators and officials of this mosque are engaged in an am-bitious enterprise. The existing mosque is to be replaced very soon by a new, glistening, white structure—a purpose-built mosque to be con-structed on the same site. The new building will have two wings joined by a dome, and four minarets, and will include a section for women and bathing facilities for both men and women. The cost has been estimated at seven million rubles, and construction was scheduled to start in late 1989. It was designed by local architects in consultation with experts from Pakistan.

The new building is yet another sign of the reviving interest in religion and spirituality. But the project may yet be held up by the shortages and delays endemic to all such enterprises in the Soviet system. If there is not yet a readily accessible translation of the Koran into Kazakh, then it may take longer than anticipated to construct a new mosque, but for the moment, the faith is strong and growing every day.

Kazakhstan has no national popular front movement such as those in the Baltic States, or even in Uzbekistan and Azerbaijan. The lack of a clear ethnic majority may be one reason why such a movement has not emerged. There are, however, some informal groups that aim to protect Kazakh national traditions and values.

"Nevada" is the organization Kazakhs have poured their national soul into. The principal aim of the movement is to ban nuclear testing around Semipalatinsk. "Nevada" was chosen as its name in the hope that a coun-terpart organization called "Semipalatinsk" would take off in the United States. The inspiration for the movement came from the Kazakh Writers Union. In a letter addressed to the Supreme Soviet, the writers pointed out that the Soviet Union rated only twenty-eighth on the list of compar-ative standards of living in developed countries, and that the average life expectancy in Kazakhstan had dropped four years. The reason this state of affairs had not been remedied, they proposed, was because of the expen-diture of funds on nuclear arms.

The Nevada movement is gathering strength. The inaugural mass meeting took place on February 28, 1989, and soon thereafter the au-thorities recognized it as an official organization. Olzhas Suleimenov, the head of the Kazakh Writers Union and deputy to the Congress of People's Deputies, is its moving force. His large office at the Writers Union houses the thousands of signatures collected on petitions protesting nuclear arms testing. They are pinned to the walls around the room and guests are encouraged to sign. Some petitions read "Nevada, movement for banning nuclear testing in Kazakhstan"; others read ". . . for banning nuclear testing not only in Kazakhstan, but in the whole world." The hint of local patriotism in the first reveals a deeper sense of attachment to Kazakhstan, which the second hurriedly tries to obscure with its sweeping attempt at internationalism. The difference here may be a clue to future developments. Nevada has provided a rallying point for Kazakhs throughout the republic. Kazakhs in Karaganda have held demonstrations against the noise and pollution from the testing site and most Kazakhs consider the movement to be theirs.

The Adilet (Justice) Society is another informal group that has gained respect and recognition not only among Kazakhs. It was formed to pursue the same goals as the All-Union Society, "Memorial," which is dedicated to exposing the crimes of Stalinism and rehabilitating the victims. Adilet has steered away from an exclusively Kazakh agenda, although it has begun to research and publicize suppressed issues in Kazakh history. From its inception, it was intended to provide a voice for all who live on the territory of Kazakhstan—especially those who were deported against their will, such as the Germans, Ukrainians, Meskhetians, Chechens, Crimean Tatars, and others.

The Kazakh writer Sain Muratbekov has devoted some of his work to the diversity of ethnic inhabitants of Kazakhstan. He explains how Kazakhs have always lived in harmony with the different people around them. He recalls his youth in the 1940s, when Chechens, Germans, and Russians arrived at their *aul:* "They all learned Kazakh very quickly; there was no nationality question in those times." He encountered difficulties only when he moved to the city, when he discovered it was necessary to learn Russian, to prevent ridicule from the city people, including the few Kazakhs who had already made the move. It was only ten to fifteen years ago that Kazakhs began using their own language again in the city, he observes. He describes these early experiences in his works.

Many of the different national groups living among the Kazakhs were deported on Stalin's orders during the Second World War, when their loyalty to the USSR came under suspicion. Entire nations, such as the Crimean Tatars and Meskhetian Turks, were deported, and others like the Chechens and the Ingush were decimated. One young Ukrainian we met told us of his family's experiences when they were deported from Western Ukraine in 1941. Several families were roused in the middle of the night and given half an hour to gather their belongings before being loaded onto wagons and deported eastward. The appalling living conditions in the early years helped to spread sickness and fatal diseases, often striking at the young children and the elderly, who rarely survived. Our young friend was born just after Stalin's death when conditions had improved. Even though Ukrainians make up 5 percent of Kazakhstan's population, the former deportees are for the most part denationalized and no longer speak the language or know the customs. Some have become virtually indistinguishable from the Greeks, Uzbeks, Kazakhs, and others around them.

There has been little organized opposition to the growing Kazakh movement from the other nationalities in the republic thus far, although the statistics on emigration suggest that the Slavs among them are electing simply to return to a homeland more congenial to their national sensibilities.

The Tatars

Among the awakening Turkic peoples, there is one that is truly a hidden nation among hidden nations. The Soviet Union's Tatar population numbers around seven million, making it the sixth largest ethnic group, after the Russians, Ukrainians, Byelorussians, Uzbeks, and Kazakhs. There are differences among branches of the Tatar family; for example, the Crimean Tatars are different from the Volga Tatars; nonetheless, the Soviet census taker has often put all the Tatars in one category. Viewed in this way, the Tatars are the largest group without the valued union republic status, which brings with it certain privileges and more representation. Union republics, however small, are allocated thirty-two representatives in the Congress of People's Deputies. Even tiny Estonia, with its population of one and a half million, is entitled to a republic's share of representatives. Autonomous republics, however large, are allocated only eleven representatives to the Congress. Access to many other resources is determined by this administrative status. That is why union republic status is a desirable goal.

And therein lies a point of conflict. When the Tatar Autonomous Soviet Socialist Republic (ASSR) was created just after the Bashkir ASSR in 1920, it put an end to hopes for the formation of a large Tatar-Bashkir republic extending over the territory of the Kazan Khanate, the Middle Volga, and the Ural region. The formation of such a republic, uniting the closely related Tatars and Bashkirs, would have provided a strong impetus for Turkic unity. This expectation was quashed, together with any hope of Kazan retaining its role as the cultural and political center for the Muslims of Russia. The newly drawn boundaries were calculated to separate the Bashkirs from the Tatars, and ensure that the Tatars would not be in the majority in their own ASSR. The Tatar ASSR measured 68,000 square miles and the Bashkir ASSR 143,600, square miles. Their capital cities are Kazan and Ufa.

At present, less than two million Tatars live in the Tatar ASSR, although another six million live elsewhere in the Russian Republic in scattered, historic colonies or within other ASSRs. Nonetheless, Kazan is once more reasserting itself as the cultural and spiritual center for the Tatars. What is more, the Tatars are pressing for union republic status for their autonomous republic, as is the Bashkir ASSR. Sooner or later, the authorities in Moscow will have to face up to this new problem right in the heart of Russia.

The Crimean Tatars are another Turkic group, deported en masse from their native Crimea in a most brutal fashion by Stalin. They have taken their destiny into their own hands, and are mobilizing their people for a return to their homeland, the Crimean peninsula. After making the headlines by staging a dramatic sit-in demonstration in Red Square in the summer of 1988, the stage-by-stage reclamation began, at first in the face of official disapproval, but gradually with some cooperation from the authorities. For many years, the Crimean Tatars were well regarded among human rights activists and dissidents in Moscow; they assumed the techniques of petition and peaceful protest to further their cause after Stalin's death. Their aim has been to seek the reconstitution of a Crimean republic, once the Crimean Tatar population has returned. Their self-help approach to their cause may well be an encouragement to other Tatars to achieve their own goals in the future.

The Tajiks

The Tajiks are the only major national group in Soviet Central Asia that traces cultural roots to the Persians rather than the Turks, although it shares much in common with its Turkic neighbors, the Uzbeks, Kirgiz, and Turkmen. The Tajiks are one of the older sedentary peoples of Central Asia. The stunning architecture of Samarkand and Bukhara, now located in the Uzbek Republic, is a product of Tajik culture. Before the 1917 Revolution, Central Asian intellectuals in this region were generally bilingual in Tajik and Uzbek, and the people lived side by side in the Muslim commonwealth without significant friction in their relations.

The Tajiks now inhabit mainly the territory of their designated union republic, to the southeast of Uzbekistan. Afghanistan lies on Tajikistan's southern border. There are 4.2 million Tajiks in the Soviet Union and around as many across the border in Afghanistan. The Tajiks have been the least Russified of all the Soviet Central Asians and are among the most religious. The Soviet invasion of Afghanistan has added a powerful spur to their increasing assertiveness over the past decade. There was already a strong anti-Soviet feeling among the Tajiks: Many of the Tajiks in Afghanistan are descendants of the Basmachi, who fought a guerrilla war against the Soviets in the 1920s. When Soviet troops marched into Afghanistan, they quickly realized that their own Tajiks would have to be withdrawn from the force, as they showed themselves to be largely in sympathy with the Afghans. Throughout the 1970s, the border between Tajikistan and Afghanistan was considered a dangerous zone, prone to ambush from both sides.

The marked increase in religious activity in Tajikistan in the past few years may be partly attributed to the war. Propaganda against unofficial mullahs, the holy men of Islam, and Islamic practices intensified in the early 1980s, but failed to stem the rising swell of religiosity in the republic. Numerous discussions on improving "atheistic upbringing" among the Party members in Tajikistan have had no effect. Throughout Soviet Central Asia, Muslims have refused to succumb to official propaganda against their traditions and beliefs. A concerted effort was made to persuade Muslims that fasting during the month of Ramadan was harmful to their health, and to prevent the payment of bride money, *kalym*, when a Muslim couple marries according to the Muslim tradition, but with very little success. In fact, holy places of pilgrimage have recently become popular venues for family visits, and observance of traditions has, if anything, increased.

Tajikistan has been the source for a call to form an independent Islamic state. In 1986, Abdullo Nuriddinovich Saidov, who had practiced as an unofficial mullah for over twenty years, proposed that an independent Islamic state be formed on the territory of Tajikistan. According to all reports, Saidov had developed a large following among people on the state farms in his district, where he had established several teahouses for the purpose of spreading the teachings of Islam. Under his influence, many people in the area renounced radio and television, stopped subscribing to Soviet newspapers and magazines, and refused to participate in Soviet festivals that were tailored as a replacement for religious celebrations.

By February 1990, Dushanbe, the capital of Tajikistan, had succumbed to a wave of violence that was sparked by the military crackdown in Azerbaijan. In response to reports of violent interethnic clashes, tanks and troops were sent into the city. Officials claimed there were several dead and over two hundred injured. The demonstrations began as rumors spread among the local Tajiks that Armenians escaping from the violence in Azerbaijan would be given preferential treatment for housing on arrival. Many Tajiks, struggling to find scarce housing in the city, were understandably incensed by the rumors.

In response, thousands gathered to demand the resignation of the entire Communist Party leadership. They also demanded a broad range of economic and ecological improvements: jobs for the thousands of unemployed in the region; better housing; the return of all proceeds from the sale of Tajikistan's cotton; the closure of a dangerous aluminum plant; and an end to the sale of pork, which the predominantly Muslim population is forbidden to eat. The protesters' demands, turned out, after all, to be much the same as elsewhere in the non-Russian republics. The statistics for poverty, unemployment, and ill-health in Tajikistan are as dismal as those in other Soviet Central Asian republics.

The Muslims of Soviet Central Asia are a force about to awaken. The barriers that were so carefully constructed to partition the peoples are steadily disintegrating, and more people of this region are learning about their history and culture and rediscovering how much they have in common. In Tajikistan, Uzbekistan, and Kirgizia, there have been serious moves toward making their languages the state language in the republic. But even the new formula proposed as a compromise in the drafts of the law—native language at home and Russian as the language of international communication—has been severely questioned among the Turkic people. Many feel that it is absurd for a Kazakh and an Uzbek, or a Kirgiz and an Uighur, to communicate in Russian, when their own languages are so closely related.

Still, the Soviet Union's Muslim-Turkic peoples have not yet spoken; but when they do, they may well prove a more formidable force than anyone imagined, for as the sense of unity and potential power of their people grows, the Turkic and Muslim peoples will no longer be satisfied with the colonial relationship they have endured with Moscow thus far. The one hope in this region of poverty, violence, and despair is the emerging national rights movement rooted in the indigenous intelligentsia and the small middle class that is beginning to appear.

Russians:
The Elder Brother

> Russia is a whole separate world, submissive to the will,
> caprice, fantasy of a single man, whether his name be
> Peter or Ivan, no matter—in all instances the common
> element is the manifestation of arbitrariness. Contrary to
> all law of human community, Russia moves only in the
> direction of her own enslavement and the enslavement
> of all the neighboring peoples. For this reason it would
> be in the interest of not only other peoples, but also her
> own that she be compelled to take a new path.
>
> —Pyotr Chaadayev, writing in 1854

WHILE RUSSIA hardly qualifies as a hidden nation, no study of the
fate of the non-Russian peoples is complete without a consideration of the
USSR's most visible nation. The Russians—the self-styled "elder
brother"—make up half of the Soviet population.

Although the USSR is said to be a state guided by the principle of an
internationalism that confers equality to all its ethnic groups, the special
status of the Russian nation is celebrated in the embarrassingly fawning
national anthems of several of the USSR's republics. The Uzbek anthem,
for example, begins, "Hail Russian brother, great is your people." In the
past, the Azerbaijani national anthem extolled, "The mighty Russian
brother is bringing to the land the triumph of freedom; and with our blood
we have strengthened our kinship with him." A non-Russian textbook
from the mid-1960s put it more explicitly. "There is a Russian people," it
announced. "You have a leader." Praise of the Russian nation was particularly pronounced in the Brezhnev years, when what some writers
have called "the Russian party" of chauvinistic Soviet bureaucrats in the
Communist apparat, the cultural establishment, and the military wielded
immense power.

Although they represent a bare majority of the Soviet Union's population, it is not merely the demographic predominance of the Russians

that lies at the core of today's state of national tensions. The Russian national identity, with its assumption of imperial rule, defines national relations in the Soviet Union and, consequently, propels the resurgence of national assertiveness among the hidden nations.

Clearly, the preeminence of Russians within the empire—their relatively privileged political, cultural, and, in the end, economic status—has come at a price. Soviet rulers have deemphasized specifically Russian institutions, while at the same time making sure that each principal institution at the all-Union level is firmly under Russian control. Now, under the pressure of the national awakening of non-Russians, this arrangement is coming undone and authentically Russian institutions are gradually beginning to reemerge.

The Russian people's aspirations and uncertainties have helped define the nature of the Soviet empire, as they did that of the czarist empire that preceded it. With a population of some 146 million, the Russians are Europe's largest nation. Their titular homeland, the Russian Soviet Federated Socialist Republic, occupies 6.6 million square miles—more than 75 percent of Soviet territory. On its own, the RSFSR would be the world's largest state. It consists of eleven time zones, separated from Moscow by as much as ten hours. Indeed, there is a bigger gap in time between Moscow and the towns and settlements on the Bering Strait where the Chukchis live than between Moscow and Washington. The Russian Republic runs some 2,500 miles from north to south and 5,600 miles east to west. Geographic and climatic conditions vary accordingly. Winters are almost uniformly harsh, falling to below 70 degrees centigrade in the tundras of Siberia. The immense, sprawling distances have left a deep imprint on the Russian national character. They have led to a great deal of local isolation, and of a belief among Russia's rulers that this vast territory can only be governed sensibly by absolute control from the center.

Unlike traditional nation-states, which sought to consolidate their ethnic group within a single territory, the Russian state was shaped from the outset by the imperative of external conquest. As the Yugoslav dissident and historian Milovan Djilas has noted:

> Russia did not follow the European path from nationhood to statehood. Muscovy came first—the Russian sense of nationhood came later. Hence the Russian people's obsessive fear that the state may disintegrate; that if the state loses its grip the Russian nation may be gravely weakened. That the Communist system, too, promotes centralization for its own reasons is a bonus and a happy coincidence.

The Russians have been a dominant force in Europe and Asia for two centuries. From a population of around 18 million in 1750 the czarist empire's population leaped to 68 million in 1850. It rose again to 124 million in 1897 and 170 million in 1914. Russian numerical strength has conferred certain advantages within the multinational Russian empire. It has been a source of Russian military strength—providing a virtually limitless pool of recruits for war and expansion. The rapid natural growth of the population, combined with immense poverty, propelled the migration of the Russian nation and the expansion of the Russian state first southward, toward the Ukraine; later across the Urals, through Siberia and to the Pacific; and still later through Central Asia.

After the period of the *ordynskoye igo* ("the Tatar yoke"), Russians poured into the areas east of the Volga. In the seventeenth and eighteenth centuries, they expanded to the northern Caucasus and Siberia, and later to the Altai country, to Kazakhstan, and through to Central Asia. Although in many of these settings they maintained relations with the indigenous peoples, the usual pattern of settlement was in growing urban clusters, usually fortress towns, which helped secure a defense in a frequently violent setting.

Having endured Napoleon's invasion, endless military intrigues, a civil war, two world wars, and long bouts with illness and famine, the Russian nation has emerged with nearly double the population of the Germans, Europe's second largest national group. This numerical advantage derives in great measure from the Russian nation's rapid population growth in the eighteenth and nineteenth centuries. But it also has been aided by the Russian proclivity toward the absorption of conquered peoples. The process, given the name of Russification, is a long-standing Russian practice—having emerged as a conscious policy in the nineteenth century. It persisted under Stalin's murderous reign and was implemented with a renewed zeal under Leonid Brezhnev.

An important factor contributing to an elastic Russian identity springs from its link to Christian Orthodoxy. The Orthodox faith provides a universalist impulse that is firmly linked to traditional Russian cultural values and forms of expression. For most Russians, any Slav who adopts the Russian language and converts to Orthodoxy is regarded as Russian. Yet this elasticity also leads to significant confusions and evasions. Indeed, many Russians to this day deny the separate identity of the Ukrainians and Byelorussians, seeing in them something less than distinctive nations, considering them peoples whose languages are vulgarizations issuing from their isolation from the Russian centers of culture and education.

The relationship of Russians to their Ukrainian and Byelorussian neighbors reflects deep-seated ambiguities and tensions. It is undeniable that these three nations at one point in history shared certain traditions and influences. The Kievan state that emerged on what is now ethnically Ukrainian territory brought to the three peoples the Christian faith and the Cyrillic alphabet. But linguistic differentiation into separate ethnic groups began, according to Roger Portal and other leading historians, as early as the eleventh century. And certainly by the seventeenth century, Russians, Ukrainians, and Byelorussians had evolved into distinct national groups.

The ambiguous attitude of the Russian imperial elite to its Ukrainian and, by extension, Byelorussian subjects can be found in these patronizing excerpts from the writing of a leading nineteenth-century architect of Russian education policy, Mikhail Katkov. In 1864, he wrote: "We love the Ukraine in all her peculiarities in which we see the token of future riches and variety in the common development of the life of our people." Katkov, a leading defender of what Lenin called the "prison of nations," went further: "We love the Ukraine, we love her as part of our Fatherland, as a living beloved part of our people, as a part of ourselves, and this is why any attempt to introduce a feeling of mine and thine into the relationship of the Ukraine towards Russia is so odious to us." In this remarkable explication, the Russian proprietary impulse is expressed clearly.

In their constant search for new frontiers, the Russians became the most relentlessly and consistently successful expansionist ethnic group in history. That expansionism left an imprint on the national consciousness and institutions. Russia had to become a highly centralized state in order to rule over the vast territory, to control the diverse non-Russian peoples, and to hold the empire in its thrall. All policies, cultural and political, issue from Moscow. The Soviet empire is, like its czarist predecessor, a "centralized despotism mightier than any other in history." The eminent historian Hans Kohn extends this pattern back to the nineteenth century: "The later Russian Empire differed fundamentally from the liberal, tolerant British Empire in its tendency to impose uniformity upon its immense domains, to Russify or later to communize them without any freedom of spontaneous development."

Czars and Commissars: Continuities in the Russian and Soviet Empires

Indeed, the principal continuities between the czarist and Soviet empires are striking and convincing. Above all, the borders of the two entities are remarkably similar. The Soviet Union is almost identical to the configuration of the Russian empire of the late nineteenth and early twentieth centuries. There is a striking continuity in the realm of ideas, as well. Where the czarist empire had a state religion in the Russian Orthodox Church, the USSR has a state ideology with many of the characteristics of religious faith. Where the Russian empire suppressed competing religious groups, Soviet leaders repress competing political movements that threaten their ideological and political monopoly. It was as early as

1511 that the monk Philotheus wrote to a Russian czar that Moscow was
the "third Rome." And just as under the czars, the doctrine of the third
Rome meant that Moscow was the center of the true faith and spiritual
heir to the traditions of Rome and Constantinople, so, under Communist
rule, Moscow became the center of international Communism—the sole
arbiter and bearer of Communist orthodoxy. Indeed, after the Bolshevik
Revolution, the "third Rome" was supplanted by the Third (Communist)
International.

The exiled Russian essayist Boris Shragin finds other important continuities between the USSR and its czarist antecedent. "The idea of 'Holy
Russia,' " he writes, "conferred a sort of plenary indulgence on the country, a clean bill of moral health despite the atrocities of its history and all
it did or suffered." So, too, he argues, has the idea of Communism's
progressive mission justified immense inhumanities.

Another continuity in the Russian tradition is the close relationship of
the state to the Russian Orthodox Church, a link that has endured to this
day. Today's Russian Orthodox Church is a pliant tool of Soviet foreign
policy, willingly partaking in the USSR's agenda of nuclear disarmament,
while refusing to speak out against the repression of democratic religious
activists and the suppression of entire churches. At home, too, the Russian Orthodox Church has been silent in the face of decades of the Soviet
state's violations of basic human and religious rights, never speaking out
in defense of religious prisoners of conscience. Its hierarchy has frequently collaborated with the Communist state, most notably in Stalin's
effort to crush the Ukrainian Catholic Church and the Ukrainian Auto-
cephalous Orthodox Church. Under the czars the mechanism of the
Church's subjugation to the state "in the name of God" was realized
through the state-controlled Most Holy Synod; today, control is exercised
through the Religious Affairs Committee of the USSR's Council of Ministers.

An impulse to militarism and expansionism, too, has been a characteristic of both states. In the case of the czarist empire, expansion was
justified as a civilizing mission—the advancement of higher moral teaching and the promotion of a better living standard—an idea echoed in
modern-day Communism's claim that it represents the force of progress.
Among the other striking continuities is a commitment to the Russification of subject nations within both empires. In the mid-nineteenth century the imperialist, Pan-Slavic ideologue Stepan Shevyrev put it this
way: "All the other Slavs should become Russian." And his fellow thinker
Mikhail Pogodin added: "He who is not ours, we shall force to become
ours."

The list of such continuities can be extended as well to the internal
regime of today's USSR and, in particular, to the idea of communal judgment and communal responsibility. The clearest evidence of this trait is

the long-standing institution known as the *mir* (literally "world"), or *obshchina*. It was ostensibly an economic arrangement reinforced by the ceding of land not to individual peasants but to communities. This peasant commune administered the land, supervised the collection of taxes, and arranged the provision of draftees into the czar's army. But it had a second role that has proved even more abiding. As the Russian émigré writer Boris Shragin argues, the mir strictly regulated private behavior, coercing individual peasants into proper conduct, retaining the right to exile unruly or unreliable members of the community, and was pliantly submissive to the local constabulary. In this way, in the nineteenth century it linked its coercive power to the means of livelihood, and diminished the sanctity of private property. Today, as well, the workplace is a source of collective pressure on the individual, a kind of moral seat of judgment. Its mechanisms are more rigorously defined in a panoply of workplace collectives, comrades courts, and state-controlled trade unions. In other words, the workplace has become an instrument of collective coercion. As such, it does not reflect the traditions of the non-Russians, but rather the long-standing prerevolutionary institutions that are deeply immersed in the Russian tradition. Interestingly, in neighboring Ukraine, where even the czars recognized that such an arrangement was alien to the native spirit, land was ceded to the individual and serfdom was not as deeply rooted.

Others have pointed out that the practice of the psychiatric incarceration of dissidents, the existence of a powerful secret police, the use of state censorship, and the institution of forced labor all had their antecedents in the prerevolutionary Russian past. Just as the Russian serfs were tied to the land and denied the right of free movement, so too under Soviet rule, an elaborate internal passport system denies Soviet citizens the right to change workplaces or residences without state approval.

While Russian consciousness was inextricably linked to the powerful and oppressive state that predated it, a clearer sense of Russianness emerged full-blown in the nineteenth century. Russian nationalism was given impetus by the proclamation in 1832 of the doctrine of "Autocracy, Orthodoxy, and Nationality." Propounded by Count Sergei Uvarov— later to become minister of education—the doctrine sought not only to make the czar and the Russian Orthodox Church the pillars of legitimacy, but to extend the sense of national consciousness, which permeated the elite, down to the masses. Historian Hugh Seton-Watson argues that, in the 1880s, Russians, like other "leaders of the most powerful nations, considered it their destiny and indeed their moral duty to impose their nationality on *all* their subjects—of whatever religion, language or culture." Consequently, Russians sought to make over the non-Russian subjects into Russians.

Russification accelerated under the rule of Czars Alexander III and

Nicholas II. The targets of this Russification campaign were above all the Slavic subjects of the czar—the Ukrainians and Byelorussians. The czarist court promulgated two ukases (decrees) concerning the banning of the Ukrainian language in its printed form: the Ems Ukase and the Valuyev Ukase. But Russification also was applied to the subject Baltic peoples; to Poles, who came under Moscow's dominion; and to Jews, whose schools were closed down and who were banned from wearing their traditional clothing.

In the end, despite attempts by the czarist state to create a more modern notion of nationalism, these ideological ambitions soon encountered the weight of Russian history and of the Russian nation's close identification with the very structure of empire.

Today, in the face of an upsurge of non-Russian nationalisms, Russians once again are confronting their sense of identity. Yet, the process of self-examination is by no means simple. As the writer Grigory Pomerants has written: "The Russian Empire antedated Russian self-awareness, and therefore every territory that Russian soldiers set foot on is considered Russian. This can be seen in the national (not only the official) reaction to the Prague Spring [of 1968] and the subsequent Soviet invasion." Such an attitude, needless to say, has profound consequences as well for the Russian view of their political institutions. In Pomerants's view: "To preserve the remnants of an imperial structure is to doom democracy (and subsequently *perestroika*) to failure in advance." The imperial system is old and decaying, he argues. It can collapse "like an old mushroom." The risks of a turn to pluralism, Pomerants suggests, "are justified and unavoidable." Indeed, the writer argues, "in practical terms, an imperial scope offers very little for the common man (the right to move from a run-down village to the Caucasus, to Central Asia or the Baltics) and demands a lot (huge military expenditures and axes drenched in blood)."

The highly xenophobic and messianic aspects of the Russian tradition have been accompanied by a large-scale identity crisis, in which the subjects of the Russian empire are frequently confused with the Russian nation itself. Nowhere is this more clear than in the very terms for Russia and Russians. English-language translations do not do the Russian-language terms justice. The term for Russia is *Rossiya*. And *Rossiya* is defined as all the territories that are a part of the empire ruled by Russians. In casual conversation, most Russians still refer to such areas as the Ukraine and Georgia as "Russia." Even the term for Russian, *Russkiy*—a member of the *Rus'* nation—is filled with ambiguity, since the center of the ancient Kievan Rus state was on what is today, ethnographically, not Russian but Ukrainian territory.

So, very early on, the line separating the Ukraine, Byelorussia, and Russia was blurred. Indeed, the Russians themselves have never experienced a prolonged period in which they lived in an authentic, ethnographically homogeneous nation-state: Their expansive state predated the full-blown formation of the Russian national consciousness. The idea of a definite configuration of a Russia proper is a modern-day phenomenon, only today given shape in the form of the Russian Soviet Federated Socialist Republic. However, until the recent rise of Boris Yeltsin, most Russians did not identify with or feel particular loyalty to the RSFSR, but rather to the broader USSR. The name "Union of Soviet Socialist Republics" bolsters the notion of elasticity and expansionism within the state structure: It is the only state in the world whose name does not make reference to a particular geographic or ethnographic entity.

A further aspect of the Russian tradition is the absence of a strongly rooted democratic orientation. This lack of democratic roots poses fundamental problems for Western policymakers and raises profound questions about the fate of even Gorbachev's limited reforms. Some argue, of course, that the maintenance of a vast internal and external empire is incompatible with the exercise of democracy. But more significant, Russian history gives little evidence of mass-based support for democratic ideas.

Writing about the Russian national character in 1978, Boris Shragin posed the issue starkly:

> The Russian people have always been obedient to authority and accepting of the status quo. Before and after the revolution their public life has been marked by a show of inviolable uniformity and unanimity. But behind this facade there is a fierce battle of private material interests, with no genuine collaboration for the common good. The general interest is represented by the autocratic state and by it alone; citizens must not "dare to have their own opinion."

A decade later, in 1987, the popular songwriter Bulat Okudzhava reflected a similar view of what was happening in a time of glasnost when he said, "We have a revolution; but there are no revolutionaries." He was making reference to the reluctance of Soviet citizens to take up the banner of independent activism. Clearly, Okudzhava's comments can no longer be applied to the highly active and well-organized non-Russians. But they can still be applied to the vast majority of Russians in the USSR, who, to date, have been comparatively quiescent.

Patriotic Russians attribute such passivity to decades of centralized control. They claim that the Russians suffer from immense disadvantages, not least of which is the totalitarian attack on their tradition and on the obliteration of their specifically national institutions. Indeed, it is worth considering the special status of the Russians. While there are Communist parties for the Ukraine, Uzbekistan, Byelorussia, and every other non-Russian republic, until mid-1990 there was no Communist Party of Russia. Indeed, it was only in December 1989 that Gorbachev took a hesitant—some say reluctant—step in such a direction when he announced the creation of a Russian Bureau of the Central Committee of the Communist Party of the Soviet Union, and put himself at its head. And while there are Ukrainian, Lithuanian, Georgian, Armenian, and other Academies of Sciences, there had been no specifically Russian Academy of Sciences.

The absence of these organizations and structures, however, did not put the Russians at a great political disadvantage. Rather, it secured Russian dominance of all-Union institutions.

At the Pinnacles of Power

Nowhere is this domination more clear than within the pinnacle of Soviet power—the Communist Party. Russian dominance has been most pronounced at the apex of Soviet power—within the Politburo and the USSR government. In June 1990, in the eighteen-man Politburo (including its six nonvoting members), fourteen were Russians. Such domination is also reflected within the Soviet military elite, where the general staff is overwhelmingly Russian. And it is present within the economic nerve centers of authority—the Council of Ministers of the USSR. Headed by Soviet Prime Minister Nikolai Ryzhkov, the leadership, known as the Presidium of the Council, consists of chairman, three first deputy chairmen, and ten deputy chairmen. These men and one woman (Aleksandra Biryukova—famous for her $160 million shopping spree on behalf of the USSR at London's Marks and Spencers department store in the summer of 1989) make all the fundamental decisions concerning the economy, ecology, and daily life of the Soviet Union. Yet, there is among them only one non-Russian. And in mid-1989, of the fifty-four ministers and heads of state committees in the central Soviet government whose nationality was known, forty-seven were Russians.

It seems astonishing that within a society that propounds its commitment to equality among the nationalities, there cannot be found a sufficient number of qualified Ukrainians, Uzbeks, Azerbaijanis, or Lithuanians to fill such fundamental posts. This dominance is not simply confined to the pinnacles of decision-making power. Even within the structures of Communist authority in the non-Russian republics, the Russian presence is widespread. In addition to the fact that in many of those republics (the Ukraine, Byelorussia, Kazakhstan, and Moldavia among them), the official language of daily discourse within the Communist Party and state has been Russian, there is an unwritten principle that the second secretary, the number two leader in the non-Russian republics, is usually an ethnic Russian, while the first secretary is usually a Russified representative of the titular indigenous nation. This practice, while no longer absolute, is still widespread and is widely regarded as a safeguard against any possible growth of something the Soviets regard with particular dread—national Communism: the notion that a constituent Communist Party might be taken over by separatist sentiments, making it independent of control from the center.

Of course, as each national Party today is, in theory and practice, subject to the discipline of democratic centralism, it is already subordinated to the Russian-dominated All-Union Communist Party. But the strategically placed, ethnically Russian second secretary plays the role of the reliable eyes and ears of the Kremlin in the hinterlands, as a hedge against the power of nationalism—a force that already has won over large segments of the Lithuanian, Latvian, Estonian, Georgian, and Azerbaijani Communist parties.

Yet while they are significantly overrepresented within the various centers of power—from the Politburo and Central Committee, to the Academy of Sciences, to the All-Union Central Council of Trade Unions, to the Soviet Council of Ministers and Mikhail Gorbachev's Presidential Council—such Russian dominance comes at a price. It would be destabilizing to a multinational system if Russians were to boldly assert their dominance. Strict control of the media long assured that such issues as ethnic representation in the Party and state were not discussed. Propaganda further assured that Russian dominance was usually couched in the highly nuanced terms of internationalism. By virtue of such argument, the Russian language is presented not as the language of the dominant nationality, but as the language of interrepublic discourse and, more significant, of interethnic communication within each republic. Even the disproportionate economic investment in the Russian Republic is attributed to the need to develop the harsh Siberian regions, which are resource-rich.

Some Sovietologists and not a few Russian nationalists have argued that overt Russian nationalist themes have been further dampened by the cooler, more modern form of rule that typifies the technocratically oriented Gorbachev *equipe*. In the face of growing assertiveness among the non-Russians, it is the Russians, they insist, who themselves are becoming a hidden nation.

Still, in the face of the upsurge of non-Russian nationalisms, there is today among Russians a growing discussion in the press of their need to create specifically Russian institutions. Already, prominent leaders and important periodicals have added their voices to a debate over the desirability of a Russian Academy of Sciences, a Russian Communist Youth League, and an RSFSR trade union confederation. Indeed, the leaders of the moribund All-Union Central Council of Trade Unions had attempted to dampen growing enthusiasm for a specifically Russian trade union body, on a par with the Ukrainian, Armenian, and other sections; they proposed creating a Russian Bureau attached to the AUCCTU. But these calls met with opposition within the trade union and the embattled union leadership not only has relented but, in a variety of cases, has linked itself enthusiastically with the most extreme Russian chauvinist forces, particularly those organized around the United Front of Workers of Russia. And growing Russian discontent led to the establishment of the Russian Bureau of the CPSU Central Committee and to the creation in June 1990 of a Russian section of the Party.

From these developments has emerged a more precise sense of Russianness, a concept that, for centuries, has been full of ambiguities. The emergence of such a specifically Russian, nonimperial nationalism could play an important role in stimulating further the decomposition of the USSR or in accelerating its devolution into a decentralized confederation. But for the moment, the emergence of nationalism among the non-Russians is feeding antidemocratic currents among the Russians.

Indeed, the greatest albatross around the neck of the Russian nation, and the principal threat to the process of reform in the USSR, is the absence of a strong democratic tradition. It is revealing itself with a vengeance in the more open atmosphere of the Gorbachev age. There is a great deal of evidence concerning many cultural and political advantages enjoyed by the Russians, who are *prima inter pares* within the Soviet empire. But many Russians do not agree. In the view of many Russian nationalists, it is a Russian-speaking, ethnically Russian, but fundamentally totalitarian antinational ruling elite that stands atop the Soviet Union. Russians and their culture, opposition Russian nationalists say, have suffered more than anyone else under Communism. That totalitarian ideology has destroyed the Russian village, drained the Russian Orthodox Church of much of its spirituality, claimed millions of Russian victims through repression, and subsumed Russianness into a bland version of national identity that cannot be fully authentic lest it awaken the slumbering nationalisms of the smaller nations in the Soviet Union. The price Russians have paid for empire, they say, is a loss of their own spiritual roots and national identity.

Bitterness and resentment in the face of growing non-Russian demands today also are emanating with increasing frequency from such state officials as Colonel General Dmitry Volkogonov, head of the Institute of Military History of the USSR Ministry of Defense and a deputy of the Russian SFSR Supreme Soviet. In an address to the Russian parliament on October 26, 1989, he recounted the broad range of problems afflicting Russians. "As a result of the symbiosis of bureaucracy, dogmatism, social inertia and mistakes by the leadership," he stated, "the Russian Federation occupies one of the last places in the Union for living standards of the population, level of education, medical provision, ecological situation, demographic situation and crime."

Although Soviet statistics contradict the general's claims, his speech was brimful of anger at indignities heaped upon the aggrieved Russian nation: "Insults against the national dignity of the Russian people have become an ugly fashion. These attacks—quite unprovoked, as they say— are being made methodically and in a more unbridled manner."

The culprits, according to General Volkogonov, were the non-Russian popular fronts, whom he accused of "political obscenities coupled with Russophobia." The Russian nation, claimed the general, was being depicted as "slow-witted, lazy, shortsighted, and lackadaisical." His intemperate diatribe was part of a growing reaction to the assertive non-Russian national movements. But if General Volkogonov had taken his argument a bit further, he could have turned from xenophobia and toward anti-imperialism, by acknowledging that the maintenance of empire by force creates an untenable drain on the economy and on the national spirit.

The Cost of Empire

In the past, other Russians have warned of the disadvantage of empire. Writers like the great novelist and controversial social critic Aleksandr Solzhenitsyn argue for a new, retrenched Russia, a Russia shed of much of its empire. For them, Russian empire has come at too high a price—the debasement and disintegration of Russianness. Such a Russia that looks at its own Orthodox roots and traditions would have no claims on the Catholics of Western Ukraine, the Baltic nations, the vast and populous reaches of Central Asia, or the Caucasus. The empire has led to the degradation of our own cultural traditions, Solzhenitsyn and some of his colleagues argue.

In Moscow, one gets the simultaneous sense of imperial grandeur and of the corruption and disintegration that are at its heart. Today's Moscow is a city of ill-constructed, long-unpainted buildings. Grim-faced, plodding citizens, many of them living on the verge of a desperate poverty, trudge along the cracking, muddy sidewalk. In winter as in summer, Russians are dressed in poorly made, ill-fitting, tawdry, and fraying clothing. To the casual observer, they appear to be dressed more badly than the unfortunate street people in the United States. The steady decline in the value of the ruble has made Soviet society increasingly barter-oriented. A common sight is of a woman hawking cheap digital wristwatches in an alleyway near the Lenin library. Or, a man carrying a latticed shopping bag filled with dozens of packages of butter, presumably to be traded for different necessities. This degrading descent into more primitive forms of economic exchange wears away at the souls of young and old alike. For the average resident of the capital of the Soviet empire, it takes a long leap of faith to believe that there is any economic benefit from the burdens of empire.

Farther off, away from the city's center, the streets are full of potholes, the concrete is broken, the sidewalks are covered with sludge. Endless miles of roads are constantly torn up for repair work that never seems to end or bring improvement. Housing, too, is decrepit. Nearly every building looks as if it has been untouched by paint for decades. The high-rise apartments in which most Muscovites live are stuffy and dilapidated, their facades and stairwells crumbling. The elevators and hallways frequently reek of urine, the result of endless drinking binges.

For many days during the summer of 1989, even the vanilla ice cream that has long been one of the few reliable staples of Soviet consumers was unavailable in Moscow; the city's drab and dreary ice cream shops simply stayed boarded up. Cheese, too, has become unavailable. Sugar is rationed. It makes little sense to the ordinary Muscovite when he is told that he is benefiting from the economic system of the vast empire and superpower at whose center his city and nation stand.

A young, thickset cab driver in his late twenties, a native Muscovite, reflects such resentments to us: "It's hard to live in Moscow. And yet the Asians and Georgians keep on coming. Where do they get their money? They come here, loaded with cash and they go after our Russian women. Why don't they keep to their own?" These are hardly the comments of a self-confident citizen who feels he has directly benefited from Soviet imperial rule. The payoff, many Russians are inclined to feel, is nowhere in sight.

Amid Moscow's gloom and harshness, amid its jarring monumentalism and gigantism, there is little question that the empire has taken its toll on this historic city of czars and boyars. Yet many experts will agree that the Russian psyche not only is highly adapted to the idea of empire but that the very stability of the state has long depended in large measure on its capacity to satisfy the Russian public's support for an expansionist imperial structure. In the absence of stability issuing from a system that has been economically backward and politically repressive, the roots of legitimacy are now to be found in the success of empire and in the USSR's status as a superpower. The sources of legitimacy ultimately stem, however, as much from the internal projection of power as from its external manifestations.

As Marxism-Leninism increasingly is identified with economic stagnation, and as Communism's crisis of confidence mounts, Russian citizens— and some leading Soviet officials—are turning increasingly to empire and Russian nationalism as the ideological pillars of legitimacy. The turn to Russian nationalism is not without precedent in Soviet history. Stalin resorted to Great Russian nationalism when he faced the Nazi invasion. In the latter years of the Brezhnev era, too, there was a notable growth in Russian nationalist sentiments, often officially and openly condoned in the Party and Red Army press. Then, the lid was slammed tight on the non-Russian nations and their cultural and national aspirations. Soviet prisons, forced-labor camps, and psychiatric hospitals were filled with non-Russian political prisoners, many of them nationalists and advocates of national rights.

In the period of Mikhail Gorbachev's rule, tens of thousands of independent, informal groups have emerged. While most have appeared among the non-Russian nations, there are growing signs of a political awakening of Russian nationalism. Of these groups, some have been openly and frequently attacked by the Soviet authorities and state-controlled media. Other groups appear to have powerful allies at the heights of the Soviet establishment. Among these, the most sensational is a bizarre, shadowy organization known as Pamyat—or Memory.

Although it has frequently been rocked by factional splits, Pamyat's enduring popularity—its rallies draw thousands of supporters and there are chapters in two dozen Soviet cities—is evidence that in Gorbachev's USSR, the ideology of fascism is alive and well. Its living embodiment is one Dmitry Vasiliyev—leader of the Pamyat organization. A charismatic orator with a flair for the dramatic, Vasiliyev is known for taking the stage at public meetings and shedding his extravagant bearded disguises.

Located on the third floor of a building on the southern arc of the Sadovoye Koltso, Moscow's ring road, Vasiliyev's five-room flat has been transformed into a museum whose symbology attests to his political and, in his words, "moral" agenda. At the door, visitors are greeted by Vasiliyev's son. In his early twenties, the young Vasiliyev wears the Pamyat group's now traditional black shirt, emblazoned with military insignia from the czarist era. On the wall, there is a poster bearing the Star of David and in it a skull. Above, in large script, is a single word: DANGER. The poster is produced by the PLO, but it coincides with Pamyat's anti-Semitic, or as Vasiliyev would have it, anti-Zionist, predilections.

Dmitry Vasiliyev greets visitors in an ornate sitting room with vaulted ceilings that Vasiliyev has transformed into an aesthetic unity that echoes with the "spiritual" heroes of his movement: Dostoyevsky; Pyotr Stolypin, the czarist interior minister, whose aborted agricultural reforms, Pamyat believes, could today save Russian agriculture; Aleksandr Nevsky, the thirteenth-century ruler of Vladimir and victor over the Swedes and Teutonic Knights (Germanic crusaders of the Middle Ages); General Suvorov; and the "holy" Czar Nicholas II. Here, amid icons and axes, Vasiliyev, a photographer by profession, has constructed a shrine to his extremist political agenda.

Where, in the past, he was known to have quoted from the program of the Communist Party of the Soviet Union, today Pamyat's leader is unremittingly harsh in his assessment of the Party's legacy and its intrusions into family life. "Do you want the Party apparatchik to crawl into bed with you and your wife? Or to tell you that you cannot go to bed because you must attend a commemoration of the Russian Revolution?" His voice booms with rhetorical anger as he speaks of Communism's destruction of family and tradition.

He is a strong proponent of a specific idea of unity. "Fascism," he observes, "means unity, unification. There's nothing bad in that." He aspires to such unity in national relations as well and laments the "artificial division" of the Russian, Ukrainian, Polish, Byelorussian, Slovak, and Yugoslav peoples, who he believes came from one entity "created by God." Such unity should extend to religion as well; every Christian Slav should be a part of the Orthodox Church. "We need to return to our original, natural state of unity," Vasiliyev argues.

The Pamyat leader is an unabashed admirer of Mussolini. "No one can aspire to anything different," he says. "After all, Mussolini spoke of the unity of the nation, the unity of national good." He reserves his contempt for Hitler, whose rule wasn't fascist, but "national socialist," Vasiliyev says, emphasizing the last word. In any event, he tells us, "no Christian nation can bring forth a concept of racialism. Only one religion has a conception of racialism, a conception of the chosen people." This "Zionist idea was imported into the ideology of the Nazis." By whom, we inquire? "By the Jew Eichmann. He was a Jew, but he killed his own," Vasiliyev charges, his voice filled with passion and grief. "You see," he says, "Eichmann was fulfilling the instructions of *The Protocols of the Elders of Zion.*"

It isn't long before Vasiliyev's oration, an exceptionally dramatic performance of rhetorical largo and sotto voce, turns to the hidden source of all that ails Russia and the world—Zionist Jews and their servants the Freemasons. There are the frequent references to Jewish control of the world economy and to the internationalization of the "Zionist idea."

There are many more such extreme claims in Vasiliyev's litany. He uses every opportunity to denounce Israel: "We are called fascists. But who today is using fascist methods in the Middle East? Israel." He bristles at charges that he is an anti-Semite: "I am not the one who is warring with the Semitic tribes. Are the Hebrews the only Semitic tribe? It is they who are killing other Semitic tribes. But does anyone dare call them anti-Semitic. . . . There is no problem of anti-Semitism in the Soviet Union today. It is an invention designed to cover up the brutal ethnocide of the Slavic peoples."

Vasiliyev likes to boast of Pamyat's international plans: "We have to unite all honest people throughout the world. Patriotic forces have to coalesce. We have to create a single all-European Pamyat front, where we can gather all patriots. I am a great admirer of [France's Jean-Marie] Le Pen. . . . I am trying to bring this idea into fruition." Above all, he is virulently anti-American: "The U.S. has little to be proud of. It expanded on the blood of the Russian nation, on our Civil War, the October Revolution, and the Great Patriotic War. Its enrichment has been paid for with bloodstained lucre."

Vasiliyev professes to be a deeply reverent man and he does indeed display a genuine reverence, indeed sentimentalism, for his faith and traditions. But there is no trace of Christian mercy in his philippics about the devastation wrought on humanity by the Zionists. Nor does he show any tolerance for views that fall outside his compact worldview. Whenever challenged with a contrary idea, his voice thunders bombastically and his piercing eyes widen and bulge. He is at once self-effacing and vain, compelling and repugnant.

Yet the movement he heads is considered by some to be extremely dangerous. Vitaly Korotich, the high-profile editor of the popular Central Committee weekly *Ogonyok* (circulation: 3.2 million), has been among the most vocal establishment critics of Pamyat and its chauvinist cohorts. In an interview in his hectic office in the huge, grim north-central editorial and publishing complex of *Pravda,* Korotich explained the danger of this virulent strain of xenophobia. "Pamyat," he says, "offers the public simple answers, simple solutions. Such simple solutions find support in the unorganized segments of society which cannot think politically. This absence of political thought is convenient for segments of the political leadership."

But there is another factor at work here. The arcana of Pamyat, its obsession with conspiracy theories—its willingness to blame Russian misfortunes on the plottings of Jewish and Masonic cabals—all are a sad by-product of the closed nature of Soviet society. As Soviet citizens gain greater access to information, the appeal of such movements may diminish. For the moment, however, the new flood of information produces incomplete and distorted views of reality. Pamyat therefore can also be seen as the political manifestation of an interest in the esoteric and exotic, which is paralleled by the widespread interest in UFOs and the occult, trends now being fed by segments of the state-controlled media. They are two sides of the same coin. Yet Pamyat's delusions have been proven in the past to be deadly.

Much Western and Soviet media attention has, of course, been paid to Pamyat's virulent and extreme manifestation of Russian nationalism. Its black shirts and anti-Semitism have made Pamyat good, bracing copy. But beyond its outward extremism, Pamyat has some strong support within the Soviet cultural establishment. It is rumored, for example, that the Moscow Party boss, Yuri Prokofyev, as well as the Leningrad Party chief, Boris Gidaspov, are Pamyat supporters. Even more ominous, many of Pamyat's objectionable antidemocratic and xenophobic views can be found in the writings of some of the USSR's most popular and best-selling writers, proponents of what today is the dominant trend in Russian nationalism.

There are several central characteristics of Russian nationalism in the era of glasnost: a nostalgia for the village, which leads to calls for increased resources to support rural life; a nostalgia for the prerevolutionary past and its concomitant concern for the restoration of important monuments; a hostility to modernization and a clear hatred for all things Western, ranging from rock and roll to imported technologies. In many of these backward-looking traits are interests that are clearly inimical to Gorbachev's reform agenda. Linked to this Russian nationalism is the idea that democracy in the Western sense is alien to Russian tradition. In the view of many of the nationalists, democracy represents disorder and disorder is a strain in Russian culture that emanates from the Jews and their agents—the Freemasons.

Anti-Semitism and Antidemocratism

The exiled Russian novelist and literary critic Andrei Sinyavsky has spent many years grappling with the question of Russian nationalism and its anti-Semitic inclinations. In his view, while there are, of course, some Russian liberals and democrats, "the greatest concentration of Russian nationalists is antidemocratic and conservative." According to Sinyavsky, "Russian nationalists have come awake. And they have taken on an openly anti-Semitic and antidemocratic character." Sinyavsky points with particular concern to the work of one ultraconservative author, the exiled mathematician Igor Shafarevich, whose book argues "that within the powerful Russian nation there is a smaller nation. The great nation is Russian, the little nation is Jewish." This "little nation," the Jews, says Sinyavsky, is accused by Shafarevich of "carrying out destructive activities. Many of Shafarevich's ideas are similar to those of Nazi ideologue Alfred Rosenberg."

Shafarevich's views are crystallized in this excerpt from an essay in which he grapples with the sources of what he terms "Russophobia" and the pressures to transform Russia into a democracy:

Whose national sentiments, then, are reflected? For anyone acquainted with the reality of our country, the answer is beyond doubt. There is only one nation of whose concerns we hear almost every day. Jewish national emotions shake both our country and the whole world, influencing disarmament talks, trade policy, and international connections of scientists. . . . The "Jewish Question" has acquired an incomprehensible power over the minds of people, eclipsed the problems of Ukrainians, Estonians, Armenians, and Crimean Tatars, while the "Russian Question" is not recognized at all.

Jews are, the nationalist Shafarevich asserts, " 'an anti-people' among the people." In the view of Andrei Sinyavsky, Shafarevich's essay is one sign of a dangerous upsurge in anti-Semitism that has accompanied the Russian national awakening. Where in the past, anti-Semitism was the monopoly of the state, now it has been handed over to the broad masses.

Running through the various strands of modern Russian nationalist thought is the nihilist notion that Russia is dying, and that no one has suffered more than Russians. In one strain of Russian nationalism, this sense of despair is linked to the idea that Communism has led to the destruction of "Russianness." In another type, there is the belief that it is the contemporary loss of discipline that has led to Russia's decline. The first strain is dissident—it is linked to such voices as former political prisoner Vladimir Osipov's and dissident priest Father Dmitry Dudko's. It is a viewpoint not dissimilar to Aleksandr Solzhenitsyn's. The second kind of nationalism helps bring together establishment-oriented Russian nationalists, national Bolsheviks, neo-Stalinist opponents of liberalization, and Communist apparatchiks.

Although establishment-oriented Russian nationalism has a number of strains, it has aptly been described by some observers as "national Bolshevism." Many Russian nationalists, who today are firmly ensconced in the Soviet cultural establishment, also believe that in order to save Russia and her empire, it is necessary to infuse the current statist system with a new nationalist ideology oriented around the Orthodox Church.

Among the many strands of Pamyat, there is a faction that, as one leader of a Moscow-based leftist informal group has suggested, is " 'black' i.e. fascist on the national question, but 'red' on the social question," that is, supportive of Soviet rule and the "socialist" system. Gleb Anishchenko, a dissident writer generally sympathetic to Russian patriotism, observed in the underground, self-published *Glasnost* magazine: "In putting the principle of nationalism at the head of the list, Pamyat is neither a Christian nor an anti-Christian organization, and neither a Communist nor anti-Communist organization." Pamyat, Anishchenko tells us, "has always carefully stressed that its platform is neither anti-Communist nor anti-Soviet. On the contrary, many of Pamyat's leaders call themselves true Communists and quote Lenin's works."

For Andrei Fadin, a contributor to the trailblazing and provocative journal *The Twentieth Century and Peace* and a research associate of the Russian SFSR Institute of Atheism, "Pamyat has little future as an organization." The authorities, he believes, simply will put too many obstacles in its path. However, "as a point of view, an outlook on life, it has great possibilities and a large base of support," Fadin contends. He worries about the characteristic style of the Pamyat supporter. "He is uninterested in compromise or accommodation. I have never met a Pamyat member who sought to understand me. They are fierce, harsh, and gruff in manner."

Fadin's assessment may in the end prove accurate. Despite some pro-

Ztectors in the Party hierarchy, the group has been viciously denounced in a number of newspapers and journals. Clearly, many reformist Soviet officials are alarmed at Pamyat's quick growth. But it is equally clear that Pamyat's nominally "loyalist" stance has won it staunch supporters among leading Russian nationalist writers who are pillars of the literary establishment. Among them are the best-selling novelist Vasily Belov and the popular "village" novelist Valentin Rasputin. Rasputin, a writer of undoubted literary ability, is likewise a purveyor of an odious imperialist viewpoint. Just after the Soviet invasion of Afghanistan in 1979, Rasputin wrote: "Is Fate not bringing us closer to the time when we shall once again go forth on the field of Kulikovo to defend the Russian soil and Russian blood?" Kulikovo is where in 1380 the Russians defeated the Tatars and for Russian nationalists possesses not simply a patriotic connotation, but is redolent of the struggle between radically different civilizations, not to say races. More recently, Rasputin has defined his ideology succinctly on the pages of *Izvestia* as "order in the soul—order in the homeland." Despite such views, Rasputin appears to enjoy Mikhail Gorbachev's support. In early 1990, he was named to the sixteen-member Presidential Council, with responsibilities for ecological and cultural issues in the part advisory, part executive body. Rasputin's colleague, Belov, one of a hundred candidates selected by the Communist Party's Central Committee to serve in the Congress of People's Deputies, gave a scandalous, anti-Western front-page interview to *Pravda* in March 1989 in which he claimed that each year two hundred thousand babies are born in the United States infected with AIDS.

"Such writers reflect our national dignity," Pamyat leader Vasiliyev believes. "They have a strong influence."

Regrettably, the writers Belov and Rasputin are not isolated extremists. The USSR's best-selling books of 1987 represented the dangerous mind-set of many Soviet citizens. The third through fifth most popular books were a novel by conservative Valentin Pikul (2,850,000 copies); Krasnoyarsk writer Viktor Astafyev's PECHAL'NY DETEKTIV (*The Sad Detective*), a novel that recounts the tragic effects of alcoholism and has helped direct Russian nationalists toward temperance campaigns (2,750,000 copies); and the Vologda-based Vasily Belov's harshly anti-Western novel VSYE VPEREDI (*Everything Is Yet to Come*) (2,700,000 copies). As John Dunlop, of the Hoover Institution, recently observed, Belov's novel portrays a "Western oriented Soviet intelligentsia as being in the clutches of a fearful Jewish-Masonic conspiracy." Belov's best-seller was published both by the monthly *Nash Sovremennik* and in its huge edition by an official organ of the Goskomizdat, the USSR State Committee for Book Publishing. It invokes a universe full of evil forces. "Satan is there," Belov's novel asserts. "There exists a powerful, determined, evil and clandestine force whose purpose is the destruction of Russia." The novel's clear message: Isn't it "better to die in a nuclear war than to live according to Satan's orders?" Not surprisingly, the best-selling Belov has defended Pamyat. As for his highly popular colleague Valentin Pikul, he is best known for an earlier novel, *At the Last Boundary*, in which the mad monk Rasputin is depicted as fronting for a worldwide Zionist plot and blamed for all the calamities that befall Holy Russia.

Two other Russian nationalist writers—Yuri Bondarev, famous for his sharp criticism of perestroika at a Communist Party conference in 1988 and notable for his apologias in the 1970s for Stalinism; and Pyotr Proskurin, who heads the archconservative RSFSR Cultural Fund—are also published in enormous editions.

Most of these reactionary writers' views are disseminated through a series of large-circulation journals and periodicals, including the monthlies *Nash Sovremennik* (1988 circulation: 240,000), whose editor, Sergei Vikulov, is also a defender of Pamyat; and *Moskva* (1988 circulation: 683,000). Additional mass enclaves of the pro-Stalinist national Bolsheviks and Russian nationalists include the youth journal *Molodaya Gvardiya* (*The Young Guard;* 1988 circulation: 700,000), whose deputy editor, Vyacheslav Gorbachev, wrote the afterword to Belov's xenophobic and anti-Semitic best-seller; and the daily newspapers *Sovyetskaya Rossiya* (the newspaper of the RSFSR Council of Ministers and of the Central Committee of the CPSU) and *Krasnaya Zvezda* (the self-described "organ of the USSR Ministry of Defense").

Whenever a journal attempts to break out of the nationalist mold, its editors pay a high price. Such was the case with the editor in chief of the literary monthly *Oktyabr*. After he published excerpts from Vasily Grossman's widely acclaimed anti-Stalinist novel *Forever Flowing* and a five-page excerpt from Andrei Sinyavsky's *Walks with Pushkin*, the editor was sacked from his post by the journal's patron, the Russian SFSR Writers' Union.

To his credit, Vitaly Korotich's pioneering journal *Ogonyok* has repeatedly spoken out against the thrall in which Russian letters are held. In one issue (No. 43, October 1988), *Ogonyok* pointed to the dominance of a small clique of writers who derive vast material advantage from relationships that date to the Brezhnev era. Among those *Ogonyok* singled out were Yuri Bondarev, whose novel *The Hot Snow* has been released in thirty-eight separate editions with a combined print run of over eight million; and Anatoly Ivanov, editor of *Molodaya Gvardiya*, one of whose novels has appeared in twenty-one separate editions.

What troubles *Ogonyok* is not simply that a small clique of writers is dominating literary life. *Ogonyok* is concerned that these huge megaeditions of favored conservative writers are crowding other, more worthy writers out of the limited Soviet marketplace. Wouldn't it be better, *Ogonyok* has provocatively suggested, to publish fewer editions of Bondarev and his cronies, while issuing at last the long-awaited and long-suppressed writings of Pasternak, Mandelshtam, Zoschenko, and Akhmatova. Meanwhile, activists from the USSR's many democratic organizations bitterly complain that the USSR's paper shortage makes it impossible to have true freedom of speech for the independent mass media.

A self-described "civil war" has broken out over the publishing practices not only of the central publishing houses, but also of an entire range of well-financed, lesser-known, specialized publishing enterprises that are firmly in the hands of the Russian nationalists, neo-Stalinists, and conservatives. Among this category of publishers are the Victory Library (Biblioteka Pobedy), the Military Library of the Schoolgoer (Voyennaya Biblioteka Shkolnika), the Village Library of the Non-Chernozem Region (Sel'skaya Biblioteka Nechernozema), and the Military-Patriotic Library (Voyenno-Patrioticheskaya Biblioteka). Those specialized libraries republish numerous titles by a narrow group of conservative Russian writers while keeping the print runs of non-Russian writers who publish in their native languages at artificially low levels. Thus, after several years of glasnost, the Russian nationalists and neo-Stalinists continue to control written popular culture, even at the level of the state publishing enterprise. In addition to its malign influence on public awareness, this arrangement confers on a handful of Russian writers immense wealth and privilege.

Exposés against such publishing practices and sharp polemics with neo-Stalinist authors have made *Ogonyok*'s editor, Vitaly Korotich, a lightning rod for attacks by Russian nationalists. These denunciations reached fever pitch at a meeting between Mikhail Gorbachev and scholars and cultural figures. Held on January 6, 1989, at the headquarters of the Central Committee of the CPSU, the occasion was used by Anatoly Ivanov, editor in chief of *Molodaya Gvardiya*, to attack *Ogonyok* for "petit bourgeois views." Korotich, too, has been denounced by chauvinist Russians as a "Jewish interloper." Korotich is not Jewish; he is Ukrainian and for many years was a leader of the Ukrainian Writers Union.

Extremist and racist views are frequently expressed by leading Russian writers. At a January 1989 meeting of the Russian Writers Union, one of the speakers advocated the creation of reservations to house the indigenous non-Russian peoples of the Russian Soviet Federated Socialist Republic. So extreme and embarrassing have the views of the Russian Writers Union become, that Moscow writers are seeking to secede from the body. "Remember," observes Andrei Fadin, "the RSFSR Writers Union includes a great number of Russians from the provinces. Many of these provincial writers have little talent and so feel locked out of the literary scene. Today, they are using anti-Semitism as a way of lashing out at the more liberal Moscow literary figures."

It is understandable that in the more open atmosphere of debate and discourse that has arisen under Mikhail Gorbachev, informal groups like Pamyat could proliferate. What is surprising, however, is that in the period of Gorbachev's self-styled liberalizing reforms, highly virulent, xenophobic, and anti-Semitic expressions of Russian nationalism continue to dominate Russian popular culture and Soviet best-seller lists. According to Andrei Sinyavsky: "In the nineteenth century, anti-Semitic views may well have been held by some in the Russian intelligentsia. But to express such views openly was regarded as something shameful. Now anti-Semitism is openly expressed in daily conversation and on the pages of the press."

Perhaps the most famous, indeed notorious, expression of reactionary Russian nationalist sentiments has been the letters of an obscure Russian schoolteacher from Leningrad—Nina Andreyeva. In March 1988 in a letter published in the Central Committee daily *Sovyetskaya Rossiya*, Andreyeva's was the first conservative voice to directly attack the Gorbachev reforms. She has since become a tribune for the voices of reaction. In a July 1989 letter published in the rightist Communist Youth League monthly *Molodaya Gvardiya*, Mrs. Andreyeva, who in 1989 conspicuously visited and signed the guest book of a private museum for Stalin, forthrightly defended the Soviet tyrant and charged that attacks on Stalin are but a prelude to attacks on Lenin and Leninism itself. She denounced the emergence of mass national movements in the non-Russian republics, charging that they are heightening ethnic tensions and advocating secession. Andreyeva's letter, which went on to claim that antisocialist forces were creating a counterrevolutionary situation, was a *cri de coeur* of the extremist antireform forces. The outspoken schoolteacher was not content to stop there in her accusations. In December 1989, she gave an interview to the Hungarian daily newspaper *Magyar Hirlap*, in which she echoed the views of Pamyat when she excoriated "Zionists" for plotting to restore capitalism in the USSR through perestroika.

Andreyeva's letters and pronouncements, of course, are hardly isolated rantings. They reflect the growing link between Russian chauvinism and opposition to political liberalization and economic reform. Throughout the Soviet Union, dozens of unofficial Russian chauvinist organizations are springing up. These groups share a common approach and a common agenda. They are for a return to strict discipline and for the restoration of strict censorship. They call for the use of force to maintain the integrity of the empire. They are deeply opposed to Mikhail Gorbachev's economic reforms. "There is a common interest for a strong central state and for a strong army among these nationalists. In this regard, their interests coincide with those of the Party bureaucracy and with the military elite that is fearful of losing its vast resources," says Andrei Sinyavsky.

Russian chauvinist groups have sprung up in the urban centers of Moscow, Leningrad, Sverdlovsk, the Volga region, the Urals, Siberia, and in several of the non-Russian republics with a heavy Russian presence—Byelorussia, the Ukraine, Moldavia, and Kazakhstan.

In May 1989, one such group met in Moscow for its inaugural conference. Called the Russian Patriotic Society, Otechestvo (meaning Fatherland), the group was sponsored by the right-wing journals *Nash Sovremennik* and *Moskva* and by the Moscow Branch of the All-Russian Society for the Preservation of Monuments, whose offices serve as the group's headquarters. The advocacy of Russian patriotism might not strike one as objectionable; yet on closer examination, Otechestvo reveals many of the characteristics of a dangerous chauvinist sect that idealizes what has been a tragic and violent Russian past. The group is steadfast in its mission to preserve Russian preeminence in their empire. The organization's founding document suggests that an equilibrium among the nations of the USSR must be maintained and that because "openness is a Russian national trait," "the Russian people [are the only ones] capable of maintaining the integrity of the huge, multinational state—as has been proved by a millennial history."

Otechestvo calls for a strengthening of "military-patriotic education" and appears to favor uncompromising economic self-sufficiency. The group's chairman, a prominent Moscow art historian, used the group's founding convention to praise Romanian dictator Nicolae Ceauşescu's headlong drive toward economic self-sufficiency, without making reference to the immense sacrifices it exacted from Romanians. What matters most, Otechestvo's leaders argue, is to sidestep the danger posed by Western "colonizers" eager to enslave the Russian nation. In the organization's estimation, the Russians are themselves not colonizers. Unlike the British Empire, for example, Russia's colonies have benefited from the relationship with the imperial center, the organization asserts. Indeed, Otechestvo argues that the non-Russian peoples have raised themselves up at the expense of the Russians. On the local level, chapters of Otechestvo organize ecological demonstrations, conduct temperance campaigns, and march under the banner of Russia's patron, Saint George, while calling for the unity of the Russian nation.

The appeal of this new nationalist organization is broad and includes some of the pillars of the Russian literary and cultural establishment; prominent military figures, up to the rank of lieutenant generals, who participated in the convention; and Metropolitan Filaret—the second most important figure in the Russian Orthodox Church.

An even more dangerous Russian group that is functioning with the apparent encouragement of leading Russian Orthodox hierarchs was formed early in 1989. Called the Union for the Spiritual Revival of the Fatherland, the organization is headed by a fanatic by the name of Mikhail Antonov. Antonov has played an important role in polemics concerning economic reform. Writing in the journal *Moskva*, a publication of the Russian Writers Union, Antonov has savagely attacked such economists as Leonid Abalkin (now a deputy prime minister), Abel Aganbegyan, and Nikolai Shmelev—all leading proponents of liberal economic reforms. He has denounced a plan calling for the creation in the USSR of free economic zones, asserting: "[It] offends me, a Russian and a Soviet citizen, offends my patriotic sentiments. We are not an underdeveloped country but a vast industrial power."

Antonov's attack underscores the unity between tradition-oriented nationalists and the opponents of perestroika within the Party apparat. Antonov is equally famous for an attack on what he calls "economic-mathematical" approaches to reform. In his view, only a program based on religious values and on Russian tradition can rescue Russia from the abyss. Antonov is not new to political extremism. In the 1960s, he was part of a tiny Russian fascist group that regarded the world as dominated by a struggle between order—represented by the Teutonic-Slavic forces in such movements as Nazism and Stalinism—and chaos, represented by the Jews. The group called for the deindustrialization of the USSR and for a return to the peasant commune—the *obshchina*.

Although Antonov's Union for Spiritual Revival includes extremists and anti-Semites among its supporters, it appears to have avoided the extreme formulations of the more celebrated and notorious chauvinist groups. In this sense, it may well be more dangerous. For it signals the emergence of a more nuanced, sophisticated group that seeks to rally leading figures of the Soviet establishment whose reputations and positions cannot afford a direct association with Pamyat.

Another group whose themes echo those of Otechestvo and the Union for Spiritual Revival is the Association of Russian Artists. The group, which includes many of the USSR's best-selling Russian writers, issued an appeal to the Russian people after it was founded in March 1989. It read: "The once powerful union of the peoples of Russia, joined together by the idea of steadfast unity, is experiencing a difficult period, during which under the guise of demagogic slogans nationalist groups . . . are seeking to break up and destroy the unity of nations."

Yet another entity, a Fund for Slavic Writing and Slavic Cultures, was launched in the same month. Although it has the cooperation of a number of prominent Byelorussian and Ukrainian writers, its imperial cast is to be found in the keynote address of the fund's chairman, N. N. Tolstoy: "Our Slavic cultures—Byelorussian, Ukrainian, and Russian—

are on the one hand original national cultures, and, on the other hand, united cultures."

Symbols of Unity?

The theme of unity is omnipresent throughout the non-Russian reaches of the Soviet Union. It is enshrined in an endless landscape of architectural monuments to the "indissoluble unity of the Russian and non-Russian peoples." Along the Georgian Military Highway leading away from Tbilisi, there is a rusting convoluted mass of steel that is intended to symbolize the bonds of friendship and cooperation between Georgians and Russians. In Kiev, the Ukrainian capital's sprawling Park of the Pioneers is disfigured by a monstrous steel sculpture of two linked steel arcs depicting the "reunification of the Ukrainian and Russian nations." War memorials too echo the theme of unity. In a park in Alma-Ata, in the shadow of China's Tien Shan Mountains, one such memorial bears the words "In front of us the enemy. Behind us is Russia. Not one step backward." Kazakhstan, native Kazakhs will remind you, is not Russia. The statue makes no sense. It is an appeal to a crude Russian nationalism that seems intrusive and oblivious to indigenous sensibilities.

In the period of growing national assertiveness by the formerly hidden nations, it is not only anachronistic but offensive to the native population to have these symbols and ornaments displayed in the non-Russian republics. This state of affairs has succeeded in making native non-Russians feel like intruders, aliens in their own land. This is especially true in the major cities of most of the non-Russian republics, where Russian culture predominates. Yet such a state of affairs is perfectly sensible to most Russians, says Andrei Fadin. In his view: "The Russian psyche is not ready to be relegated to minority status. Russians have never felt themselves to be a minority anywhere they have gone and they have been unwilling to subordinate themselves to other cultures. They have felt themselves, everywhere, to be the vanguard of a great nation." The symbolism of the sculptures celebrating the inextinguishable Russian presence is an external reflection of their psyche. As Fadin notes: "The Russians have always felt the central power behind their backs, standing behind them."

Despite a confluence of symbols celebrating the Russian imperial presence and despite historic Russian national self-confidence, the growing assertiveness of the non-Russians has contributed to heightened anxiety by Russians, who have rarely been forced to confront the essence of their colonial relationship with the other half of the empire that is the USSR. The reaction of Russians, of course, has not been uniform. Some Russians who live in the non-Russian republics actively participate in the work of the indigenous popular fronts. Not a few have emigrated from Russia and even developed a sense of loyalty to the non-Russians. Some work hand in hand with nationalist non-Russian deputies in the Interregional Group of Deputies. Still, the rhetoric of most Russian groups betrays the growing sense by Russians that they are today under siege.

To respond to this sometimes perceived and sometimes very real fact, some Russian nationalist organizations have established sections in such republics as Byelorussia, Kazakhstan, and the Ukraine. Where non-Russian nationalities have been particularly forthright in pressing their cultural and political rights—as in the Baltic States and in Moldavia—Russians have taken to organizing what are referred to as "inter-fronts" or "inter-movements." Their aim is to resist efforts to force them to learn the languages of the national republics to which they have migrated and to act as a counterweight to non-Russian separatists. The inter-movements and inter-fronts are considerably complicating the efforts of the non-Russians to reassert their language rights, to create rules of the terms of republic-wide citizenship, and to press for full autonomy or even independence. In the case of Estonia and Latvia, where the Estonians and Latvians barely make up the majority of the population, these Russian nationalist movements have a great potential for destabilizing the peaceful evolution toward decentralized self-rule. In a number of cases, they have organized effective political strikes, challenging Baltic moves toward independence.

But, perhaps the most significant new organizations are those that aim to mobilize the Russians' discontent over economic difficulties and place all blame on the economic reforms of perestroika. These groups are looking for scapegoats on whom to pin Russia's growing woes. The most important such group is the United Front of Workers of Russia, which was founded as a nationwide organization in September 1989. The United Front is an umbrella organization uniting groups that make populist appeals and manipulate group hatred in an effort to build a base among disgruntled and increasingly restive Russian workers. Although it pretends to be a grass-roots body, the United Front can trace its origins to sections of the Communist Party apparat. Its founding convention, held in the Russian city of Sverdlovsk, was organized with the cooperation and material support of officials from the All-Union Central Council of Trade Unions (AUCCTU)—the conservative trade union group that has long sought to restrict independent worker organizing and which sat at management's side in negotiations with striking Soviet miners in July 1989. The AUCCTU has long been a home port for the most moribund segments of the Communist Party, including apparatchiks now under siege as a result of political and economic reforms initiated by Mikhail Gorbachev. In creating the United Front, local AUCCTU leaders joined with hard-line Party leaders like former Politburo member and deposed Leningrad Party boss Yuri Solovyev, Nina Andreyeva, and a host of local

Party hacks who suffered defeat in the March 1989 elections for seats in the USSR Congress of People's Deputies. In March 1990, Gorbachev named one of the leaders of the United Front of Workers to his influential Presidential Council.

Conservative Communist Party leaders clearly see the United Front as a grass-roots, mass-based alternative to the growing number of democratically inclined organizations. As the Soviet economy continues to unravel, the front and its allies in the inter-front and inter-movement in the Baltic States appear to offer simple and comforting populist solutions and hateful slogans in the face of worrying change.

For the moment, in areas where independent worker activism has emerged as a result of strike movements, the appeal of the ultranationalist United Front has been blunted. In other working-class enclaves, the extent of its popular support is not yet clear. Still, there is no doubt that with the emergence of a more assertive brand of nationalism and patriotism among the non-Russian peoples of the USSR, Russian nationalism is emerging once again as a potent force within the Soviet national equation. In part, the appeal to this latent nationalism is being made by leading opponents of Mikhail Gorbachev's policies. By co-opting some of the United Front's leaders into his inner circle, Gorbachev may be trying to co-opt the group and deny his opponents an important ally.

Over the years of Soviet rule, the Communist Party has adopted various strategies in managing and manipulating the far from latent power of Russian nationalism. Lenin, the USSR's founder, warned against the danger posed by what he called "Great Russian chauvinism."

It was Lenin's profound fear of Russian nationalism that led him to urge a revolving leadership for the USSR. But it was Stalin who shaped the future of Party *and* state relations. Under him, the promotion of Russian nationalist themes and the suppression of the non-Russian republics reached their apogee. It was as if Stalin, a Georgian by nationality, had sought to demonstrate his Russianness. His open embrace of Russian nationalist symbols was most pronounced in the period of the Second World War. With the Soviet Union under attack, the Party turned to its strongest source of ideological legitimacy—films like Sergei Eisenstein's *Ivan the Terrible* and *Aleksandr Nevsky* were produced as big-budget mass spectacles; the leaders of the Russian Orthodox Church were given access to the Soviet media to mobilize the nation against the heathen onslaught.

Without question, the rapid rise of national demands among the non-Russians, and the relative relaxation of public discourse under Gorbachev, have emboldened various Russian nationalist tendencies within the Soviet establishment. Some have even been encouraged—whether consciously or accidentally—by Mikhail Gorbachev himself. After all, it is the general secretary who gave support to a highly public, state commemoration of the Millennium of Christianity in 1988 (an event attended by then Soviet President Andrei Gromyko and Raisa Gorbachev) and who has endorsed high-profile media coverage of the Communist authorities' rapprochement with the pliant Russian Orthodox Church. Gorbachev's impromptu speech in Krasnodar, in which he waxed poetic about the Russian character and referred to Russia as "the last haven, the last reservoir of spirituality," also encouraged the further growth of nationalist trends. And he has gone out of his way to maintain cordial relations with Russian nationalists in the literary community. In 1989, when Gorbachev traveled to Finland, he included the anti-Semitic and anti-Western novelist Vasily Belov as part of his entourage. When he traveled to China, the Soviet head of state took with him Valentin Rasputin, a writer whose anti-Asian credentials are well known. In March 1990, Rasputin's brand of Russian nationalism was given a further boost by Gorbachev, who named him to his inner Presidential Council.

Gorbachev's longtime conservative rival, Yegor Ligachev, regarded as a voice of the disgruntled Party bureaucracy, also has made public gestures in the direction of Russian nationalists. In July 1988, he paid a highly public visit to an exhibit of the paintings of the Russian nationalist Ilya Glazunov, known for his epic paintings of heroic figures from Russia's past and for his portraits of Brezhnev and Andropov. In 1989, Glazunov gave an interview to *Ogonyok* in which he railed at the reemergence of an artistic avant-garde, openly calling it the "Abram-garde," in an odious anti-Semitic aside.

This is not to suggest that Mikhail Gorbachev is a Russian nationalist. But it is quite likely that Gorbachev as well as his right-wing opponents within the Politburo are fighting for the "hearts and minds" of this potent national force. An editorial in 1989, on the occasion of the "Day of the Union," underscored this. After having paid obligatory lip service to the worth of all the USSR's national cultures, *Pravda* waxed rhapsodic about the necessity of safeguarding Russian bilingualism, leaving unstated the obligation of Russians who live in non-Russian republics to learn a second language, indigenous to that republic.

In a period when the Communist Party leadership acknowledges that it faces a grave ideological and economic crisis, the strong appeal of traditional Russian nationalism beckons as an inviting and dangerous source of instant legitimacy. That nationalism, however, is also a potential source of instability. For any attempt by the Soviet authorities to play the "Russian card" will contribute to mounting resentment and assertiveness among the non-Russians. Russian nationalism clearly is a sharp and dangerous weapon. But in a multinational state in which Russians are soon to become a minority, it is a double-edged sword.

In the end, the attitude of Russians toward their non-Russian neighbors is central to the peaceful resolution of the "nationalities question."

Indeed, there are not a few signs of sympathy among democratically inclined Russians with the demands of the non-Russian movements. In the fall of 1989, a small Russian Anti-Colonial Society was formed by Russians in Leningrad. And in Moscow, ferment in the non-Russian republics is regularly covered in underground journals like *Glasnost,* which devotes extensive attention to the plight of Crimean Tatars, the travails of Armenians living in Nagorno-Karabakh, and the struggle of the Ukrainian Uniate Catholic Church.

Glasnost editor Sergei Grigoryants has even served in prison as a consequence of his travels to Armenia and his trailblazing reports on the national movement there. In his modestly appointed, three-room Moscow flat, Grigoryants exudes intensity. Half Russian and half Armenian, Grigoryants is culturally Russian. He worries about the absence of a democratic nationalism in Russia. The Russian ethnic affairs expert and member of the USSR Congress of People's Deputies, Galina Starovoytova, agrees and finds:

> The position of the Russian people in the Russian federation is paradoxical: The largest ethnic group and the largest republic do not have . . . a Communist Party, an academy of sciences, or a capital, since Moscow is the capital of the Union. . . . Russia should solve its problems not only for its own development, but also for the sake of the freedom of other ethnic groups, since an ethnic group that oppresses others cannot be free itself.

In the view of Sergei Grigoryants: "We in the human rights movement have tended to concentrate on transcendent issues of democracy and fundamental rights. We have in a sense forsaken the question of Russian national traditions, of Russian culture, and so on." This absence of clearly Russian concerns helps explain why many Russians have thus far remained largely on the sidelines in the mass struggle for democracy or democratization. "The non-Russian national movements," he continues, "are wielding powerful unifying symbols that are fundamentally cultural and deep-seated." In their modernness, dissidents like Grigoryants have tended to shy away from appealing to the powerful impulses of Russian national identity. "We ought to be reviving and helping to define a democratic specifically Russian tradition in the way the Balts or Armenians are doing," Grigoryants notes, signaling that democratic Russian patriots may be ready to challenge Russian chauvinists and neo-Stalinists who are exploiting Russian anxieties.

But others believe that such an appeal may fall on deaf ears. Indeed, those looking for a democratic Russian tradition have little to point to. There is of course the tradition of limited rule as exemplified by the Westward-looking Novgorod republic of the fourteenth and fifteenth centuries. And, it goes without saying, there have been outstanding individual Russian liberal thinkers, such as the nineteenth-century critic Aleksandr Herzen. In our own time, there are many noble Russian men and women actively engaged in the human rights movement whose commitment to democracy is personified in the moral authority of the late Dr. Andrei Sakharov. Yet their voices are isolated and on the periphery of the Russian tradition. Indeed, the late Dr. Sakharov's principal constituencies were to be found among the national democratic movements of the Baltic republics, Byelorussia, and the Ukraine. "With the exception of the period between the February and October revolutions in 1917, Russia never had a period of democratic rule," says Andrei Sinyavsky. "There is no strong democratic tradition to which one can appeal. First there was the czar, later came the commissars. Even serfdom is a relatively recent phenomenon," Sinyavsky observed pessimistically.

One group of young social democratic Russian intellectuals, formed around the Club for Democratic Perestroika, is fearful that the rise of nationalism will derail the democratic course initiated by Mikhail Gorbachev. They have set up a discussion group and a publication to counter official Soviet doctrine on national issues. Called *The USSR—Our Common Home*, the journal circulates in an underground edition that is influential far beyond its small numbers. Its ranks include a new generation of experts on Soviet ethnic issues. Andrei Fadin is one of the young intellectuals who plays a key role in the club's work. In the early 1980s, his views were adjudged heretical and he was sentenced to imprisonment. Today, Fadin works out of a tiny office in a former church that is now part of the Institute of Atheism of the Russian SFSR Ministry of Culture.

Fadin believes that Russians will not willingly surrender the non-Russian territories. "There's bound to be a backlash," Fadin observes. "I think the imperial and antidemocratic tradition will in the end win out. There are around twenty-five million Russians who now live in the non-Russian republics. The dissolution of the empire will raise the question of their fate. I just don't see how Russians will let the non-Russians go. The Russian psyche is not prepared to accept minority status. It's alien to Russian experience."

The writer Grigory Pomerants, too, believes that the Russian nationalist tradition can create problems in the transition to democracy. "The politics of pluralism," he claims, "clash in part with the traditional blend of nationalism and imperialism." In Andrei Fadin's view: "For two hundred years Russia has sought to be a great power. And because this goal has been attained by virtue of the blood and sweat of the masses it has entered into popular political consciousness." Fadin goes on: "To the extent we can distance ourselves from this imperial tradition, we can become a normal nation." But he argues that if Russians fail to "shake the psychology of the 'Third Rome,' we will never see the rise of normal society here." Fadin is convinced that the Soviet economy will no longer permit the USSR to remain a great power without exacting more and more economic sacrifices from the citizenry. "Any great sacrifice will necessarily call forth the need for mass mobilization under the banner of empire and world superpower status."

Fadin believes that the Communist Party is today searching for an ideology. "This ideology certainly will be the result of a compromise between economic realities and the need to safeguard some ritual forms and procedures of the old order." The young writer notes that "a vacuum has been created; one of power and ideology." That vacuum has allowed various tendencies, some of them odious and long hidden beneath the surface, to resurface within the Russian nation. Still, although he concedes that the Soviet Union could move to a more federal or even confederal arrangement in the years ahead, Fadin believes that "the real problem is that big empires don't fall apart neatly and peacefully. And this is particularly problematic in an empire that is also a nuclear superpower."

As 1990 began, Russian nationalists gave a sign of the growing consensus within their movement. While stressing the importance of respect for the spiritual heritage of the Russian nation and demanding greater autonomy for the Russian Republic, they virulently attacked liberals and reformers and denounced the Party leadership for economic ineptitude. More significant, just as movements for national independence were becoming increasingly vocal in the Baltics and the Caucasus, the Bloc of Russian Patriotic-Public Movements came out firmly for the preservation of empire, demanding that the USSR maintain its unity so that it can retain its status as a superpower.

And Mikhail Gorbachev, too, showed some signs that he may in the end be willing to articulate Russian national interests if it means hanging on to power. In consenting to the creation of a Russian Buro of the Communist Party's Central Committee and later, a Russian Communist Party, he was circling the wagons in a reliable configuration to face the growing revolt among non-Russian Communists that is most advanced among the Lithuanian Communists. By deciding to chair the Russian Buro, Gorbachev was also indicating that in the end he may be forced to retreat to Russia itself, while the non-Russians in the Party and outside spin further and further out of Moscow's orbit.

Yet Gorbachev's inclination to co-opt Russian nationalism is meeting with a fierce challenge from the "left." Responding to growing signs of a Russian turn inward, the charismatic populist reformer, and Gorbachev rival, Boris Yeltsin indicated his support for the emergence of "an independent Russian republic" that "as an independent state would sign agreements with other republics, also as independent states." Yeltsin suggested that it would then be up to each sovereign republic to decide whether it should be part of a federation, or a confederation, or be fully independent.

Yeltsin's narrow victory was in part a hopeful sign of the beginnings of a Russian retreat from empire. In late February 1990, for example, a public-opinion poll conducted primarily in Russian cities by the Soviet Academy of Sciences Institute of Sociology indicated that 52.4 percent of those polled supported the right of union republics to secede. Another 14 percent partly endorsed this right and only 7 percent were clearly opposed. Yeltsin played to these sentiments, emphasizing his desire to promote the interests of the Russian Federation first. In seeking to diffuse Russian concerns about the fate of the twenty-five million Russians who live outside the Russian Republic, he ran on a platform that called for a "law of return." Such a law would give to all ethnic Russians citizenship in the Russian Republic, which in turn would protect their material interests and assure them of a residence and a job in the event they left a non-Russian republic.

Still, Yeltsin was elected president by a narrow majority in the Russian parliament. And in the weeks after his election he was forced to accept a political opponent as Russian prime minister.

Thus, at the beginning of the 1990s, Russians were becoming a nation deeply divided and increasingly polarized over its role in history. On one side were Boris Yeltsin and other proponents of a turn inward, away from domination of other nations. On the other side were the dangerous forces of anti-Semitism, anti-Western xenophobia, and hostility to democratization, and their proponents within the army and the Communist Party apparat.

The Future of the
Empire:
Prospect and Policy

America's historic failure [has been the inability] to factor the power and persistence of nationalism around the
world into its foreign policy.

—William Pfaff, *Barbarian Sentiments*

I s THE Soviet Union an unstable state teetering on the verge of disintegration or collapse? The very fact that such a proposition can be seri-
ously considered is one measure of the breadth and depth of the national
revival among the hidden nations of the Soviet Union.

Today, there is no doubt of the intensity of discontent among the
non-Russian peoples of the USSR. In any openly and fairly contested
election, the Communist Party apparat would be routed by the pro-
independent popular fronts that have emerged in the Baltic States, Armenia, Georgia, Azerbaijan, Moldavia, and Uzbekistan. With somewhat
less certainty, similar claims can be made about the popular fronts of
Byelorussia and the Ukraine. Indeed, in the light of Mikhail Gorbachev's
call on the Communist Party to compete electorally, these national movements had a chance to test the depth of their support throughout the
USSR in elections to republic parliaments, and city and town councils
held in early 1990. The results were a confirmation of the growing strength
of the national movements. They swept elections in Lithuania, Estonia,
and Latvia; won many seats in the urban centers of Byelorussia; took
decisive control of legislatures in Western Ukraine; and won control of the
Ukrainian capital of Kiev. In Georgia, the authorities postponed elections

in the face of nationalist opposition to the very idea of conferring legitimacy to a process whose rules were set in Moscow.

Judging by the speeches, publications, and positions of the national movements in the non-Russian republics, there is little question that the forces of nationalism and patriotism are important proponents of democratic change in the USSR. More and more, these non-Russian movements are pressing for the devolution of power from the central state apparatus, for a democratically elected legislature, for an end to the Communist Party's once constitutionally guaranteed "leading role," for a pluralistic and free press, for freedom of association, and for a market economy. In this, such movements have much in common with the liberal nationalism that swept Europe in 1848 and little in common with the revanchism, imperialism, and fascism that provided the coloration of the European nationalisms of the 1920s and 1930s. In this regard, the non-Russian national movements differ profoundly from their Russian counterpart, where irrationalism, the appeal to hatred, and support of the totalitarian status quo still predominate, and where the democratic voices, though on the ascendant, are still somewhat weaker.

The Democratic Tradition

Democratic rule is not unknown to the non-Russian republics, which have experienced periods of independence. Multiparty parliamentary democracies, a free press, independent trade unions, and free public organizations existed previously in the Baltic States. The Estonian Republic, founded in 1920, saw fifteen years of a vigorous, democratic multiparty system that drew its inspiration from the United States, French, Weimar, and Swiss constitutions. Lithuania's independence between the two wars included six years of democratic rule. In Latvia, interwar independence led to twelve years of democracy, with power changing hands peacefully between social democrats and conservatives. In the Ukraine, too, the independent state administration—the Ukrainian Central Rada (Ukrainian for Council)—was formed in 1917 by political parties that were broadly supported by the army, workers, and the peasantry. Then, they received over 70 percent of the vote in democratic elections to the All-Russian Constituent Assembly. In that December 1917 vote, the Bolsheviks received only 10 percent of the Ukrainian vote. There is a record of strong commitment to a multiparty parliamentary system in Western Ukraine, today's center of intense proindependence sentiments. For decades, the Western Ukrainians from Galicia participated in the Austro-Hungarian and later Polish parliaments. In Georgia, too, the modern period of independence (1918–21) was associated, albeit for a brief three

years, with the moderate rule of the Mensheviks, who tolerated a high
degree of political pluralism and economic diversity, despite an unremit-
ting ideological commitment to class struggle and to the expropriation of
the large estates of the nobility.

After World War I, the then independent states of Azerbaijan and
Armenia, too, were characterized by democratic governance. In Azerbaijan, coalition governments briefly reflected the often contradictory
interests of nationalists, Mensheviks, Muslim socialists, and conservatives. Independent Armenia, ravaged by famine and disease, managed to
preserve a freely elected multiparty legislature.

The rich democratic political thought that arose during these periods of
independence has long been suppressed in the Soviet state's propagandistic educational and academic system. But that body of thought is making an appearance in rapidly proliferating samizdat and even in some
official publications issued beyond the control of local state censorship.
The basic writings and constitutional documents from the periods of non-
Russian independence are influencing a new generation of political leaders, making an important contribution to the rebirth of free political
thought decades after they first appeared.

The democratic complexion of the non-Russian movements has been
shaped even more fundamentally by their experience of decades of totalitarian rule. For the Balts, the preferred model today appears to be the
neutral democracy of Finland and Austria. For the Ukrainians, the influence of the democratic process in neighboring Poland and Hungary is
playing a decisive role. The Turkic peoples of Azerbaijan, Uzbekistan,
Turkmenistan, and Kazakhstan are keenly interested in learning more of
the polity shaped by their ethnic cousins in Turkey. And, certainly, the
toppling of Nicolae Ceauşescu's murderous regime by a mass movement
demanding *"Libertate! Libertate!"* initially sent a prodemocratic message
to fellow Romanians who make up the majority of Soviet Moldavia's population.

Despite the vast privations of Soviet-style Communism, the last decades have seen the emergence of a substantial, indigenous middle class.
Although by Western standards that class lives on the margins of material
comfort, its members are outward-looking and interested in interethnic
cooperation and dialogue. They also provide an important social base for
democratic orientations. Among this middle class are the new entrepre-
neurs who are transforming the face of Rustaveli Boulevard in Tbilisi and
rebuilding the ancient caravansaries of Baku into prosperous restaurants
and tourist attractions; the artists and musicians cooperatives that are
forming in Lvov, Yerevan, and Alma-Ata; as well as the plentiful cultural
and scientific intelligentsia. As the strength of this new social stratum
grows, so too will its support for the proindependence national movements. Moreover, the fact that the intelligentsia of the non-Russian re-

publics is playing a leading role in their peoples' mass movements is contributing to their demonstrable tolerance for free expression, their support of an end to censorship, and their advocacy of an independent and pluralistic press.

And then there is, to borrow from Marxist parlance, the "objective" democratic role of the new, rudimentary institutions of civil society that have arisen as part of the non-Russian national rebirth. Thousands of ecological, political, human rights, trade union, cultural, and educational organizations have sprung up as part of the wide-ranging popular mobilization. Those organizations, free of the fetters of Communist Party dogma, are creating pluralistic interest groups, sometimes with competing and even contradictory interests. What is emerging in the Soviet Union, too, is the process of coalition building. In it, important compromises are made, agreements reached, and tactics agreed to, all in behalf of a unitary goal—national self-determination based on radical economic and political decentralization.

The activists from these proindependence national movements and not the stodgy apparatchiks of the Kremlin are the principal hope for democratic reform of the world's last remaining empire.

A Changing Population

The non-Russian national rights movements have mobilized broad masses into political movements, have provoked massive general strikes and work stoppages, and have formed and sustained democratically accountable organizations independent of the state. These peaceful movements of peoples are major factors in Soviet life and are certain to be of great consequence for the Soviet Union's superpower status. The movements are therefore going to play a decisive role in the nature of United States-Soviet superpower relations, as well as in East-West relations. The prospect of a further growth of national and nationalist movements, their consolidation of local power, and even their eventual cooperation is not fanciful; it is likely. As was the case with such Eastern European democratic and human rights movements as Poland's Solidarity and Czechoslovakia's Charter 77 before the democratic revolution of 1989, non-Russian democratic movements are lending each other technical, material, and moral support.

Demographic and migratory processes also are contributing to the growing strength of nationalist and separatist tendencies within the non-Russian movements. Census statistics for 1989 show that two broad trends are emerging: One is the proportional decline of the ethnically Russian population; the second is the return of large numbers of Russians to their ancestral home, the European part of the Russian Republic.

Statistics show that in the decade between 1979 and 1989, the population of the Russian SFSR grew by 8 million as a result of natural increases and by 1.77 million as a result of migration. By contrast, the population of the non-Russian republics increased by 14.5 million. More significant, in the southern republics of the USSR—in the Caucasus, Uzbekistan, Kirgizia, Tajikistan, Turkmenistan, and Kazakhstan—there was a natural population increase of nearly 13.2 million and a net outmigration (primarily of Russians and other Slavs, back to their native republics) of 2.2 million citizens. The consequence of this process is that there is now a significantly lower proportion of Russians and Russified Ukrainians and Byelorussians living in the southern republics. Even the rapid increase in the proportion of Russians in the Ukraine, so evident in the 1950s, 1960s, and 1970s, has ceased. And the trend toward "indigenization" appears to have reached even the Baltic republics. While in the first six months of 1988 the population of Latvia saw the in-migration of 6,700 new citizens (most of them Russians), in the first six months of 1989, 1,610 more people left Latvia than migrated in. As native Latvians are least likely to want to leave their native republic, it can be surmised that the flow of Russians out of the republic is increasing, while the number of Russians wishing to come to this economically prosperous Baltic redoubt is on the wane.

In the southern republics of Muslim Soviet Central Asia and in the Caucasus, the Russian presence is clearly and dramatically in decline. Between 1979 and 1989, this drop was precipitous. In Georgia, the Russian proportion of the population declined from 7.4 to 6.2 percent; in Azerbaijan, it fell from 7.9 to 5.6 percent; and in Armenia, from 2.3 to 1.6 percent. In Uzbekistan, the proportion of Russians declined from 10.8 percent in 1979 to 8.3 percent by 1989. In Kirgizia, it went from 25.9 percent in 1979 to 21.4 in 1989; in Tajikistan, from 10.4 to 7.6 percent; in Turkmenistan, from 12.6 percent to 9.5 percent; and in Kazakhstan, from 40.8 percent to 37.6, with the Kazakhs emerging as the largest ethnic group in their republic. As with the Baltic States, in the Ukraine, Moldavia, and Byelorussia, the rapid growth of the Russian population began to slow in the 1980s.

As the numerical and proportional strength of the non-Russians increases, particularly in the south, so too do their assertiveness and rising national consciousness. And as the urbanization rates and education levels of the non-Russians continue to rise, so too do their capacity for independent organizing and their demand for increased rights. From Baku to Tashkent to Alma-Ata, the non-Russians with whom we met spoke of the palpable, exhilarating sense of a growing presence of their non-Russian countrymen in the city streets, in schools, and in workplaces.

Most of the two million Soviet citizens—the vast majority of them

Russians—who left the southern non-Russian republics in the 1980s returned to the homeland of their ancestors, European Russia. It can be predicted with some measure of certainty that the migration of Russians out of the non-Russian republics will accelerate in the next few years, in good measure because of new language legislation that was enacted in these areas at the close of 1989. The effects of that diminished Russian presence are likely to be profound. With fewer Russians in the work force of the non-Russian republics, the need for the Russian language may be considerably lessened. The authorities' argument for the Russification of the workplace will be weakened, too. Coupled with growing non-Russian militancy about language rights, the cultural environment will become less comfortable for those Russians who are unwilling to learn indigenous languages or to absorb traditions.

Changes in language laws in the non-Russian republics are already affecting demographics. An article in the September 16, 1989, issue of *Izvestia* reported that in the first six months of 1989, 10,000 non-Tajiks, all of them non-Tajik speaking, left Dushanbe, the capital city of Tajikistan. In a city of 582,000, that represents approximately 2 percent of Dushanbe's population. The *Izvestia* article made it abundantly clear that the principal reason for the migration out of the city was the recent decision by the Tajik legislature to make Tajik the republic's official language. This trend, no doubt, was further propelled with the outbreak, in February 1990, of anti-Armenian demonstrations and violence that broke out among Tajiks in Dushanbe. The protests were a further sign of growing claims by the indigenous non-Russian populations that they are entitled to live in their capital city.

Another factor that is contributing to the trend toward Russian migration out of the non-Russian republics is a growing shortage of labor in the Russian SFSR. That labor shortage has arisen because of the low birth rate among ethnic Russians, whose population is growing at a pace that is among the slowest in the USSR. This birth dearth, which became pronounced in the 1960s and 1970s, has opened up job possibilities in European Russia. In cultural, social, and economic terms, these job prospects are preferable to those in the ethnically Turkic and religiously Islamic Soviet south.

As a result of these factors, the Soviet republics are going to find their populations growing more nationally specific. The process begun by glasnost, perestroika, and the national renaissance among the non-Russians is therefore likely to grow in intensity and, if it does not meet with brutal repression, to move from strength to strength. And such demographic and migratory trends are likely to reawaken the idea of nationalism long dormant within the imperial Russian nation. As Russians come home in increasing numbers, they may look inward, back to their own innate traditions and values. Signs that the Russians have already begun to turn homeward can be seen in their retreat from Afghanistan and the neighboring states of Poland, Hungary, Czechoslovakia, and even Bulgaria. This turn inward is also part and parcel of Boris Yeltsin's campaign to win greater sovereignty for the Russian Republic.

The radical shift in Russian priorities and in Russian identity will meet will resistance from powerful antidemocratic, proimperialist, "great power" ideologies of such groups as the international fronts and movements, the United Front of Workers of Russia, and the Pamyat Association.

The West has only reluctantly considered the dilemmas of the shifting, some say collapsing, Soviet empire. Rather than welcoming the emergence of mass-based movements pressing for decentralization and democracy, and contributing to the restoration of a civil society, the Western democracies have met the renaissance of the USSR's non-Russians with a combination of institutional inertia, hands-off caution, and fearful antipathy. The U.S. State Department, for example, has retreated from the forthright defense of the sovereignty of the Baltic States it has maintained since their incorporation into the USSR, and instead urges Baltic proindependence groups to exercise extreme caution and restraint. When, in March 1990, the democratically elected Lithuanian parliament proclaimed an independent republic, no Western state extended recognition. The United States government also shies away from any open discussion of Mikhail Gorbachev's "nationalities problems." As with any imperial structure in the process of unraveling or mutating, questions of instability and turmoil have greeted the rise of the hidden nations. Certainly, the West is not only refraining from encouraging the secessionist movements in the USSR, it is generally pretending they are not there.

Within the Western press, expressions of sympathy for the goals of the popular fronts appear to be limited to the Baltic States, whose claims to national sovereignty are not any more compelling than those of other nations absorbed by force into the Soviet Union. Why should the claims of independent states that were invaded by Russian armies in the aftermath of World War I be any less legitimate than those who lost their sovereignty as a result of World War II? If, for example, the United States limited its support of the right to national sovereignty only to states recognized in 1939, it would have opposed the decolonization of Asia and Africa. Nation building, in the end, is never a final, absolute process. Nations and the states they create are constantly mutating, evolving entities. Their configurations are never permanent or ideal. The unifying principle of Western support for national self-determination should therefore not be the permanence of existing state configurations, but support only for movements that are committed to a peaceful struggle to achieve their national aims.

Current official Western attitudes are inadequate and shortsighted. They amount to standing idly by while a rival nuclear superpower undergoes a period of profound uncertainty and potentially turbulent crisis. The Western democracies ought not promote the disintegration of the Soviet Union or independence for this or that non-Russian republic, a process that will unfold of its own accord. But they also must not limit their engagement to protests of the excessive use of force or to the violation of human rights. It clearly *is* in Western interests to play an active role in creating positive incentives for the evolution of the Soviet internal empire into a more stable, confederal entity or into a commonwealth of nations. The United States and other Western governments ought, therefore, to express at the highest levels clear support for emerging democratic movements throughout the USSR, including non-Russian movements, provided they are committed to peaceful, evolutionary change.

While Poland's Solidarity was initially welcomed as a mass-based popular movement in 1980, and its suppression in December 1981 was correctly greeted with the imposition of harsh Western economic sanctions, most of the mass-based non-Russian movements have been greeted with a deadening silence. The reasons for that are many. Not least among them is the view of Western policymakers that the reform process initiated by Soviet leader Gorbachev deserves to be supported strongly and that the emergence of nationalist and separatist groups is an unnecessary and unwelcome complicating factor that strengthens the hand of hard-liners who seek to displace Gorbachev and the Communist Party's reform wing. They argue that non-Russian nationalisms are adding yet another unstable element into an already volatile mix of Eastern and Central European peoples pressing toward democracy and independence.

Some Western voices have raised fears that ethnic tensions in the USSR may result in the "Balkanization" of the Soviet Union. The term refers to the process of feuding among the small new states that emerged in the midst of the collapse of the Ottoman Empire in the years leading up to the First World War. Some policy experts fear that the series of microstates that would emerge in the wake of the dissolution of the Soviet Union would offer a new ground for instability and ethnic violence.

The very notion that the attainment of national independence will lead to a state of constant tension among the many peoples of the USSR, the specter of Balkanization, is a fear without foundation. Democratic national rights advocates insist that relations among most of the proindependence movements are cooperative and mutually supportive. In their view, today's ethnic tensions in the USSR, like the Balkanization in the period before the First World War, are an instability that is the result of the denial of national sovereignty. In the USSR today as in the Balkan States in the early twentieth century, the sources of antagonism, violence, and extremism are not to be found in the small nations of the region, but in the fact that entire peoples were denied their sovereignty by empires.

Actually, ethnic violence in the USSR has not been of a scale to warrant such conclusions. While such violence has made for sensationalist news headlines, it has in fact erupted mainly in remote, economically backward outposts, where the influence of popular fronts is quite limited or officially blocked. Proportionately fewer people have died in ethnic strife in the Soviet Union than have in the terrorism and violence in Great Britain resulting from the struggle in Northern Ireland; or in Israel, from the Palestinian uprising. Significantly, there have been only a handful of instances of urban terrorism. Nor has there been any call to violence by popular fronts or other, more radical nationalist movements. Indeed, the mass-based movements organized by national rights and nationalist groups have been nonviolent and have used peaceful means of suasion: elections, political campaigns, independent publishing, boycotts, strikes, and demonstrations. Groups like the popular fronts, moreover, are safety valves for popular discontent; and because they articulate deeply felt national discontents, such groups can be seen as an important factor in preventing violence. The ethnic violence that has erupted in the USSR is, in the end, evidence of a dehumanized and atomized segment of society, whose only sense of mastery and omnipotence is through the violence of the mob. To this anarchic violence, the national movements counterpose the opportunity of constructive participation in civil society, which they are helping to restore. Even in the case of the anti-Armenian pogroms that tragically erupted in Baku in January 1990, it became clear that the vast majority of the leaders of the local popular front were working to protect the lives of local Armenians from the violence of a growing lumpenproletariat—Azerbaijan's poorest of the poor.

Indeed, many violent interethnic conflicts, such as those in the Fergana Valley and Samarkand in Uzbekistan, Osh in Kirgizia, and Novy Uzen in Kazakhstan, stem largely from socioeconomic immiseration. In other intergroup conflicts in Georgia, Armenia, and Azerbaijan, the violence is not economically based, but has involved disputes over local autonomy. Nonetheless, even those violent confrontations do not represent real ethnic conflicts. Rather, they reflect the accumulated discontents and problems that have built up among the peoples of the USSR because of the denial of national sovereignty. They are frustrated because they do not have the final say in determining their internal affairs, are restricted in setting the terms of local citizenship, and are forced to live with the consequences of territorial and economic decisions made in Moscow.

Many proindependence activists believe that violence is often fanned by the actions of the local Communist apparat and by provocateurs encouraged by the Soviet authorities. Others suggest that violence directed at innocent civilians (as in Tbilisi in April 1989 and in Armenia in May 1990) is an attempt by the Soviet military to provoke violent public protest and pave the way for introducing martial law. Many observers now believe that the introduction of martial law in Azerbaijan in January 1990 was not motivated by a desire to stem anti-Armenian pogroms. The pogroms, in fact, had already subsided when Moscow sent in its troops. Rather, martial law was introduced to suppress the proindependence opposition, which was emerging as the dominant political force in Azerbaijan.

Notwithstanding local ethnic conflicts, today most of the non-Russian nationalities feel comfortable with the notion of outright independence. They would, after all, prefer the option of choosing allies and alliances for themselves. And certainly all non-Russian groups, and increasing numbers of Russians themselves, seek greater autonomy for their own republics in matters of cultural and economic life, if not in terms of national defense. All such aspirations, including those of many radical separatists, could adequately be addressed in a truly confederal or commonwealth structure. Even in the aftermath of violent conflict between Armenians and Azerbaijanis and anti-Armenian pogroms in Baku, the Armenian National Movement—the mass-based national front—denounced the introduction of Soviet troops into the conflict. The Armenian nationalists preferred to negotiate directly with the Azerbaijani Popular Front rather than submit to the Kremlin's heavy hand.

Paradoxically, even the fears of doomsayers about the agenda of the non-Russian movements would be better served by a policy of active interaction with their emerging leaders. United States government institutions like the U.S. Information Agency and its West European counterparts should be in the forefront of sponsoring major exchange programs between the leaders of the cultural, ecological, trade union, and political organizations and their Western counterparts. American and Western private sector organizations, too, should take an active role in meeting with their non-Russian counterparts. To date, there have been few such exchanges. Programs to bring non-Russian scholars to the West for academic years abroad, or for research at leading Western think tanks, should also become a consistent part of Western exchange programs with the USSR.

Western skeptics who are troubled by an unwieldy set of new independent states and doubt the efficacy of a confederal or commonwealth arrangement must keep in mind the alternatives. Suppressing the national aspirations of the peoples of the USSR could well contribute to lasting instability on the borders of the new Europe. As complex as a new postimperial Soviet landscape might be, it is clear that unless a new deal is struck, based on self-determination and democratization, pressures within the USSR will further build and could even threaten the fragile stability of the democracies that are taking shape in Hungary, Poland, and Czechoslovakia.

Gorbachev's Design and Party Policy

In the last year, Soviet leader Mikhail Gorbachev has begun to shape his own, inadequate version of just such a new deal. Since the summer of 1989, he has been compelled to begin articulating a national and ethnic policy in response to the resurgence of nationalism and national consciousness among his once hidden nations. In his still-emerging approach, Gorbachev has shown a reluctance to resort to widespread repression in the face of growing nationalist demands, and has chosen to respond instead with a policy of concessions to such pressures. This approach reflects his grudging acknowledgment that a widespread crackdown would have unpredictable consequences. It would only postpone an inevitable day of reckoning for the shaky Soviet empire and could put an immediate end to his attempt to restructure the Soviet economy with the help of Western investment, defeating his aim of integrating the USSR into the Western-dominated world economy. Indeed, even when Gorbachev has resorted to the use of military force, as in Azerbaijan in January 1990, he has done so in settings where group violence has made such action plausible in the eyes of some in the West.

In the face of rising local assertiveness, Gorbachev and his Politburo colleagues have therefore agreed to concede fundamental mistakes that arose out of what is now disparaged as "unitarism and administrative-command forms of management." In contrast to such hypercentralized distortions, Gorbachev and the Central Committee are now stating they intend to offer the non-Russians a new deal based on limited, but very real, decentralization, primarily in the economic and cultural spheres. The cornerstone of that new deal may turn out to be a new treaty of the union, to replace that agreed to in 1922. The enactment of a new treaty would be part of a wide-ranging process aimed at relegitimating and reanimating Soviet institutions and national arrangements, a stated aim of perestroika. The reform process also will include the new law outlining a procedure for the secession of republics from the USSR, legislation that Gorbachev promised while on a visit to Lithuania in January 1990.

Gorbachev's own views on the question of centralization have evolved over the recent years of upheaval. In his first three years in power, he evaded any systematic pronouncements on the national question. By 1988, he began to concede that the current state of national and ethnic relations in the USSR was an issue of fundamental importance. He, likewise, began to speak out in dire tones of disapproval about the dangers posed by growing ethnic tensions and violence. By 1989, with his power bolstered by purges of some of his leading opponents, Gorbachev was convinced that he had to address the question of a fundamental restructuring of this unstable factor in Soviet political life. In his report to the

Central Committee at the Party's two-day plenum on "nationalities," in September 1989, Gorbachev took his first major step as he outlined his conception of the Leninist form of national self-determination.

This address on the most fundamental issue facing the USSR was carried on Soviet television and featured on the front pages of the USSR's press. In it, Gorbachev noted that

> in present-day conditions, [national self-determination] finds its optimal expression in self-management, which ensures the preservation of national distinctiveness and the right of each people to enjoy all the benefits of sovereignty and to decide independently questions of its economic, political, and cultural development. At the same time, self-management presupposes a voluntary unification of the republics and national formations in the name of the solution of tasks common to all and their organic involvement in the development of the whole country.

This distinctive paragraph, while a departure from past Party pronouncements, is nonetheless full of internal contradictions. It asserts the primacy of national sovereignty, while at the same time arguing that aspects of that sovereignty already have been voluntarily surrendered by the Soviet republics. The Soviet leader appears to be claiming that a "voluntary" arrangement of economic interdependence was shaped between the non-Russians and the Kremlin. But the problem with his argument is that economic, political, and cultural relations among the USSR's peoples were shaped during the years of Stalin's absolute rule, the very period that Gorbachev has consistently denounced as contrary to Lenin's teachings.

At the Communist Party plenum, Gorbachev sought to put the best possible face on national relations. He declared that the Soviet Union had made important improvements upon the czarist imperial pattern. Above all, Gorbachev asserted in his address of September 19, 1989, "it is worth recalling that czarist Russia did not have the Ukraine, Byelorussia, or Georgia, but only provinces of the Russian empire." Those peoples were not "regarded as whole nations" but as mere "subjects of his majesty the emperor."

Although Gorbachev conceded that there were marked discrepancies in the level of economic development between the historic, predominantly Russian industrial areas and the backward non-Russian regions, he tried his best to place even this phenomenon in a positive light by reaching far into the past. "Whereas in 1926 the maximum industrial production per capita of old industrial regions exceeded that of the ethnic outskirts by 38 times," he declared, "in 1941 the ratio shrank to 4.1 times and now stands at only 2.3 times."

Gorbachev doesn't begin to explain that much of the industrialization

in the Soviet south was brought about in large measure through the
migration of Russians and other nonindigenous peoples. It is primarily the
Russian workers who moved into the cities of the less developed non-
Russian regions, thus systematically excluding the non-Russians from a
fuller participation in the clear material and educational benefits of city
life and industrialization.

Gorbachev's remarks also fail to explain the persistent lag in the urbanization of the Ukraine, an intended consequence of the planned economy. Indeed, Soviet development policies were structured to expand the
industrial might of the Russian Republic at the expense of the Ukraine,
whose natural resources and gross national product were diverted outside
the republic. After the Second World War, Stalin's contempt for the
Ukrainians, fueled by his anger at the resistance to Sovietization by the
fiercely independent Western Ukraine, led to a policy of calculated economic underdevelopment for what had once been a relatively prosperous
outpost of Central Europe.

Gorbachev's optimistic reading of the future development of Soviet
republics also does not address the question of how, in a period of economic decline and mounting environmental catastrophe, Soviet authorities propose to resolve the long-standing underdevelopment of many of
the non-Russian republics.

While Gorbachev and the Communist Party are correct in noting the
gross inequalities of colonial czarist rule, they are wrong in claiming that
seventy-three years later the legacy of czarism is still responsible for the
inequities that persist to this day. In the period of seventy-three years,
great new economic powers have risen around the world—Korea, Tai-
wan, Singapore, and Brazil, for example, have all radically transformed
their economies, becoming international economic success stories. The
war-ravaged states of Italy, Great Britain, France, Japan, and West Germany all rose from the ashes to take their place as leading forces in the
world economy in a matter of a few decades of the end of World War II.
All this has been accomplished in unpredictable and vastly divergent
settings of postwar misery, political instability, social upheaval, and the
undisciplined lurches of the market system. The regional economic landscape in the United States, too, has been drastically transformed with the
development of the West and Southwest. If all these basic changes could
have been achieved as a result of the vagaries of market forces, equally
drastic changes could have been attained by the USSR's more directed
economy. Indeed, to take Communist ideology at face value, the Soviet
system was a tabula rasa on which any developmental pattern could be
drawn thanks to its centralized, voluntaristic economic system. According
to the standards set by the Soviet rulers themselves, the patterns that
exist in Soviet society today, therefore, can only be the legacy of Communism and not that of czarist rule.

But the fundamental issue for the leaders of the nationally conscious movements in the non-Russian republics is not so much the very grim reality of increasingly apparent inequities of income, education, health care, and development, but the lack of control by the non-Russians over their own economic and social fate. On this key matter of social and economic self-determination, Gorbachev's September 1989 address contained within it a series of ideas that are unsatisfactory and even distressing for the non-Russian popular fronts. Referring, apparently, to the Baltic States, Gorbachev put the issue thus: "Tendencies toward autarky and attempts by the relatively prosperous republics and oblasts to isolate themselves and shut themselves off from others would be extremely dangerous in present-day circumstances. This could turn out to have exceedingly negative consequences for those who embark on such a path."

His voice rising in visible agitation, the Soviet leader went on: "We must speak of this once more at the plenum of the Central Committee before all the peoples of the Soviet Union so that they don't succumb to demagogues who conceal the possible results of the implementation of slogans served up under the 'pleasant sauce' of independence, secession, and so on."

Lest his outburst against the forces of nationalism have escaped his audience, the general secretary went on to warn that "only adventurists would take it upon themselves to break up our society with all its closely intertwined economic, political, social, spiritual, human, and family ties."

The plenum at which these remarks were made was filled with a number of important developments. Announced and planned more than a year before, the meeting had been postponed on a number of occasions. The Communist Party had spent the last three years grappling with the reemergence of the hidden nations and with the volatility of interethnic relations, and had put off this important policy statement as the contours of nationalist upheaval began to take shape. On September 20, 1989, however, the Central Committee of the CPSU at last felt ready to adopt its most fundamental statement on nationalism, separatism, and growing ethnic ferment. It was styled in the stilted prose associated with the Communist Party as the "Nationalities Policy of the Party Under Present Conditions (CPSU Platform)." And, in this case, style seemed to presage content for the document was a profound disappointment for those non-Russians who had hoped for a radical change of direction. As Gorbachev's address itself suggested, the Communist Party statement proved to be an incomplete, infuriating, and at times contradictory document.

While it determinedly and unmistakably criticized the practices of the past, ultimately the Party showed its inclination to repeat formulations that had justified the abuses of national rights in the Stalin and Brezhnev years. In its broad considerations of the question of ethnic relations, the CPSU restated the hoary claim that the formation of the union socialist state [in 1922] . . . made it possible through joint efforts to implement the country's industrialization and the socialist re-organization of the countryside, aiming at elimination of the backwardness of outlying districts and equalizing the peoples' level of economic development and material provision. An integral national economic complex took shape. The social structure of the Soviet nations underwent a qualitative change. In the spiritual sphere, opportunities were created for preserving and developing national individuality. At the same time, integration processes proceeded con-ditioned both by economic needs and the unity of aims and ideals which objectively led to the formation of *a new social community—the Soviet people.* [Italics in original]

This last term, "the Soviet people," or "the Soviet nation," as it might have been translated, was an echo of an idea deeply rooted in the Brezh-nev era. It carried with it the bad odor of social engineering, voluntarism, assimilation, and the negation of cultural tradition. Like the Party views of the Stalin, Khrushchev, and Brezhnev eras, the new CPSU document reasserted the special place in the Soviet system of only one nation—the Russians. "Russia," the document said, "was and remains the consolidat-ing principle of our entire union, and . . . [has] made a decisive contri-bution to the elimination of the backwardness of the outlying national districts."

A portion of the document placed particular emphasis on the special problems of the Russians, who face "acute socioeconomic and ecological problems" and confront the need for "the rescue and restoration of his-torical monuments and the preservation of national cultural assets." Such specific language was a major concession to what has been called the "Russian Party." The "Russian Party" is a term coined by dissident critics during the Brezhnev era to denote the bedrock of the CPSU that consists of proimperialist forces, including the most reactionary segments of the USSR Writers Union and the propaganda sections of the Soviet armed forces.

On the fundamental issue of the ownership of local natural resources, the CPSU platform statement on the nationalities offered nothing new. It declared that "the land, its minerals, timber, water, and other natural resources are the property of the union republic and the USSR." The document concluded that the central authorities, and not the republics, have the final say in the disposition of natural resources—a conclusion that will heighten resentment among the national movements.

The ownership of natural resources is a key factor in the issue of economic autonomy of the republics. Without unambiguous control over the natural wealth they possess, and the right to withhold such wealth from all-Union use if it is priced below true value, the idea of economic self-determination for the republics is an empty fiction. How can a re-public be responsible for *khozraschet,* for economic self-accounting, if it does not have absolute control to determine at what prices it can sell its products, and if it does not have the right to sell its natural resources on the international market. All these essential economic rights appeared to be excluded by the Party's nationalities document.

The national rights of army recruits were also denied in the document. While the CPSU's assertion of the "multinational basis" of the Soviet armed forces cannot be held unreasonable if the Party is to maintain the integrity of the Soviet Union, it does not address the growing number of complaints from the non-Russian republics over the a priori assignment of indigenous peoples to tours of military duty far outside their own republics. The Party made no concessions to the demand of leaders of the popular fronts, who wanted their recruits to be given the opportunity to maintain links with their native cultures in the culturally and linguistically Russian armed forces. On the basis of this document, it was clear that the Communist Party intends to continue to use military service as an instrument for the Russification of young recruits.

Most significant, the Party steadfastly rejected any suggestion that the Communist parties in the republics should be independent of the control of the central Party. "Federalist ideas in the building of the CPSU are fundamentally unacceptable," the Party document intoned. "Communists must consider it their duty to prevent any demarcation on national grounds either in the Party or in labor collectives and social formations and must combat manifestations of nationalism and chauvinism, first and foremost, in their own national milieu." The document thus enshrined the role of the CPSU as the principal instrument for maintaining the cohesion of the empire.

Surprisingly, while national ferment had been most apparent among the non-Russians, the Party document made no mention of the Lithuanians, Estonians, Latvians, Ukrainians, Moldavians, Byelorussians, Uzbeks, Tajiks, Azerbaijanis, Georgians, Armenians, or Kazakhs. The document specifically avoided any direct reference to the Baltic republics, where political challenges to the empire have been most pronounced. Nor was any direct mention made of the Caucasian republics, which have been the scene of intense protests and ethnic strife. Such an oversight can hardly be accidental. It almost appeared as if the CPSU was going to considerable lengths to indicate that its positions would not be influenced or driven by the mobilization of the non-Russian peoples. Indeed, as far as the language of the Party document was concerned, the non-Russian peoples remain hidden nations in what was touted to be a fundamental expression of Party policy on nationalities.

Conspicuously absent in the CPSU assessment of the "nationalities question" was any reference to the role of mass-based popular fronts, which have become the motor force in the political and cultural awakening of the hidden nations. The popular fronts, therefore, cannot take comfort in the new document. No acknowledgment is given to their legitimate place in the debate on ethnic, cultural, economic, and political matters.

On the question of language, the Party document appeared even to take a significant step back in contrast to the demands of the non-Russian movements. It expressed sympathy with the idea that the Russian language should be given special status as the *obshchegosudarstvenny yazyk*—the common state language. Curiously, despite Gorbachev's constant reference to a "Leninist" solution of the "nationalities question," he appeared to discard Lenin's unequivocal opposition to making Russian the state language on the ground that that would be too coercive a policy.

The Communist Party offered only a few concessions to the peoples of the Soviet Union. It did outline a new, improved deal for many of the smaller peoples, emphasizing the rights of a number of the so-called punished peoples, nations that were repressed by Stalin for their putative collaboration with the Nazis. But it sidestepped the precarious place in Soviet society of the Jews, whose needs and sufferings are nowhere referred to in the document.

Although the document failed to make an outright call for the right of the punished peoples to return to their ancestral homelands, it gave further impetus to their claims for repatriation.

The Party also acknowledged the inequities among peoples, but disappointingly rejected any concrete remedies that would involve the devolution of power. In answer to calls for such decentralization, the Party document and Gorbachev emphasized the complex pattern of economic interrelatedness that has emerged as a consequence of Soviet rule. One can expect these themes to dominate the Soviet media in the months and years to come, as part of a glasnost-styled public relations campaign to sow doubts within the public about the efficacy of independence and to bolster divisions within the popular fronts.

The biggest losers in the Party's new platform appeared to be the Baltic States, whose demands for full autonomy were dismissed or, even worse, ignored; the popular fronts, whose place in the debate on national relations was slighted; and all the non-Russian movements that had been pressing for greater equity for their national cultures.

The Party plenum on nationalities had long been anticipated by reformist-oriented non-Russians, including the growing category of nationally conscious Communist Party members. One such man, a leader of the Ukrainian Popular Front, the Rukh, spoke to us with great distress about Gorbachev's program for the non-Russian peoples. "I'm profoundly disappointed. He just doesn't seem to understand the depth of our discontent. The new Party program is just a rehash of the old formulas," the people's deputy from the Ukraine asserted to us in disgust. "It says absolutely nothing new on the issue of economic autonomy. And in the case of its emphasis on a 'state language' for the USSR it is positively retrograde. The Russian language is de facto and de jure the state language for the Soviet Union. It enjoys so many advantages that it doesn't need constitutional protections," the deputy argued. "I'm not sure whether Gorbachev even has an idea of what the broad masses in the Ukraine are thinking. Certainly, the document doesn't seem to indicate that he does." By April 1990, this nationally conscious Communist Party member had had enough. He resigned from the Party along with hundreds of other prominent Ukrainian activists.

Yet even as the Communist Party began to enunciate its new line on the nationalities, its positions were beginning to be challenged by unfolding events. Although the Party document countenanced no redrawing of the USSR's boundaries, the legislatures of Azerbaijan and Armenia each passed laws (later voided by the USSR's Supreme Soviet) that peremptorily sought to absorb Nagorno-Karabakh into their own patrimony. Nor did the Baltic States temper their demands for greater autonomy. Indeed, within days of the Communist Party plenum's strong assertion of the indivisibility of the Party, the Communist Party of Lithuania began debating and in late December 1989 announced its secession from the CPSU. Within two months of the Party plenum, the Lithuanian parliament by a vote of 243 to 1 had also rejected the "leading role of the Communist Party" and declared Lithuania a multiparty state. It was soon thereafter followed by its Estonian neighbor. And by February 1990, Mikhail Gorbachev himself was grudgingly conceding the reality that the Soviet Union was, de facto, no longer a one-party state.

Even the Supreme Soviet, the USSR's conservative-dominated, if unpredictable legislature, rejected as "insufficiently radical" the government's draft legislation on economic autonomy for the national republics—legislation that had been patterned on the decisions of the Party plenum.

In the face of such radical rethinking on the part of the republics, why did Gorbachev support such a fainthearted program for the nationalities?

Gorbachev is attempting to maintain an exceedingly complex balancing act. His economic reforms already are creating a good deal of social turmoil, and promise even more. A sign of leniency on a question that most Party leaders see as potentially incendiary would further worry conservatives and could result in renewed efforts by those hard-liners to oppose or depose Gorbachev. And it was those very conservatives, led by former KGB chief Viktor Chebrikov (purged at the plenum), who had drafted the basic document on nationalities.

Still, by all accounts, Gorbachev has maintained his political balance, using every instance of instability to consolidate or extend his personal

power. In this rapid concentration of power, he has transformed the
Soviet parliament, the Soviet government, the Central Committee and
Politburo of the Communist Party. He even has placed himself in the
position of head of the newly constituted Russian Buro of the Party's
Central Committee.

Now, despite his immense base of support within the upper rungs of
the Party and state elite, Gorbachev risks alienating the leading forces for
change in Soviet society. He is in danger of making enemies of many of
the USSR's best and brightest, who have for the first time become active
in Soviet political life through the tens of thousands of independent groups
that have sprung up to advance the cause of the formerly atomized non-
Russian nations.

Other Voices

One aspect of the Gorbachev line on ethnic issues has been clearly
defined. In the weeks and months before the Communist Party's position
paper on nationalities was issued, the Soviet press and more significantly
Soviet television were filled with propaganda against the national movements.

We viewed a number of these programs during our visits to the
USSR. One such program—a documentary about a festival honoring the
Russian writer Mikhail Sholokhov—emphasized the commonality of
Ukrainian and Russian culture in the Don region. The subtext of the
documentary was that these two cultures were part of an inseparable
continuum, and their peoples had been fused together through common
labor and common struggle in war and revolution. The documentary
clearly was aiming for a significance beyond the depiction of folk life in
this colorful region.

Another program featured the leading dance and folk ensembles of
each of the fifteen national republics. The narrative, again, emphasized
the purity of folk cultures and the links between the working people of
these diverse nations, whose lives and values were reflected in the dances
and songs.

But we also saw the "dark side" of national relations: a highly tenden-
tious television news documentary that served as a transparent diatribe
against the Moldavian Popular Front. Aired in July of 1989, the half-hour
report demonstrated how "unworkable" the idea of forcing the inhabitants
of Moldavia to speak Moldavian in their workplaces would be. It included
a denunciation of the alleged irredentism that lurks beneath the surface of
the Popular Front's demands.

The program included interviews with thickset Communist Party officials, interspersed with comments by Russian workers and scenes of

mass demonstrations by the Moldavian Popular Front. If the effect was to scare Russians about the upsurge in national assertiveness, then the program succeeded admirably. The only voices that are given short shrift in the documentary were those of the leaders of the Moldavian Popular Front, an organization that now has hundreds of thousands of supporters. They were relegated to a minute-long interview with one of their local supporters.

In the past, such programs, which have been paralleled by equally crude attacks on "fascist" Ukrainian and Baltic nationalists and Muslim "extremists," would have been the first signal of a new wave of police repression. These days, media attacks thankfully are ends in themselves, part of the glasnost era's battle of ideas, in which one side has near total control of the state's monopolistic mass media.

Yet, the propagandistic diatribes that are part of the Gorbachev approach to the nationalities are increasingly being challenged by the democratic wing of the Russian community, which is speaking out for a new constitutional arrangement. In an interview that appeared in the fall of 1989 in the popular proreform weekly *Ogonyok*, Dr. Andrei Sakharov expounded on his views of ethnic and national relations in the USSR, coming out for a confederal system:

> I support confederation. The republics—union and autonomous, the autonomous oblasts, and the national territories, all should be given equal rights within today's territorial boundaries. All of them should receive the maximum degree of independence. Their sovereignty should be minimally limited to questions of mutual defense and foreign policy, transport, communication . . . perhaps, one or two other points. The main point: in everything else they should be totally independent and on such a basis should enter into relations within an all-Union agreement.

In what was one of the Soviet human rights advocate's last major public pronouncements before his death, Dr. Sakharov urged that the USSR enter a period of the *"démontage* of the structure of empire." He suggested that the establishment of full rights of self-determination for the USSR's various republics and other territories would resolve the ethnic conflicts in such regions as Nagorno-Karabakh. "Nagorno-Karabakh," Dr. Sakharov suggested, "would not belong either to Armenia or to Azerbaijan—it would in and of itself have the right to enter into economic arrangements with whatever other parties it chooses."

Though today such a solution might strike some as utopian and unacceptable to the Kremlin, many of the views advanced by Dr. Sakharov— when his was a distinguished but lonely dissident voice—are now part of the reforms sweeping the Soviet Union. Sakharov's prescriptions may, in a few years' time, seem exceedingly mild.

Dr. Sakharov clearly did not fear that the growing strength of the national rights movements threatened to plunge the USSR into anarchy. He worked closely with those very movements and came to appreciate their commitment to democracy and peaceful change. Indeed, he proposed a formula by which the demands of the movements could be constructively absorbed into a state structure that would resemble those of such multinational polities as Switzerland and Belgium.

The question of how to respond to the growth of ethnic assertiveness in the Soviet Union is certain to be a central issue in United States and Western foreign policy in the 1990s. The reemergence of the hidden nations of Asia and Europe poses profound challenges and opportunities. Already some voices within the United States and other Western foreign policy establishments have argued that the emergence of nationalism in the Baltic States, Armenia, Georgia, and Azerbaijan, and the signs of its revival in the Ukraine, are dangerous to the future of glasnost, perestroika, and democratization.

These theorists have not taken into account the kinetic power of reform that already is surging through the USSR. The reforms that already are in motion cannot be pushed aside or ignored. Glasnost, perestroika, and democratization cannot be separated from national ferment.

It is illusory to expect that perhaps the most deeply felt political emotion—nationalism—can be suppressed in the context of political relaxation. Glasnost and democratization are only possible with the reemergence of the nationalisms of the hidden nations. The reemergence of those nationalisms is proof that glasnost and democratization are genuine. Perestroika and Soviet economic development, too, will not occur unaccompanied by the revival and satisfaction of limited national aspirations on the part of the non-Russian nations and the Russians themselves. Rather than undermining the process of democratization, by calling for the decentralization of economic and political power, the emerging non-Russian nations are pressing for the attainment of those very goals. Nor can the USSR move in the direction of a multiparty democracy if citizens are denied the right to organize around perceived interests, whether local, ethnic, or transnational.

It is very clearly in Western interests that the process of far-reaching reform in the USSR be peaceful. However, any veering away from reform at this juncture is likely to lead to dangerous instabilities. The years of political relaxation have created a climate of rising expectations that must now be fulfilled.

There is, as well, a strategic dimension to the rise of nationalisms in the USSR. For the process of national rebirth has military implications that are beneficial for the Western democracies. The growth of separatist tendencies within the Soviet empire is already calling into question the loyalty of the non-Russian recruits in the Red Army. The Red Army is, in its internal life and culture, a quintessential Great Russian institution. Its language of operation is Russian. Its general staff and officer corps are almost exclusively composed of Russians and Russified Slavs. Although it is Soviet practice to forbid the formation of ethnically based units, the representation of Russians is particularly pronounced in the high-technology-oriented services—the Soviet Navy and Air Force.

For the non-Russians, the Soviet military and the military units of the Ministry of Internal Affairs are increasingly viewed as an alien force. This view has its origins deep in history. For the Ukraine, Armenia, Azerbaijan, Georgia, Soviet Central Asia, and the Baltic States all were conquered by the predominantly Russian Red Army. As in Eastern Europe, it was the Red Army and not authentic indigenous revolutions that brought Communists to power in the non-Russian republics.

There is, today, a growing campaign of draft resistance that has involved thousands of Latvians, Estonians, and Lithuanians and over fifteen hundred Georgians. Draft evasion, too, is said to be on the rise in the Ukraine. In the Baltic States, Moldavia, Georgia, and Azerbaijan, demonstrations against the induction of non-Russians for military service outside their republics have been on the rise.

Well before the introduction of martial law in Baku, Azerbaijani activists reported that in late 1989, as a result of protests that began in October, not one of their youth had been sent out of the republic for military service. Reuters reported that in the fall of 1989 the head of the republic's military draft had called for the establishment of Azerbaijani national divisions. And, according to the newspaper of the Ministry of Defense, *Krasnaya Zvezda*, 20 percent of Latvians are now serving in the Baltic region. This clear reversal of the long-standing military practice of "extraterritoriality" is a clear concession to growing ethnic opposition to military service.

There is also significant evidence that nationalist sentiments are affecting an increasing number of recruits, many of whom have been active participants in the massive patriotic demonstrations and general strikes of the last few years. Their politicization has created growing conflicts with ethnic Russian recruits. Such conflicts have led to the mistreatment, and even murder, of non-Russian soldiers from Latvia, Estonia, Lithuania, Georgia, Azerbaijan, and Soviet Central Asia.

As far as the Red Army is concerned, there are two severe consequences of this growing non-Russian nationalism. On the one hand, questions of loyalty are likely to act as a strong constraint against any revival of Soviet military expansionism. On the other hand, the growing unreliability of Soviet recruits can act as a constraint against the widespread use of military force against the increasingly assertive national movements. Certainly, at the very least, rising ethnic assertiveness injects an element of uncertainty into the calculus of Soviet military power and its application at home and abroad.

If Russian chauvinism, with its profoundly antidemocratic and anti-Western subtexts, becomes the last refuge of Soviet imperialists, then international peace is likely to be threatened. Consequently, it is in the best interest of the West to engage in cultural and political dialogue with Soviet citizens and to launch initiatives that strengthen democratically oriented, anti-imperial Russian nationalist groupings and movements.

Clearly, the Western democracies will be unable to stage-manage or wish away the rise of nationalism in the USSR. But the West can use its limited leverage in influencing the natural course of events in the USSR if it elects to offer consistent moral and material support to those indigenous movements in the USSR that favor democracy and reject chauvinism.

Western actions and policies with regard to the Soviet Union, of course, will develop within the context of ethnic influences on the foreign policies of the democracies. The presence in the United States of Jews, Lithuanians, Armenians, Ukrainians, and Russians also is certain to be a factor shaping relations with the USSR.

The right to national self-determination and to the defense of indigenous cultures is enshrined in the democratic traditions of the United States and other Western democracies, and in the international covenants that the West is committed to upholding. The noble Wilsonian tradition of support for the rights of oppressed nations is a far more compelling and honest principle than the opportunistic Leninist doctrines of support for revolutionary national liberation struggles.

From today's vantage point, it appears that in the long term, national assertiveness in the USSR can only lead to one of three resolutions. The course of events could lead to the return of severe political repression, to the end of perestroika and glasnost, and to their replacement by the Brezhnev-style politics of neo-Stalinism. Such a scenario would very likely be fueled by an increasingly xenophobic Russian chauvinism. A second possible scenario would involve the complete collapse of the USSR into many independent nation-states, the largest and most powerful of them, Russia itself. The third scenario envisions the emergence of a genuine confederation or commonwealth, built on real autonomy of national republics, including a flowering of the native cultures and economic diversification—a low-budget Eurasian version of the European Community.

Of these variants, those that result in outright independence or independence within a highly decentralized confederation are consonant with Western values and principles. The variant that foresees outright independence and separate statehood for the USSR's many potential nation-states is least likely to be attained by peaceful means, if only because the

Soviet authorities would block any attempts at secession that would be accompanied by the creation of independent standing armies. The confederal variant, by contrast, embraces the national interests of the non-Russian and Russian peoples, without risking extreme political strife, turmoil, and civil war. Indeed, even if confederation or commonwealth proved in the long term to be an unworkable formula, it could be accepted by many nationalist activists as an important transitional phase on the road to full sovereignty.

A New Europe

As Eastern Europe continues to move further and further from Soviet domination and creates the economic and political preconditions for a European integration based on democracy, the Soviet empire and the Russians, in particular, ought to be compelled to make a fateful choice. Soviet leaders must decide whether to join in this integration or to stand on the sidelines and risk being swept aside as a perennially backward economic entity.

The Western democracies must be resolute in making Russia's choice clear. As the British journalist and historian Paul Johnson has suggested in a provocative essay in the London weekly *Spectator* (November 11, 1989):

> If Europe is an entity "from the Atlantic to the Urals," then the Russians belong there. But this acceptance must be qualified in two vital ways. First, if Russia is to become again a part of Europe, in an institutional sense, it must renounce its global aspirations. It cannot be both part of the European Community and a world superpower, deploying its armies in the heart of Asia and the Far East. . . . It must choose, and if it opts for Europe it must decolonize. Moreover, it must decolonize not merely in Asia—from Vladivostok to the Caucasus. It must also decolonize in Europe. Not merely the former satellites, but the Baltic peoples, possibly the Ukrainians and the White Russians too, the Georgians, Cossacks [the author here is probably referring to the Kazakhs] and the Armenians, and others must be given choices and, if they opt for independence, sovereignty.

Until 1989, and the explosion of peaceful democratic ferment in the USSR and in the Soviet bloc, such proposals were confined to the realm of fantasy. Today, they can very well be regarded as part of an emerging prodemocratic realpolitik that recognizes that real stability cannot be achieved unless the world's last empire is peacably dismantled.

Certainly, American and other Western policymakers must be sensitive to Soviet fears that the West might exploit the sensitive and combustible issue of national ferment. But as the late Dr. Andrei Sakharov and, more recently, President Carter's national security adviser Zbigniew Brzezinski have argued, confederation is a constructive, nonconfrontational approach to helping the Soviet empire evolve out of its ethnic dilemma.

Throughout 1989 and 1990, the Soviet press was filled with discussions of the need to renegotiate the terms of the Soviet "federation." Such a "renegotiation" was touted as a useful way of strengthening the "union" of republics. Yet, such a discussion need not be confined to a pro forma exercise in internal and external public relations. It could be given real substance and impetus by the idea of confederation.

In contrast to the Communist Party's formulations on the "union" (made at the Party plenum on nationalities in September 1989), the idea of confederation could be counterposed as a form of authentic self-determination for increasingly assertive non-Russian nations. Such confederation would, however, gain authentic support if it was based on the principles of democratic elections, a free press, and the devolution of power to each of the USSR's constituent republics. The prerogatives of the central government could be determined by a new treaty ratified by the USSR's constituent republics and limited to defense (or coordination of defense), the formulation of foreign policy in the area of strategic alliances, and, perhaps, the codification of a unitary system of communications and transportation. Under such a formula, everything else, including laws on the press and freedom of association, cultural and language policies, internal security and economic rights and forms of ownership, would all be local, or rather national, prerogatives.

In such a system, commerce among the republics could be regulated by the exigencies of the marketplace. Prices would be set by world rates, and the diversification of the economies of the various republics would be based on an interplay of market demand and the long-term economic policy of democratically accountable governments.

Such a policy would include the right of republics to regulate the standards of immigration, citizenship, and voting rights, and would place responsibility for the protection of indigenous languages and cultures in the hands of each republic. These unprecedented liberties would contribute to the development of a healthy diversity in a formerly monolithic society. It also would satisfy most of the concrete grievances of the non-Russian nations and their national movements and relieve much pent-up nationalist pressure.

A voluntary confederation or commonwealth could bring the formerly hidden nations of the USSR into a state of cooperation similar to that which will emerge in the European Community in 1992. Indeed, the European march toward economic integration is simultaneously a source of anxiety for the Soviet authorities and an attractive model of how for-

merly hostile and historically antagonistic nation-states can shape a constructive and mutually advantageous relationship.

There are many reasons why the idea of a confederation might begin to
look attractive to Soviet leaders. In Western Europe, the cultural and
economic independence of nation-states has led to an unprecedented,
voluntary movement toward cooperation, integration, and amalgamation
in 1992. The tranquility of relations among Western European states,
coupled with their economic successes, must be viewed as an increasingly
attractive model of ethnic and national relations by the embattled leaders
of the Soviet Union, much of whose energy these days is sapped by the
constant need to cope with new outbreaks of nationalist protest and unrest.

The idea of confederation has been made more realistic by the amazing
confluence of events in Central and Eastern Europe. The democratic
revolution that has swept Poland, Hungary, East Germany, and Czechoslovakia, and the unprecedented Soviet tolerance of the evolution of
those countries away from the Soviet orbit, have bolstered the confidence
of national rights advocates in the USSR. Such Soviet conduct is evidence
that the current leadership is prepared to sacrifice a good deal of control
if it can help relieve popular anger and mounting discontent.

The Soviet tolerance shown to the Eastern bloc countries is a tacit
admission of the failure of the Communist command system. The rising
tide of national ferment is now eroding the links that have held together
the Soviet Union. And confederation is a sensible and necessary step away
from the disintegrating empire.

The West has a role to play in propelling just such a step. It should be
prepared to reward Soviet moves toward confederation and a consensual,
rule-of-law polity based on cultural and political pluralism. But even as
the West seeks to engage Soviet leaders in a dialogue with its increasingly
restive nations, there must also be a wide-ranging dialogue and engagement with the emerging democratic movements among the USSR's many
peoples. That dialogue should include the opening of many more Western
consulates in the non-Russian republics; first, in the Ukraine and
Byelorussia, which already are represented in the United Nations.

Any Soviet hesitancy in moving toward confederation should be overcome by Western incentives. It should become the declared policy of the
United States and other Western democracies to assist in initiatives that
promote the economic and cultural diversification and decentralization of
the Soviet Union. To that end, Western assistance that is offered to the
USSR to help it emerge from its economic crisis should have the explicit
aim of empowering the non-Russian peoples.

Western responsibility should extend to the promotion of the free flow
of information to all the peoples of the Soviet Union. A greater interest

should be shown in the cultures and traditions of the USSR's hidden nations. The works of Ukrainian, Armenian, Lithuanian, Georgian, Kazakh, and other non-Russian writers and artists are little known and deserve access to a broader Western public.

Western radio stations should follow the example of Radio Liberty, the Voice of America, and Radio Vatican and establish services that broadcast in the native languages of the non-Russian peoples. For example, although the highly regarded programs of the USSR Service of the British Broadcasting Corporation play a vital role in disseminating information, because they are provided only in Russian they are equally an unwitting instrument in the Russification of the non-Russian peoples. Even Radio Liberty's non-Russian services are woefully understaffed. The Ukrainian Service, for example, which serves a potential audience of nearly forty-five million, has a professional staff smaller than that of Radio Free Europe's Bulgarian Service, which reaches a potential audience of about ten million Bulgarians.

For the moment, Western radio broadcasts have an important role to play in publicizing the positions of the wide range of national rights movements that have emerged in the USSR. Those organizations, while no longer subjected to police state repression, are still denied access to the USSR's mass media and in most cases for the moment do not have the right to print their own publications. Their views should be made known by the Western radio services.

Outreach efforts by the Western radio services also should embrace democratic *Russian* groups and movements. The battle over the hearts and minds of Russians will be decisive to the prospects for democracy in the Soviet future. The weak indigenous democratic traditions of Russia, coupled with the demonstrated strength of fascist and chauvinist sentiments, suggest that democratic Russian patriotism is a much needed tendency. The promotion of an authentic Russian nationalism, one that seeks the creation of an ethnically Russian nation-state, would contribute mightily to the peaceful dismantling of the last empire.

The emergence of independent political and cultural life should be regarded as the underpinning of other internal democratic reforms. The prospect of stability and democracy in today's USSR is integrally linked to the emergence of a civil society and not merely to reform at the highest levels. Such a civil society has never before existed as a fully developed entity, either in the USSR or in its precursor, the czarist state. It did, however, exist in Georgia, Armenia, and the Ukraine, where distinct cultures were initially protected from total control by their insularity and by the imperfection of, first, the czars' and, later, the commissars' centralist ambitions. Civil society, moreover, was extinguished far later in Western Ukraine and the Baltic States, which were absorbed by the USSR during the Second World War. It is no accident that these areas on the empire's periphery are today in the forefront of the struggle for democratic change.

Nonetheless, despite these important traditions, Soviet citizens are embarked upon the building of a new, democratic society from the roof down. The first contours of a civil society are emerging. And they are emerging precisely as a consequence of the forces of patriotism and nationalism, which already have surfaced in Eastern Europe.

In Poland, during the 1980s, deep anti-Russian, anti-imperial, and nationalist sentiments combined seamlessly with pluralistically oriented social movements to rebuild civil society. The reemergence of Poland's civil society required painstaking effort, a commitment to long-standing struggle and sacrifice. It probably could not have been realized without moral and material support from outside to the democratic groups that functioned in the Solidarity-led underground. Nor could it have succeeded without the impetus of a mounting economic crisis that removed the last pillar of Communist legitimacy. The government could no longer deliver adequate food, provide shelter, ensure job security, and improve living standards.

In most parts of the USSR, the Communist Party has controlled all institutions and all social initiatives for nearly three quarters of a century. The Party-state apparatus still does not confer legal status on most independent groups, even the most politically innocuous. More significant, the Party prevented independent organization by creating totalitarian institutions like the state-controlled trade unions, cultural associations, Communist Youth Leagues, and other entities that served not only to exert social control but to ensure that rival groups would not emerge. Totalitarianism, therefore, differed from its authoritarian counterpart in not merely repressing or intimidating any potential adversaries, but in denying them the very right to exist.

Until 1986, no independent organizations could function openly. Democratic activists were subjected to severe repression. Today, according to the Soviet press, there are tens of thousands of informal associations. While many of them are purely apolitical and some are even frivolous, a large number, particularly in the non-Russian republics, are the rudimentary institutions that are helping to break the monopoly of the state in daily life. As part of this blossoming of independent civil society, there has emerged a broad range of interest groups: ecological associations, independent trade unions, cultural organizations, political parties, and an ever growing community of samizdat periodicals.

Although they share many common aspirations for national self-determination, autonomy, and independence, these groups also reflect competing interests, above all because they are democratically accountable to their memberships. The interests and agendas of new ecological groups are, in the end, likely to meet with opposition from workers whose economic interests may be threatened if an environmentally hazardous factory is shut down. Religious movements may, in the end, clash with the libertarian values of independent cultural groups seeking to expand the horizons of artistic freedom. Yet, it is precisely from this contradictory interplay that independent societies arise.

The Road to Decolonization

If the current Western enthusiasms for Gorbachev stem from the Soviet leader's liberalizing reforms and commitment to democratization, then the principal mass movements that support these processes also should be encouraged.

One important source of support can be offered by Western nongovernmental organizations. With the loosening of controls and the flowering of independent life, now is precisely the best time for true people-to-people, institution-to-institution contacts, cooperation, and even material assistance.

Exchanges should be matched with training initiatives, and even open material assistance. Authentically independent groups are craving the knowhow and are eager to learn about the way institutions function in a democracy. Those groups, moreover, need a broad exposure to the technical experience of their Western counterparts. Western trade unions must reach out to the nascent trade union movements like the Lithuanian Workers Union, the independent coal miners strike committees in the Donbass and Kazakhstan, and to new Solidaritylike trade unions from Western Ukraine and Byelorussia. Western ecological groups can share their expertise with Soviet environmentalists from the Ukraine's "Green World" Society, from the ecological movement in Armenia, and from the antinuclear "Nevada" Movement in Kazakhstan. Political parties should reach out to the vast array of Christian Democratic, liberal, social democratic, and conservative political groups that are well developed in the Baltic States. Similar assistance should be extended to the political parties that are emerging now in other Soviet republics as a result of the Communist Party's abandonment of its monopolistic control of political life. Assistance also could be provided to the emerging independent non-Russian press and to the increasingly independent radio and television broadcasting that is appearing, first of all, in the Baltic republics. As democratic coalitions take power in various republics, regions, and cities, they discover that few newspapers belong to the state. Rather, such mass media are the private preserve and the property of the Communist Party. The need to create independent media is now one of the highest priorities of these movements. Thus, assistance can be patterned on the successful support provided by Western nongovernmental institutions to the democratic movements in Poland, Czechoslovakia, and Hungary, which have taken over the reins of government in their renewed democracies.

In this context, Western governments should make clear that the suppression of the new democratic entities that have emerged throughout the USSR would set back East-West relations and preclude broad economic cooperation. Such a clear statement of policy, coupled with the promise of a new economic relationship linked to further democratization, could have an immense impact on Soviet behavior.

The nurturing of rudimentary civil society throughout the USSR will ensure that the movement of the USSR away from its imperial structures can proceed peaceably, through negotiation among democratic groups and representative institutions. Such democratic groups, if strong and well-established, can help create a climate of stability and civility and protect the rights of ethnic minorities in what are likely to be turbulent and tumultuous transitions to a postcolonial order.

Just as there is a vital role to be played by the West in assisting nascent civil society as it emerges in the USSR's fifteen republics, so, too, can democratic groups in Hungary, Poland, and Czechoslovakia aid the transition to democracy in the USSR. Activists from Solidarity already have begun to reach out to their Ukrainian, Lithuanian, and other non-Russian neighbors. Their path of resilient, peaceful struggle for democratic change in their own societies is a model for how the peaceful decolonization of the USSR can be achieved. The millions of spiritually wounded non-Russians, as well as Russians themselves, can learn much from the experience of Poland's Solidarity, Hungary's Alliance of Free Democrats and Democratic Forum, the Czech Civic Forum, Slovakia's Public Against Violence, and nascent free trade unions and strike committees that have emerged throughout Eastern Europe.

The first priority must be to provide help to those organizations building cooperation and dialogue among the various national groups. As Zbigniew Brzezinski has noted in an influential essay on "Post-Communist Nationalism," published in the Winter 1990 issue of *Foreign Affairs*, Communist rule eliminated some of the forces in society most associated with an international outlook, in particular the business class. The restoration of forces that have an ecumenical and transnational democratic outlook is essential to the creation of cooperation among what are certain to be increasingly independent national republics.

A trend of intergroup cooperation already is emerging. At the founding congress of the Ukrainian Popular Movement—the Rukh—there were delegates representing the republic's Jewish and Russian communities. And there were fraternal delegates from Baltic, Armenian, and Azerbaijani popular fronts. Cooperation among democratic national rights advo-

cates is particularly advanced in the Soviet parliament, where the locus of
activity has been the Interregional Group of Deputies, the liberal faction
created by Dr. Andrei Sakharov. Other trends in group cooperation include the emergence of a Baltic Council that coordinates activities among
Latvia, Lithuania, and Estonia in their march toward independence; a
Union of Democratic Forces that acts as a coordination group for popular
fronts and other democratic organizations of Russians and non-Russians;
and efforts at dialogue and negotiation among Armenian and Azerbaijani
nationalist leaders.

If Western commercial interests are to play a constructive role in
Soviet society, they also must be well aware of the strong sensitivities of
the non-Russian peoples about their embattled native languages, reli-
gions, and traditions. Under no circumstances should Western investments in the non-Russian areas be used to perpetuate the institutions of
the central state apparat or be used to strengthen the hand of Russification.

Western economic investment can promote democratic change if, in
the development of joint ventures, emphasis is given to the devolution of
power to the constituent republics. Such joint ventures could help to
diversify the economies of the non-Russian republics, which are remarkably one-dimensional as a result of the Soviet imperial economic system.
For example, Azerbaijan produces *all* of the USSR's air conditioners, and
most of its oil refining equipment. On the one hand, that makes the
republic dependent on pricing decisions taken in Moscow. On the other,
it makes the entire Soviet oil industry and Soviet consumers and office
workers seeking relief from oppressively hot summers subject to Azerbaijani producers and workers. Such an extreme division of labor in the
end needlessly exposes many of the national republics to the vagaries of
Soviet and international demand. If, for example, cotton were to suffer a
precipitous drop in demand, it would have disastrous consequences for
the economy of the Soviet Central Asian republics.

In the years ahead, the Soviet republics will have to make a transition
to the market. The market, according to Prime Minister Nikolai Ryzhkov,
may, as a result of economic reforms, account for as much as 70 percent
of Soviet output. But because of the imbalances that have arisen as a
result of centralized planning, there will also have to be some reparations
and adjustments to compensate for past inequities. A free fall to the
market could have wrenching and potentially destabilizing consequences
for these national movements. Therefore, while the West should continue
to pressure the Soviets to create free markets, its enthusiasm for such
economic reform should not permit this process to move forward without
taking into account the need to right current regional economic imbalances.

In the end, most of the non-Russian national movements, given a fair pricing mechanism linked to world prices and adjustments for unjust capital outlays, are in favor of economic autonomy based on market mechanisms. Such autonomy would do away with the widespread suspicions, particularly in the Soviet Central Asian republics and the Ukraine, that their own economies are being drained and their people exploited for the sake of the Russian majority.

Restructuring the Soviet empire will be a difficult and ambitious project. Its success must be made a high priority by all who support the cause of democracy and peace. Yet, these days, predictions of the Soviet Union's future are either too cautious or too pessimistic. Those who are cautious overstate the improbability or impossibility of reform. They argue that the USSR can tolerate democracy and sovereignty among newly "Finlandized" states on its periphery, but cannot survive a similar process within its own borders. Efforts aimed at sovereignty after the Eastern European pattern are thought to be quixotic dreams that will inevitably be stifled, perhaps without the resort to widespread repression. For such cautious voices, the popular fronts emerging within the non-Russian republics will, in the end, back away from the goal of seceding from the last empire and replacing it with independent nation-states.

The pessimists see the Soviet future as one of accelerating economic collapse occurring in the context of increasing, sometimes violent ethnic unrest. For them the ethnic violence that has erupted in Armenia, Azerbaijan, Uzbekistan, and Kazakhstan is a portent of revolutionary violence. In the end, pessimists insist, ethnic unrest will lead to an orgy of state repression ushered in by a tyrannical, probably Russian nationalist, and, possibly, military dictatorship. Or even, some doomsayers more ominously argue, the USSR will collapse into a group of extremely unstable, warlike, nationalistic states.

In one important way, the views of those who see little prospect for significant change intersect with the views of the pessimists. Proponents of both viewpoints conclude that the West has no role to play in the unfolding events other than as a passive spectator. In the first argument, intercession or participation is unnecessary as the Soviet leadership will never renounce its internal empire. In the latter, Western intercession is ill-considered as the process inevitably will end with a reversion to prior patterns of Soviet conduct or with extreme instability.

And while in politics, and certainly in Soviet politics, little can be completely excluded, the emergence onto the Soviet political scene of the once hidden nations makes these two scenarios less and less likely. On the one hand, the rapid emergence of mass movements deeply rooted within the intelligentsia and among workers creates a powerful lobby for the fundamental devolution of power to the republics. On the other hand, the ability of the non-Russians to build the rudiments of an independent civil society and to unite their society's most creative and talented forces makes it unlikely that they will be the victims of a wide-ranging crackdown. After all, Mikhail Gorbachev and others committed to economic growth and technological progress are not likely to attack the principal forces capable of ensuring such growth and progress. In instance after instance, Gorbachev has threatened, warned, and condemned moves toward independence by the non-Russians. Yet, in the end, he has acquiesced to the rising demands of the non-Russians. He has accepted the secession of the Lithuanian Communist Party from the CPSU, has given the green light to a more radical devolution of economic power to the republics, has agreed to the registration of rival political parties, and has a mechanism, albeit flawed, for the orderly secession of republics from the union.

In the foreseeable future, therefore, the struggle of the once hidden nations for national self-determination, autonomy, and independence will unfold along a peaceful, evolutionary pattern. Such a process, moreover, is likely to strengthen international stability, inasmuch as it represents the mechanism for realigning an inherently unjust imperial order and supplanting it with a democratic and forward-looking confederation of sovereign nation-states. Whatever other blights it has brought upon the Soviet people, the Soviet system has not been able to stifle fully the growth of a nationally conscious indigenous intelligentsia among the non-Russians and has been unable to stem the entry of the non-Russian workers onto the political stage. Historians reexamining the post-Stalin era will no doubt conclude that it was these two factors that created the preconditions for the mass-based movement for national sovereignty, pluralism, and democracy that is changing the face of the USSR.

The reemergence of the non-Russian peoples onto the political map is likely to continue along a well-established path. That path begins with the mobilization of the indigenous literary and cultural intelligentsia. These writers, artists, and filmmakers press for a revival of the national past, for the restitution of the classics of the national literary tradition, for a reevaluation of past periods of national independence, and for legislation that would make the indigenous national language the republic's language of government, education, and commerce. The next stage in this path includes calls for the social, economic, and political autonomy of the republic. Those calls are raised by broader segments of the intelligentsia, oftentimes supported by radicalized workers and liberals within the Communist Party, all of whom take part in a popular front. With the emergence of such popular front movements, a mass base is created. Such popular fronts frequently enter into local electoral politics and proceed along a course of escalating demands that initially are articulated by a narrower group of dissident democratic activists. In time, such demands include the revival of national symbols of state independence (flags and

crests) and culminate in calls for outright independence. The impetus
toward independence is diverse. In the case of Lithuania, Latvia, and
Estonia it has been encouraged by the atmospherics of electoral politics,
a relaxation of censorship in the mass media, and the perception that the
local Communist Party and the authorities in Moscow are not prepared to
resort to repression and force. In other republics, as in the case of Georgia, Armenia, and Azerbaijan, support for independence is given impetus
in a climate of ethnic violence. In these settings, the introduction of
martial law or other acts of repression by the central authorities is deeply
resented and leads to calls for outright secession. With the emergence of
local nationalisms, the non-Russian movements are beginning to show
signs of coordination and cooperation. That cooperation is most pronounced in the Baltic States. But there also are trends toward contact and
dialogue among the popular fronts of Byelorussia and the Ukraine, signs
of growing Pan-Turkic cooperation in Soviet Central Asia, and even halt-
ing efforts at dialogue between the Azerbaijani and Armenian national
movements.

Almost all the non-Russian national movements are to be found somewhere along this continuum (see chart on page 268). Indeed, as one or
another non-Russian republic moves further along this continuum, it becomes an example, if not a model, for the actions of the other non-Russian
movements.

Mikhail Gorbachev has as yet not found any formula for reversing this
process of national mobilization and deepening radicalization. Indeed, his
ethnic policies have been reactive: The Kremlin has been responding to
events and not initiating them. Yet, in other spheres of Soviet political
and economic life, Gorbachev has demonstrated a willingness to make
bold and unexpected moves. In the years ahead, it is still possible he will
respond with similar boldness to the mounting calls for independence
among the non-Russians.

For the short term, however, Gorbachev appears to have drawn a clear
line on the question of independence for the Soviet republics. He is
prepared to fight it primarily by political and economic means.

On April 3, 1990, the Supreme Soviet passed by a virtually unanimous
vote a law on the procedures for resolving the question of a USSR republic's secession from the Soviet Union. The law created a series of
cumbersome and onerous steps that create delays on the path to secession
for any independence-minded republic. The main features of the law—
the USSR's first to spell out the process of separation from the "union"—
include a mandatory referendum requiring an affirmative vote by no less
than two thirds of the vote by a republic's permanent residents; in the
event of such an affirmative vote, a transitional period of up to five years,
during which property, financial, and credit relations are to be settled;
during this five-year "waiting" period, the option of a second referendum

if requested by one tenth of the republic's permanent residents; in such a second referendum, a necessary second two thirds majority to confirm secession. When all these steps were completed, the USSR Congress of People's Deputies would still have the right, as TASS has reported, to "confirm the process to reach agreement on the interests and to satisfy the claims of . . . the seceding republic . . . the USSR and union republics . . . and ethnic groups."

In passing this law, Gorbachev was making it clear that the move toward independence would not be smooth or swift. But it was equally clear that the Soviet president was seeking an orderly, if exceedingly difficult, peaceful procedure for resolving one of the USSR's most divisive and critical issues.

Yet for most independence-minded non-Russians the Supreme Soviet's action was greeted with cynicism. In their view, the decision taken was the action of an illegitimate, "rump parliament." For one thing, the sitting USSR Supreme Soviet had been elected in early 1989 at a time when a third of all seats were apportioned not by universal adult franchise, but by Communist Party-controlled "public organizations." For another, many opposition candidates who had been nominated by legitimate public meetings had their nominations overturned by the action of Communist apparatchiks. Thus, unlike the more freely contested elections for the legislatures of the USSR's republics in 1990, the March 1989 elections to the USSR's legislature were tainted and illegitimate.

The procedure for the adoption of so fundamental a law as that on secession was characterized by extreme speed of action and lack of national debate. The law was quietly drafted and passed within a matter of a few weeks. Although new legislatures already had been elected in most of the USSR's republics by the end of March 1990, these were not given the opportunity to comment on and to debate a law that would have immense implications for the sovereignty of their republics.

Thus, the action of the Supreme Soviet quickly came to be resented by proindependence forces throughout the USSR as in violation of democracy. Significantly, to underscore this illegitimacy and to highlight their claim of involuntary incorporation into the Soviet Union in 1939, the deputies to the Supreme Soviet from the Baltic republics refrained from voting in the legislature.

In the end, Gorbachev's secession law is likely to heighten public indignation and not to dampen or put off secessionist sentiments as the Kremlin might have hoped. In fact, its imminent enactment helped precipitate the Lithuanian parliament's declaration of independence and contributed to the Estonian legislature's announcement that it was beginning a process that would lead to full independence.

In seeking a way to postpone or make too cumbersome the process of secession, the central Soviet authorities instead poured more oil onto the flames of nationalist discontent—putting secession and national independence at the center of the political discourse and public awareness.

By the spring of 1990, Mikhail Gorbachev, recently returned from a triumphant visit to the United States, was surveying a Soviet Union in which centrifugal forces were going from strength to strength.

In the Ukraine, thousands of ordinary citizens gathered daily in front of their legislature in Kiev to voice support for the nationalists and democrats who now controlled as much as 40 percent of the seats and had won 60 percent of the races in which they had competed. Amid growing disenchantment with the timidity and conservatism of many Communist Party holdovers, Ukrainian insurgents were threatening to launch a wide-ranging campaign for the recall of parliamentarians who refused to press for Ukrainian autonomy.

The appeal of Armenian separatists was growing in the wake of the killing of twenty-six Armenians in an attack by the Soviet military on May 27, 1990. On June 1, leaders of the radical Armenian Pan-national Movement organized a demonstration of hundreds of thousands in Yerevan's Freedom Square. Speakers denounced the army and "the center" for seeking to provoke violence "to find a pretext for . . . declaring a state of emergency . . . with the simple intention of saving the regime."

In Lithuania, in the face of a harsh economic blockade, that republic's internal solidarity and support for independence showed no sign of abating. Indeed, Moscow's economic pressures had driven the Baltic States into closer coordination of their path to independence.

In Kirgizia, ethnic rioting and pitched battles in June 1990 had led to the death of more than one hundred Kirgiz and Uzbeks, to the wounding of another five hundred, and to the torching of hundreds of residences and government and Party buildings. But politics in Kirgizia was not only a case of random ethnic rioting. On May 26, 1990, informal cultural and political groups had gathered in Frunze, the Kirgiz capital, to launch the Kirgizstan Democratic Movement. According to a report in the paper *Sovyetskaya Kirgiziya*, "the association aims to promote the radicalization of political and economic reform in the republic . . ."

In Georgia, where elections were likely to be held in the fall of 1990, nationalists dominated the republic's political life, and the only question was whether those forces favoring participation in the Soviet-imposed electoral process would predominate over those who favored launching an entirely independent electoral process, untainted by association with the Soviet system.

There were also clear signs of renewed coordination among proindependence forces. In May 1990, representatives of the Ukrainian Rukh, the popular fronts of Byelorussia, Latvia, Azerbaijan, and Georgia,

Lithuania's Sajudis, and Uzbekistan's Birlik gathered in Kiev. Russian democratic forces were represented by People's Deputies Yuri Afanasyev and Galina Starovoytova. The groups agreed to create a new umbrella organization called the Union of Democratic Forces and set up an information-consultation committee that will gather once a month to improve coordination.

As part of the growing awareness that none of the republics can go it alone, leaders of the Azerbaijani Popular Front appealed to all democratic groups in the Caucasus to abandon interethnic violence and to cooperate in establishing "a common Caucasian home." Yusuf Sametov, of the front's executive council told the Turkish newspaper *Tercuman*, "Moscow can crush us like flies if we continue to act separately. However, we can withstand Moscow's pressures if we act together."

But perhaps the greatest catalyst in advancing the cause of the reform of the USSR's imperial structures was the remarkable shift in the politics of the Russian Republic, where more than half of the USSR's citizens live. There, in a stunning victory over Mikhail Gorbachev's candidates, Boris Yeltsin was elected Russia's president. Yeltsin immediately used his new position to attack the central USSR government. "The Union government and leadership are currently losing the confidence of the people," Yeltsin proclaimed. He promised that under his rule, Russia would have "its own independent domestic and foreign policy."

Within days of his victory, the Russian Congress of People's Deputies proclaimed on June 8, the "priority of the Constitution of the Russian Federation on the entire territory" of the republic, and it endorsed, by an overwhelming vote of 544 to 271, the principle that laws of the USSR that are in conflict with the sovereign rights of Russia "are suspended by the republic on its territory."

The sentiment for self-determination proved infectious in the Russian Republic's Congress of People's Deputies, where Yeltsin and his faction indicated that they intended to establish "plenipotentiary representation" in the other republics, to claim for the Russian people the exclusive right to dispose of natural resources of the Russian Federation, to recognize the sovereign rights of the republics, and to support the right of Russia "to secede freely from the Soviet Union."

On June 12, at a meeting of the USSR's Federation Council, which brought Gorbachev and the leaders of the USSR's fifteen republics together for discussions, the Soviet President announced that he was interested in taking steps to alleviate the acute pressures tearing at Soviet unity. As reported by the Associated Press, Lithuanian President Vytautas Landsbergis noted that President Gorbachev told the fifteen republic presidents that they should nominate representatives to work out the draft of a new union treaty for the USSR that "would have elements of a federation, a confederation or some pluralistic relationship." At the very least, the Soviet president appeared ready for what he called "the deep revamping of our federation."

Where this new opening will lead is difficult to predict in its details. But Gorbachev's conciliatory stance was a further sign of the growing power of the resurgence of nationalism and ethnic pride throughout the USSR and of the emergence of the hidden nations onto the stage of history.

Postscript

In the weeks since the bulk of this book was set in type, the many simultaneous crises that are tearing at the Soviet Union have intensified.

Most notably, the Soviet Communist Party has begun to splinter amid growing signs that Mikhail Gorbachev is diminishing the Party's power while augmenting that of the office of Soviet President. The 28th Party Congress, concluded in early July, was a grim display of routinized thinking. Commentators and analysts both in the West and in the USSR noted the growing detachment of Party apparatchiks with regard to the day-to-day concerns of Soviet citizens. Even Aleksandr Yakovlev, one of President Gorbachev's closest friends and political colleagues, admitted before young Communist leaders to the low intellectual caliber of the Party leadership. Thus, while Mikhail Gorbachev's political victory over conservative Yegor Ligachev was seen by some as a major setback for conservative forces within the Party, reformists in the USSR saw the 28th Congress as evidence of the Party's irrelevance and began a swift exodus from its ranks. Among the most prominent Party members to quit were Boris Yeltsin, Moscow Mayor Gavriil Popov, Moscow Deputy Mayor Sergei Stankevich, and Leningrad Mayor Aleksander Sobchak. It was an exodus paralleled months before by that of disenchanted Party reformers in the non-Russian republics.

Ironically, just as the central Party was losing its significance, Gorbachev added insult to injury by increasing the presence of non-Russians in the once all-powerful Politburo. As a sop to the non-Russian, Gorbachev approved the creation of a Politburo expanded to twenty-four members and including the first secretaries of pro-Moscow Communist parties in the fifteen Soviet republics. Yet, with the withdrawal from the Politburo of such powerful figures as Foreign Minister Eduard Shevardnadze and Aleksandr Yakovlev, it was clear that power had shifted elsewhere—to the Presidential Council.

By late July 1990, seven Soviet republics—Lithuania (which declared outright independence), Estonia, Latvia, Uzbekistan, Moldavia, the Russian Federation, and the Ukraine—had proclaimed sovereignty and the primacy of their laws over those of the USSR. Many in the Party apparat supported these declarations, a tribute to the mounting strength of anti-Communist and proindependence sentiments. Such anti-Communist sentiments crystallized in a one-day strike on July 11 supported by hundreds of thousands of miners in the Ukraine, Russia, and Kazakhstan. The strike was organized around slogans calling for the expulsion of the Communist Party from the workplace, the surrender of power by the center to local control, the introduction of a market system, and free trade unionism.

One of the most radical declarations of sovereignty was issued by the Ukrainian Parliament, which established the right of the Ukraine to create its own currency, raise its own army, collect tariffs, and erect enforceable borders. The declaration proclaimed that the Ukraine would have its own internal defense forces, answerable only to the Supreme Soviet, and served notice that the Ukrainian citizens would fulfill military service on their own territory. Most significantly, the parliament declared its desire to see the Ukraine as a neutral state which rejects the "production, deployment and use of nuclear weapons."

In Russia, the struggle between a moribund, proimperialist Party apparat and the Russian government and parliament, tenuously in the hands of democratic activists and reformists who support Boris Yeltsin, was beginning to intensify.

In mid-July, Oleg Rumyantsev, a political activist elected in March 1990 to Russia's Congress of People's Deputies, visited the United States. Rumyantsev, a political ally of Boris Yeltsin, has been named by the Russian leader as Secretary of the Constitutional Committee of the Russian Parliament and charged with organizing the work of writing Russia's new Constitution. Rumyantsev predicted that a new Constitution would emphasize specific guarantees for the Russian Federation's state sovereignty and predicted that Russia would seek to work out the terms of a future confederation or, more likely, a commonwealth, through multilateral treaties with other sovereign *and democratically elected* republics.

"There will never again be an election for a new USSR parliament. Nor will we ever see the election of a Soviet President," Rumyantsev predicted. He suggested that Boris Yeltsin and his colleagues "will not allow Gorbachev to rush through a new treaty of the union that negates the independence and sovereignty we have proclaimed." There is no need for a unitary Soviet state, Rumyantsev argued. A commonwealth, served by a secretariat modeled on the European Community could fulfill the necessary role of coordinating a limited range of economic and international policies on behalf of the sovereign states that will emerge out of what is now the Soviet Union.

In the face of growing radicalism among newly elected parliamentarians, it was clear that the struggle of the hidden nations would orient itself increasingly to obtaining power through parliamentary means and peaceful public protest.

Appendix

NATIONAL COMPOSITION OF POPULATION OF SOVIET UNION
1979 AND 1989
(UNION-REPUBLIC NATIONALITIES ONLY)

	1979	1989	PERCENTAGE INCREASE
Total population of whom	262,084,654	285,688,695	9.0
Russians	137,397,089	145,071,550	5.6
Ukrainians	42,347,387	44,135,989	4.2
Uzbeks	12,455,978	16,686,240	34.0
Byelorussians	9,462,715	10,030,441	6.0
Kazakhs	6,556,442	8,137,878	24.1
Azerbaijanis	5,477,330	6,791,106	24.0
Armenians	4,151,241	4,627,227	11.5
Tajiks	2,897,697	4,216,693	45.5
Georgians	3,570,504	3,983,115	11.6
Moldavians	2,968,224	3,355,240	13.0
Lithuanians	2,850,905	3,068,296	7.6
Turkmen	2,027,913	2,718,297	34.0
Kirgiz	1,906,271	2,530,998	32.8
Latvians	1,439,037	1,459,156	1.4
Estonians	1,019,851	1,027,255	0.7

Reprinted with permission from *Radio Liberty Report on the USSR:* October 20, 1989. *Rahva Haal*, 9/19/89

LINGUISTIC AFFILIATION OF NATIONALITIES OF
UNION-REPUBLIC STATUS, 1979 AND 1989

	PERCENTAGE REGARDING LANGUAGE OF NATIONALITY AS NATIVE TONGUE		PERCENTAGE CLAIMING A GOOD KNOWLEDGE OF RUSSIAN AS A SECOND LANGUAGE	
	1979	1989	1979	1989
Russians	99.8	99.8	0.1	0.1
Ukrainians	82.8	81.1	49.8	56.2
Byelorussians	74.2	70.9	57.0	54.7
Uzbeks	98.5	98.3	49.3	23.8
Kazakhs	97.5	97.0	32.3	60.4
Tajiks	97.8	97.7	29.6	27.7
Turkmen	98.7	98.5	25.4	27.8
Kirgiz	97.9	97.8	29.3	35.2
Azerbaijanis	97.8	97.6	29.5	34.4
Armenians	90.7	91.6	38.6	47.1
Georgians	98.3	98.2	26.7	33.1
Lithuanians	97.9	97.7	52.1	37.9
Latvians	95.0	94.8	56.7	64.4
Estonians	95.3	95.5	24.2	33.8
Moldavians	93.2	91.6	47.4	53.8

Reprinted with permission from *Radio Liberty Report on the USSR:*
October 20, 1989. *Rahva Haal*, 9/19/89, and 1979 census results

SHARE OF NATURAL INCREASE AND NET MIGRATION IN TOTAL POPULATION INCREASE IN UNION REPUBLICS, 1979–89

| | POPULATION | | INCREASE | OF WHICH | | | |
| | | | | Natural Increase | | Net Migration | |
	January 17, 1979	January 12, 1989		Absolute	Percentage of Total	Absolute	Percentage of Total
USSR	262,436,000	286,717,000	24,281,000	24,450,000	100.7	− 169,000	−0.7
RSFSR	137,551,000	147,386,000	9,835,000	8,067,000	82.0	+ 1,768,000	+18.0
Ukraine	49,755,000	51,704,000	1,949,000	1,796,000	92.1	+ 153,000	+7.9
Byelorussia	9,560,000	10,200,000	640,000	648,000	100.1	− 8,000	−0.1
Moldavia	3,947,000	4,341,000	394,000	450,000	114.2	− 56,000	−14.2
Lithuania	3,398,000	3,690,000	292,000	193,000	66.1	+ 99,000	+33.9
Latvia	2,521,000	2,681,000	160,000	67,000	41.9	+ 93,000	+58.1
Estonia	1,466,000	1,573,000	107,000	53,000	49.5	+ 54,000	+50.5
Georgia	5,015,000	5,449,000	434,000	486,000	112.0	− 52,000	−12.0
Azerbaijan	6,028,000	7,029,000	1,001,000	1,267,000	126.6	− 266,000	−26.6
Armenia	3,031,000	3,283,000	252,000	573,000	227.4	− 321,000	−127.4
Uzbekistan	15,391,000	19,906,000	4,515,000	5,022,000	111.2	− 507,000	−11.2
Kirgizia	3,529,000	4,291,000	762,000	918,000	120.5	− 156,000	−20.5
Tajikistan	3,801,000	5,112,000	1,311,000	1,413,000	107.8	− 102,000	−7.8
Turkmenistan	2,759,000	3,534,000	775,000	859,000	110.8	− 84,000	−10.8
Kazakhstan	14,684,000	16,538,000	1,854,000	2,638,000	142.3	− 784,000	−42.3

Percentages have been calculated from absolute figures (reprinted with permission from *Radio Liberty Report on the USSR*: November 10, 1989).

CHARTING POLITICAL FERMENT: A STATUS REPORT

REPUBLIC	LITERARY AND CULTURAL FERMENT	ETHNIC VIOLENCE	MASS-BASED POPULAR FRONT	MAJORITY SENTIMENT FOR INDEPEN-DENCE	NATIONALIST CONTROL OF REPUBLIC PARLIAMENT
RSFSR	X				
UkrSSR	X		X		
Uzbekistan	X	X	X		
Kazakhstan	X	X			
Byelorussia	X		X		
Moldavia	X		X		
Georgia	X	X	X	X	
Azerbaijan	X	X	X	X	
Armenia	X	X	X		
Kirgizia	X	X			
Turkmenistan	X				
Tajikistan	X	X	X		
Lithuania	X		X	X	X
Latvia	X		X	X	X
Estonia	X		X	X	X

Status as of June 1990

Sources

Much information in this book was gleaned from the exceedingly valuable *Weekly Report on the USSR,* produced by Radio Liberty Research. Among Radio Liberty's outstanding experts on nationalism and ethnic issues in the USSR are Enders Wimbush, Bohdan Nahaylo, Paul Goble, and Roman Solchanyk.

Two periodicals that consistently cover nationality issues at a high standard are *Problems of Communism,* which is edited in Washington, D.C., and *Soviet Analyst,* published in London, England.

The daily reports on the Soviet Union by the U.S. Foreign Broadcast Information Service and the more concise, but equally valuable, BBC Summary of World Broadcasts help specialists keep up with the growing mass of Soviet articles, newspaper reports, and official statements on ethnic affairs and national issues.

We also have made extensive use of original editions of *Pravda, Izvestia, Sovyetskaya Rossiya, Literaturnaya Gazeta,* and *Literaturna Ukraina.*

Basic demographic information has been obtained from official Soviet census statistics for 1970, 1979, and 1989. The data from 1989 were reprinted in Radio Liberty's *Weekly Report on the USSR.*

General studies of Soviet nationalities include Helene Carrere d'Encausse's pioneering work *Decline of an Empire: The Soviet Socialist Republics in Revolt* (New York: 1979); Rasma Karklin's incisive ethnosociological investigation *Ethnic Relations in the USSR: The Perspective from Below* (London: 1986); and Enders Wimbush's wideranging anthology *Soviet Nationalities in Strategic Perspective* (Beckenham, England: 1985).

Readers in search of a deeply pessimistic reading of the chances for national self-determination by the non-Russians can turn to Alexander J. Motyl's *Will the Non-Russians Rebel?: State, Ethnicity, and Stability in the USSR* (Ithaca, N.Y.: 1987).

The National Question: A History of Peoples

A comprehensive account of independent nationalist and patriotic political activism before the era of glasnost is found in Ludmilla Alexeyeva's *Soviet Dissent: Contemporary Movements for National, Religious, and Human Rights* (Middletown, Conn.: 1985).

For general observations about the totalitarian Soviet system there is no better guide than Mikhail Heller and his study *Cogs in the Wheel: The Formation of Soviet Man* (New York: 1988).

Discussions of public opinion among Soviet citizens are well represented in *Politics, Work, and Daily Life in the USSR*, edited by James R. Millar (New York: 1987). The reports of Radio Liberty's *Soviet Area Audience* and *Opinion Research* surveys also offer guidance on public attitudes toward issues of ethnicity, nationalism, and empire.

Harry Shukman has edited a concise *Encyclopedia of the Russian Revolution* (Oxford: 1988), which gives a survey of the state of national movements and ethnic politics in the Russian empire before and during the Bolshevik Revolution, as well as detailed information on the first years of Soviet rule.

A Soviet encyclopedia filled with valuable information on the peoples of the USSR is Yulian V. Bromley, editor, *Narody Mira* (Moscow: 1988).

Readers interested in the writings of V. I. Lenin on the Russian empire, national self-determination, and the peoples of the USSR should turn to a volume of his essays, *National Liberation and Socialism* (New York: 1968).

Perhaps the most valuable study of Marxist-Leninist doctrine dealing with ethnic and national issues is Walker Connor's *The National Question in Marxist-Leninist Theory and Strategy* (Princeton, N.J.: 1984). From it we derived many of our quotations on the privileged status of the Russian nation in Soviet doctrine.

Readers wishing to examine further the role of nationalism in the Russian empire and, later, the Soviet empire can turn to the definitive scholarship of Hugh Seton-Watson. His book *Nations and States* (Boulder, Colo.: 1977) is an authoritative general work on the subject.

Hans Kohn's *The Idea of Nationalism* (New York: 1944) is a classic history of the roots of nationalism in Western tradition.

A *tour d'horizon* of nationalism is found in Alfred Cobban's *The Nation State and National Self-Determination* (New York: 1969), which has an especially valuable discussion of multinational states and of the forces that shaped the idea of the nation-state.

S. Enders Wimbush and Alexander Alexiev's (editors) valuable *Ethnic Minorities in the Red Army* (Boulder, Colo.: 1988) is an important compendium on the nature of ethnic tensions in the Red Army, as well as a broader discussion of the public implications of Soviet demographic changes.

The Rulers and the Ruled: The Economics of Equality

The comprehensive source for Soviet social and economic data is a book titled *Narodnove Khozyaystvo SSSR za 70 let: Yubileynyy statesticheskiy sbornik* (Moscow: 1987). The book *Pechat v SSSR v 1987 godu*

(Moscow: 1988) contains detailed statistics on the publication of books, journals, newspapers, and pamphlets on an all-Union and republic-by-republic basis.

Readers interested in more academic explorations of social and economic inequities in the Soviet Union should turn to Vsevolod Holubnychy's trailblazing essay, "Some Aspects of Relations among Soviet Republics," which is reprinted in *Vsevolod Holubnychy: Selected Works*, edited by Iwan S. Koropeckyj (Edmonton, Canada: 1982).

Ukraine: The Pivotal Nation

The most reliable history of the Ukraine is Orest Subtelny's *The Ukraine: A History* (Toronto, Canada: 1988). This magisterial survey is crisply written and characterized by prudent judgments about a people whose history is only dimly understood and has long been the subject of highly partisan interpretations.

Bohdan Krawchenko's *Social Change and National Consciousness in Twentieth-Century Ukraine* (New York: 1985) is a thought-provoking discussion of the social and economic forces that have shaped Ukrainians and their society in the period of Soviet rule.

Aspects of the Ukraine's subordinate status within the Soviet Union are discussed in Ivan Dzyuba's *Internationalism or Russification?* (London: 1968). Though written from a Marxist perspective, this book remains one of the most incisive critiques of the Ukraine's quasi-colonial status in the USSR.

Extremely detailed discussions of the Ukraine's contributions to the Soviet economy are contained in Z. L. Melnyk's "Capital Formation and Financial Relation" and V. N. Bandera's "External and Intra-Union Trade and Capital Transfers," *The Ukraine Within the USSR*, edited by Iwan S. Koropeckyj (New York: 1982).

An extensive view of the Ukraine at the height of the Brezhnev era can be derived from Peter J. Potichnyj, editor, *The Ukraine in the Seventies* (Oakville, Canada: 1975). The anthology contains considerations by leading scholars of social and economic trends in the Ukraine, the rise and decline of Party First Secretary Petro Shelest, and the fortunes of Ukrainian dissent. A brief volume edited by Bohdan Krawchenko, *Ukraine After Shelest* (Edmonton, Canada: 1983), carries some of the themes in Potichnyj's anthology through the early 1980s.

Those interested in reading about the impact of Chernobyl should turn to David R. Marples's *Chernobyl and Nuclear Power* (New York: 1986) and Iurii Shcherbak's *Chernobyl: A Documentary Story* (London: 1989).

Robert Conquest's *The Harvest of Sorrow* (New York: 1986) is the definitive study of Stalin's forced famine in the Ukraine.

The Ukrainian Weekly, a newspaper published by the Ukrainian National Association in Jersey City, N.J., is the single most accurate and comprehensive source of up-to-date information on developments within the Ukraine. The *Weekly* has an excellent, well-informed staff with an extensive range of contacts in the Ukraine.

Another source of up-to-the-minute information on the activities of independent groups in the Ukraine is the Ukrainian Press Agency, based in London, England. The agency has the advantage of a network of correspondents in Poland, Moscow, Lvov, and Kiev who provide reliable information on demonstrations, strikes, electoral politics, and political developments in a rapidly changing setting.

The Baltic States: Renaissance in the West

The best contemporary study on Estonia is Toivo U. Raun's *Estonia and the Estonians* (Stanford, Calif.: 1987), one of the first publications in the Studies of Nationalities in the USSR series sponsored by the Hoover Institution.

Readers interested in current affairs in the Baltic States should consult independent newspapers published in those countries: *Atgimimas* for Lithuania, *Atmoda* for Latvia, and *The Estonian Independent* and *Estonian Life* for Estonia.

Press releases issued by the Lithuanian Information Center in Washington, D.C., the American Latvian Association in Rockville, Maryland, and the Estonian National Council in Rockville, Maryland, have provided a comprehensive source for current news.

Problems of Communism has published a number of illuminating articles by, among others, V. Stanley Vardys, "Lithuanian National Politics" (July–August 1989); Juris Dreifelds, "Latvian National Rebirth" (July–August 1989), and Rein Taagepera, "Estonia's Road to Independence" (November–December 1989).

The Caucasus: Three Nations in Ferment

Because of the diverse character of the Caucasian states there are very few studies of the region as a whole. *Glasnost* magazine, edited by Sergei Grigoryants in Moscow, and published in English by the Center for Democracy in the USSR in New York, contains many articles dealing with events in Armenia, Azerbaijan, and Georgia.

Ronald Grigor Suny's *The Making of the Georgian Nation* (Bloomington, Ind.: 1988) offers the best study of Georgia, its history and politics up to the time of publication of this book.

David Marshall Lang's *The Armenians: A People in Exile* (London: 1988) takes a somewhat subjective look at the Armenians. It, nonetheless, contains much valuable information and some illuminating insights.

Information on Azerbaijan may be found in sources cited in the chapter on Central Asia.

Soviet Central Asia: The Muslim Factor and the Turkic Continuum

The starting point for any discussion of the peoples of Soviet Central Asia should be Alexandre A. Bennigsen and S. Enders Wimbush, *Muslims of the Soviet Empire: A Guide* (London: 1985), an invaluable directory to the various languages and cultures within this region. Bennigsen and Wimbush have also written a historical study of the region, *Muslim National Communism in the Soviet Union* (Chicago: 1979); and their *Mystics and Commissars* (London: 1983) provides a unique view of a traditional trend within Islam.

Central Asian Survey, the journal of the Society for Central Asian Studies, published in Oxford, England (editor, Marie Broxup), provides a wealth of information on the history and politics of Soviet Central Asia. The *Central Asian Newsletter*, also published by the Society for Central Asian Studies, compiles news on recent events and excerpts from current newspapers in the region that illuminate the situation.

Martha Brill Olcott's *The Kazakhs* (Stanford, Calif.: 1987) is a masterly study of the development of the Kazakhs and their recent history. Alan W. Fisher's *The Crimean Tatars* (Stanford, Calif.: 1987) has some of the same information for that nation.

Russians: The Elder Brother

James Billington's *The Icon and the Axe: An Interpretive History of Russian Culture* (New York: 1970) is the best single source for the diverse and complex Russian intellectual and cultural traditions that contribute profoundly to the nature of the Soviet empire.

Boris Shragin's neglected *The Challenge of the Spirit* (New York: 1978) is an important source for the continuities between the Russian and Soviet empires. The book also offers critical insights into the Russian liberal democratic tradition in its long struggle against chauvinism and imperialism.

Richard Pipes's *Russia Under the Old Regime* (New York: 1974) is an excellent introduction to the roots and structure of the Russian empire and of the continuities that persist to this day.

A brief, thoughtful look at the leading actors in shaping the Russian empire is contained in Marc Raeff's *Understanding Imperial Russia* (New York: 1984).

The Paris-based Russian quarterly journal *Syntaxis* is an important source for debates on the nature of Russian nationalism. It is edited by Maria Rozanova and Andrei Sinyavsky.

The Future of the Empire: Prospect and Policy

There are as yet few in-depth discussions of the policy implications arising from the rebirth of the national movements in the USSR.

The most influential essay on this matter is Zbigniew Brzezinski's article, "Post-Communist Nationalism," which appeared in the Winter 1989/1990 issue of *Foreign Affairs*.

Gail Lapidus's article "Gorbachev's Nationality Problem," which appeared in the Fall 1989 issue of *Foreign Affairs*, is also a thoughtful contribution to the debate. Although its conclusions do not all coincide with those of the authors of this book, Professor Lapidus provides a serious and lucid overview of the course of Gorbachev's nationality policy and urges broader "political, cultural, and economic contacts with the nations that make up the USSR."

Paul Henze's article "The Last Empire" (*Journal of Democracy*, Spring 1990) is a thoughtful discussion of the future of the USSR and of how progress toward democracy can relieve ethnic tensions.

Index